The Wright Stuff

The Wright Stuff

Rick Glanvill

Virgin

This edition first published in Great Britain in 1996 by
Virgin Books
an imprint of Virgin Publishing Ltd
332 Ladbroke Grove
London W10 5AH

First published in Great Britain in 1995 by Virgin Publishing Ltd

A catalogue record for this book is available from the British Library.

ISBN 0 7535 007 60

Typeset by TW Typesetting, Plymouth, Devon
Printed and bound in Great Britain by
Cox & Wyman Ltd, Reading, Berks

For Oliver.
Eye on the ball, son.

Contents

Illustrations

Acknowledgements

The first person I'd like to thank is Ian Wright. But I can't, because his manager wouldn't let me near him. I'll show my gratitude anyway, for all the years of pleasure he's given us in this sometimes mundane English game, and all the flak he's taken – in and out of the game.

Ian has many friends. Some of them spoke to me, some of them wouldn't; some would only speak 'off the record'. Likewise his relatives. I accept and respect their decisions.

To Ian's great teachers – Eric Summers, Syd Pigden, Peter McCarthy in particular; to the players, coaches, managers and staff who have contributed to Ian's story, especially Steve Coppell, Graham Taylor, Alan Smith, Cyrille Regis, Eddie McGoldrick, Peter Prentice, Billy Smith, Mickey Wakefield, Lee Lang, Henry Laville, Mike Saunders and others, I extend many thanks.

My researcher Karen McCarthy deserves credit for her sensitive work and useful suggestions. The Teamwork agency also contributed helpful material. Also the many Arsenal and Crystal Palace fans whose reminiscences and opinions were invaluable.

Thanks also to my agent Cat Ledger, and Mal Peachey at Virgin.

Finally to Yael, who was so massively supportive, and Oliver, who simply wanted to know where daddy was.

1 Paris in the Spring

'The stone that the builder refused will always be the head cornerstone.'

Bob Marley

N THE END, as in the beginning, there were tears. At the Cup Winners' Cup Final in Paris on 10 May 1995, the final kick of a fruitless campaign, and perhaps the most unlikely and spectacular strike in the history of the tournament, shattered the belief system, the 'foundation of hope' manager George Graham had ground out at Arsenal in nearly nine years at the helm.

'If you lose hope, or lose belief, you may as well get out of football', he had proclaimed somewhere along the road to European Cup Winners' glory the previous year. But by May 1995 Graham had already retreated from the game in a hail of FA bullets and 'bung' allegations.

That the projectile scoring a direct hit on his beloved Arsenal battleship should have been fired by the mercurial Moroccan Nayim – an ex-Tottenham staffer for chrissakes – supplied that ironic twist which history dictates must accompany the end of empire. Nayim's bolt from the blue came down with snow on it to bury Graham's old boys.

In Paris, the Highbury team's fabled 'mental qualities' were largely absent. If they'd played to the usual pattern and sneaked a last minute goal as Zaragoza had, it would have been business as usual: 'lucky old Arsenal!' As it turned out, the Highbury smash-and-grab merchants were the ones who ended up haunting the pitch like bedraggled redcoats.

Some players sobbed. David Seaman, memory of whose heroism against Sampdoria in the semi-finals made his complacent miscalculation of Nayim's effort all the more impossibly grotesque, was deserted by the old guard, left to stand alone for some minutes until Stephan Schwarz strode over to comfort him.

But for one among them it was second time around: Paris in the spring had broken Ian Wright's heart in successive seasons. The striker had never known tiredness like he felt now. It was overwhelming. Seconds before he'd felt capable of going on for hours. Suddenly, he felt like a machine switched off when running at full power.

In 1994's Cup Winners' Cup semi-final at Highbury, the French capital's finest, Paris Saint-Germain, had watched as Ian pointlessly executed an impetuous tackle in a meaningless position. His rash challenge was to lead to his suspension from the final against Parma in Copenhagen and the denial of a sensational climax to a three-year-old Arsenal career.

Now one year later in Paris, face coursing with tears, shirt tugged out, he was inconsolable. These people were thieves of time, his time. And time has always been Ian Wright's master.

Outside on the boulevards, Arsenal fans were dazed. Someone had torn up the bloody script. It was wrong; this wasn't the kind of thing that happened to Arsenal. Some supporters, silver lining-seekers, were pleased: 'Thank god, now we'll *have* to rebuild the team.' Mindful of Paul Merson's recent drug and drink confessions, one ran up to the coach carrying players' wives back to the airport. 'Oi!,' he yelled, banging balefully, crazily, on the steamed-up window, 'Oi! Mrs Merse! Mrs Merse! Get your 'usband back on that bloody stuff now!'

In the dressing room, the atmosphere was deathly. There was no champagne. Ian Wright wasn't going to shake the bottle out of a window and spray it on the Arsenal faithful like he had last season. Everybody felt for Dave Seaman, who was in tears. He takes things like that very hard. He'd pulled off some brilliant saves and then blamed himself for the goal. Everybody was consoling him while at the same time trying to get over the fact that they'd lost. It was just very quiet.

While everybody was trying to bolster everybody else, Ian was particularly subdued. The coaching staff were coming round trying to get players' heads up. Everyone was gutted and Ian was the same. They couldn't believe they'd lost like that.

But Arsenal are professionals. For a moment they were down. But they had suffered big defeats before and risen again to regain their composure and hunger. Ironically, as a goalscorer, Ian even appreciated Nayim's finish. It was the sort of spontaneous effort he might have scored himself – the sort he had been scoring all his life in fact.

In truth though the great survivors had been choked. Arsenal is not a popular name beyond the environs of London N5 and the lips of their satellite supporters around the country. Plenty of English people watching the Zaragoza game, and the Reds' many enemies in the press, will have felt the Arsenal had finally had a taste of their own medicine. The Spanish had spiked the Gunners' guns.

What a season it had been – nothing like the usual Highbury version – with scandals, 'bungs', mid-table mediocrity ... and Wrighty getting his lowest tally in the League since he joined. It was time for change and renewal. Let's have a team that plays football, came the cry from supporters sick of Tottenham getting all the media attention.

George Graham had constructed a side that was ruthlessly efficient, acquisitive of silverware and not always great to watch: the Steffi Graf of soccer. Traditionally, Arsenal are a high-profile club with a sniffy, aristocratic air. Even when they play well, they are rarely credited with excellence and they are frequently pilloried when there is the faintest whiff of disaster or scandal.

In recent years, Ian Wright has simultaneously challenged the image of 'boring, boring Arsenal' and suffered the worst slings and arrows of outrageous press coverage. He is a 'Wright Nutter' and 'Public Enemy Number One'. And despite nurturing influence through his friends in the press, Ian doesn't seem able to shake off that image. The player most likely to score a dazzling hat-trick is also the man most liable to aim a punch at your centre back.

'When fans meet me in the flesh they know I'm not this person that I'm perceived to be,' Ian has claimed. He feels he is misrepresented by the media, and it's tempting to go along with that.

But, by his behaviour, he hasn't always helped his own cause and he seems unwilling or unable to redress the balance by putting across his more attractive qualities: his warmth, loyalty, keen sense of humour and sensitivity. To football supporters outside Highbury, he's simply the cocky brat who's always in the press and into the bargain the guy most likely to sink your team.

His advisers, those who mould his media image as a tough guy, haven't really helped either. The hatred of thousands of opposition fans is, in a weird sort of way, the ultimate mark of respect. But it's not the sort of respect Ian wants. He wants to be liked.

In 1995, Ian has reached the stage in his career when most footballers mellow and display largesse. Players of his stature generally move in to the public arena as commentators or chat show guests. Ian's problem on that front is threefold. Firstly, he's no Gary Lineker. Secondly, he's still too ragamuffin for a *Match of the Day* presented by Desmond Lynam. And thirdly, Ian speaks his mind, no matter how controversial his opinions.

Ever since he can remember, Ian Wright's been running. Running on the tarmac of south-east London, running away from inadequacy and privation, running past defenders. But when you're running so much you have to know when to stop, and that's proved difficult for Ian on occasion.

There are some things Ian won't run from, like injustice or his responsibilities as a father, as a family member and as a role model for the youth of his community. He won't run from confrontation either.

His career has been a battle fought not on the playing fields of Eton, but on the less salubrious pitches of Eltham, Blackheath, Lewisham and Rotherhithe, and against a society that he often feels has been stacking the odds against him.

As a youth, he was rejected by numerous clubs, and so came late to a game that likes to groom and nurture the model professional from an early age. A self-made star, Ian might not be the model pro, but he is an icon to thousands.

In fact, there are few sights more bowel-loosening for opposition fans than that of the Arsenal striker galloping like an SAS corporal surging behind enemy lines, with their sedentary back four looking about as effective as the Maginot Line.

The fans and players look to the linesman: the flag stays down. Damn. Appeal anyway. One on one with their 'keeper. Ian waits. The goalie jerks . . . Ian shoots the other way. Dead. The net bulges. Ian runs to the corner flag. Brings a little Jamaican dancehall to proceedings, performs a victory 'bogle'. Fires imaginary guns like a Mafiosi gangster, runs back and thrusts a taunting arm past the enemy's fans.

Ian has two commodities rare in the English game: flair and audacity. But there's a catch – Who Dares, Whines. The Wright stuff often does the wrong thing. Ian's spitefulness is almost as celebrated as his unquestionable brilliance. He's not alone in that: Denis Law, George Best, Stan Bowles ... Maradona! All had their nasty alter egos. Why is Ian's so celebrated?

Does the answer lie in the nature of the man himself, or English football's reluctance to induct him into the Hall of Fame?

Some say Ian hasn't done himself any favours in this department. But perhaps we won't allow him to. It's been a battle for Ian to get where he is and sometimes it's difficult to know when to lay down arms: it doesn't necessarily pay to appear defenceless in the face of a relentless onslaught.

Andy Massey, a white guy who grew up on the same Honor Oak estate in south London and played for Millwall Football Club, knows the score. 'When they see him on the box, people go, "Oh you flash black bastard!" And I go, "No, he ain't, he's just like one of us." 'That's how he is. He ain't acting. That's how he's always played football, and that's how he's always been.'

Ian is one of life's high achievers, but he has never ditched his principles. He has risen from estate guttersnipe to burnished idol of football fans around the country, blemished sporadically by a petulance born of the driving desire to make something of himself – not just some*thing*, in fact, but some*one*.

He has become public property, but much of his life remains intensely private, the subject of conjecture and rumour. It's fitting that one of his heroes is Michael Jackson. Like the world's favourite singer, Ian has never really grown up – he too cheats time. Ian has survived controversy with his dignity intact.

But this is not the traditional story of the poor black kid rising from the ghetto to find fame and glory. Ian Wright's family were badly off by any financial yardstick, but in other ways they were rich. Ian's mother Nesta Wright had true pride in her family and brought them up to be strong individuals. In Ian, she produced a man who places a premium on loyalty; whose life has been shaped by his powerful convictions; who is quick to let people into his heart and equally swift to eliminate them; who never forgets the dignity of humanity.

'I draw my strength and desire from the fact I came into the game late. You want to show people, prove you are good enough. You have a lot of time to make up,' Ian once said.

'All the people who rejected me when I was younger must look at it and know they were wrong. That is the sort of thing that pumps you up when you start to do well.'

Perhaps that's as much Ian's problem as his strength: too much anger to work out; too many people putting him down; too much negativity.

Perhaps he simply wants success too much. A couple of years ago, the *Sunday Times* invited Ian amongst other celebrities to contribute a rap for a feature they were running. Ian's was a rare *cri de coeur* that's quite revealing:

I'm no saint, I'm no sinner
And everybody knows
When you got a reputation it's hard to explode;
'Cos the media are watching
And everybody sees
If you've nothing good to say . . . just keep the peace.
I'm no angel, I'm no devil
But you can surely see
When I'm out beneath the lights, you get everything from me;
'Cos the better you can get
The more the pressure will increase.
If you've got nothing to say . . . just keep the peace.

The boy's a rare British commodity. If you melted Ian Wright down, you'd be left with the essence of whatever it is that makes a winner. But we don't like 'winners', do we? We like good losers.

And Ian has never been a good loser . . .

2 Roots Man

'Dread he got a job to do and he's got to fulfil that mission.
To see his hurt would be their greatest ambition. But he will
survive in this world of competition. Cos no matter what they
do, Natty keep on coming through. And no matter what they
say, tragedy deh everyday, Natty Dread rise again . . . Have no
fear, have no sorrow . . . No matter what game they play, we've
got something they can never take away. And it's the fire, it's
the fire that's burning down every day . . . No water can put out
this fire.'

Bob Marley, 'Ride Natty Ride'

I T'S A POPULAR BANALITY in football that someone like Ian Wright
has 'come from nowhere'. Not only is the statement
materially impossible, it is also an insult. Ian Wright's family,
especially his mother, would despise the notion that the
Wright household amounted to nothing, provided no root.

In fact, Ian Wright's home, his 'yard', and his family have provided him with a founding stability in a life that has had its share
of upheaval. It ingrained in him principles of trust, respect and
humanity that persist to this day if you look behind the contorted
face of the back pages of the newspapers.

Ian may have travelled a long way from his south-east London
council house to the billboards of the nation and the stadia of the
world; but in some ways, he's hardly moved an inch.

Not many people realise there's a hospital in Woolwich, let
alone a military hospital. But it was in the austere Victorian wards
of the British Hospital, Samuel Street, where Nesta Jane Wright
gave birth to a tiny, 'bitty' son she named Ian Edward. It was
Sunday, 3 November 1963. Destiny can be cute. Ian was born so
near to Woolwich Arsenal it almost seemed inevitable he would
later play for the club called after the area, even though it moved
premises north of the river just before the First World War.

On 6 November 1963, Nesta's sister, who had arrived and
settled in the same area of south-east London from Jamaica with
her sibling, produced another boy, Patrick. The two youngsters
grew up pretty much as twins – closer than cousins, less hostile

than brothers – and even lived together in a large, bustling house on Manor Avenue in Forest Hill.

It probably never crossed the minds of the two proud mothers that the fruits of their wombs would, between them, eventually have Saturday night television stitched up: Ian Wright gracing the pastures on *Match of the Day* and Patrick Robinson providing the amiable bedside manner as Martin 'Ash' Ashford in the popular BBC soap, *Casualty*.

Patrick suddenly veered towards a Charles Atlas physique in his teens, whereas Ian's bantam-weight build meant that the nickname he acquired on the estate as a tot – 'Little Ian' – still stuck years later.

Ian was the third addition to a family that would eventually number four children. Nesta already had two sons when he was born, and a sister for them all, Dionne Marie, was to follow in the summer of 1969. Ian's father, Herbert 'Buster' McLean, a maintenance electrician in a local cable factory (and also father of Ian's brother Morris, born 16 April 1962), wasn't around long enough to be the kind of dominant father figure that Ian responded to (and sometimes found) over the next three decades of his life. Morris would have to do, and he was just a year and a half Ian's senior.

Typically for the sort of Caribbean family that migrated to the UK in answer to the call from the 'Mother Country' – invited by poster campaigns throughout the Caribbean to help overcome the labour shortage in booming Britain – the Wright family structure was overwhelmingly matriarchal. Nesta, an assertive, ebullient and strict mother, imbued a strong sense of self-worth and ethics in her offspring that was to instruct Ian in later life.

Buster McLean and she had knocked around together for a couple of years before Ian was born; this was in the days when Nesta first arrived from the Caribbean and settled in Forest Hill, near the South Circular Road, and her boyfriend lived in Lewisham.

Something of a playboy with his dashing good looks, Buster found the matriarchal set-up in her Honor Oak home stifling. Nesta's dexterity as a mother provided ample excuse for him to move on to pastures new. Moreover, she was so loving and protective towards the children, Ian in particular (and perhaps dismissive of his father's usefulness) that Buster drifted away leaving Nesta to cope.

Anyway, he'd done his bit – and perhaps more than Nesta and Ian realised. Back home in East Kingston, Jamaica, the McLeans, are well known for their footballing prowess. Three cousins of Buster McLean – Alvin, Bunny and Lloyd – have graced the national team there, which is traditionally regarded as exhibiting almost as much individual skill as the Brazilians while lacking the rigid team coherence that might catapult them on to the world stage.

In the late forties and fifties in the Caribbean, the McLean family enjoyed a similar reputation to the one south London's flying Wallace brothers (members of whom played for Southampton, Manchester United and Leeds in the eighties and nineties) do here. The fact that their adeptness with a football has been passed on to Ian Wright should be a source of pride to the Jamaican game.

The line continues: Ian's children, Bradley and Shaun, are showing inordinate promise for their age. Shaun attends the Tottenham Hotspur School of Excellence (at last his bitter north London rivals may have cause to appreciate Ian Wright's talents) and plays for the youngest team at 10-Em-Bee – his father's old side. At fourteen, his signature is courted by Nottingham Forest amongst others.

Now retired after his fortieth English winter, Buster still lives just round the corner from the Honor Oak estate, though all the Wright family except Ian's children – his grandchildren – have moved away. A framed photograph of Ian, dressed in his Virgin-sponsored Crystal Palace kit, takes pride of place on his mantelpiece amongst pictures of his five other children. Scattered around the walls is evidence of a hobby at which he's quite proficient, oil painting.

At 65, lighter-skinned and an inch or two taller than his famous son, Buster has the same wiry physique, eyes and shape of face, same raffish charm, same amiable nature. He's a dapper dresser too; he says he has to keep up appearances for when people see 'Ian Wright's dad' walking past.

Buster saw Ian regularly in the early days; even after he and Nesta were finished, Ian would visit him in Birmingham where he went to live when Ian was a toddler until he was four years old.

After his return to the area, Buster couldn't avoid bumping into all the people he knew in the tight-knit community of Honor Oak. These days, he rarely if ever sees his son, and life as an electrician hasn't always been easy, but Ian's success is clearly a source of moist-eyed pride for him. He recalls with huge affection the livewire kid romping round the tenements with a ball and a smirk.

In fact, the notorious Brockley estate has unearthed a few gems over the years. Around Ian's time, Steven Anthrobus, who carved a career for himself as a pro footballer at Fulham and elsewhere, was a star player on the hard-contested Turnham concrete. David Rocastle, three years Wright's junior, leapfrogged his friend to make it at Arsenal some years before Ian and was part of a large family well-known to the residents – Rocastle's older brother Stephen showed considerable promise until he suffered a serious illness and his uncle Sam was also an important figure in the local football leagues.

But the Honor Oak estate has an otherwise mundane history. It rose from the ruins of the pre-war slum clearances. Residents arrived from Rotherhithe, Deptford and elsewhere, installed by Lewisham Council from 1936 onwards. Many were the families of dockers.

Sydenham-born Syd Pigden, a robust, avuncular septuagenarian, who taught and coached Ian Wright during the many years he organised sport in the borough, describes what he saw when he first arrived at Turnham School, which nestles on the fringes of the estate: 'It was literally a deprived area. People used to keep coal in the bath – they'd never had one before. To these people it was affluent; it's not if you go there now. Many of the fathers were casual dockers.

'With the advent of the dock labour scheme, most moved away. Younger families came in who had relatives on the estate. There were lots of big families. The Richardsons related to the Cheesemans, the Cheesemans to the Sanders and so on. There were cousins galore. But life was very poor.'

Prime Minister MacMillan arrived in the fifties and announced that people had never had it so good, and so, fleetingly, it seemed. But even as they enjoyed the rare adventure of full employment, the estate dwellers had to improvise to enhance their quality of life. Such experiences invariably centred around the estate: focal point for fun, scrapes and skirmishes.

Turnham Road curves round to encircle the estate. Running between the tenement blocks was another road and in the fifties Pigden and the other teachers used to stage the annual sports day there. Skittles were set up with a sign saying 'Closed for the day'. Kids sat on verges and railings while their peers charged or jumped around.

'If they fell over in the road,' recalls Syd Pigden chirpily, 'the mums never used to worry, they'd just dust them off . . . not sue the school. It was a community and it was fun. It was nothing for a parent to say a kid was going to hospital and ask if she could have a shilling for the fare. You knew people, they knew you. None of this hostility there is now.'

In the late-fifties, Afro-Caribbean families began arriving in the area. The virulence of antagonism towards migrants of the time is well-documented, but it is worth restating in the context of that small pocket of Lewisham where Ian Wright was to grow up.

Like most immigrants, Caribbean arrivals tended to cluster together in their new country. This enabled them to reproduce the atmosphere, the food, language and culture from back home, and allowed for more solidarity whenever the 'host' population got shirty. In an alien society, it also provided the basis for a strong sense of community.

The newcomers were confronted with signs explaining properties were available for rent except to 'Dogs, Irish or Coloureds'. Lacking the financial clout to buy their own places until the communities later established partnership funding schemes, the black migrants gravitated towards the tenement housing no one else wanted. British racial discrimination was never more rife than in the late fifties and early sixties and, in particular, it flourished in areas of council housing.

Resentment simmered, as it continues to do, around the allocation of housing according to those in worst need. But with three young children – and a daughter still to come – and many of the usual residential doors shut to her, Nesta Wright was clearly in need of housing. She was living in Greenwich at the time when Ian was born, but when she was offered a place on the Honor Oak estate it was readily taken up.

The estate was administered by the London County Council, later the Greater London Council, who insisted on prompt rent payments as well as exacting standards of hygiene – each tenant had to sweep outside their door every day, for example. When Nesta moved in, she must have been impressed by its pristine look and the formal, well-organised atmosphere.

But appearances can be deceptive. The estate had its share of problems typical of any concentration of people: family feuds, alcoholic fathers, criminals, custody battles – even some kidnappings. At one stage, if you wanted to buy furniture on the never-never and gave a particular block on the Honor Oak estate as your address, you were guaranteed to be turned down flat.

Behind the twitching curtains, another form of malevolence often prevailed.

'When the coloured families came there,' says Syd Pigden, 'we had to be very careful in the playground – not so much in the classroom – particularly if you had a virulently racist father or mother. Luckily, Ian came when that had largely died out.' Extinct or not (and that's very doubtful), in the late sixties discrimination served to corral migrant families together through lack of opportunity. The estate became home to more and more Afro-Caribbean families.

Then as now, Turnham School's intake had a high black contingent that required new pastoral approaches. According to every reliable survey, Caribbean parents are, if anything, keener on traditional teaching methods than most others. Turnham trod the line between a fervent disciplinarian element and a moderately progressive approach towards ethnic minorities.

For some time, Brockley had been known as a black area, a focal point, and that reputation was enhanced as the community matured through the seventies. That said, there was racial tension throughout south-east London at the time, even though it was Brixton that grabbed the headlines.

The climate in and around Honor Oak was typical. Black and white kids would mix for sport but not on the social side after school, when they tended to gravitate into separate groups after the watershed age of fifteen, sixteen.

As Ian was growing up, there were often incidents of a racial nature. Houses were daubed with offensive slogans; kids were attacked in the street; sexual jealousy was the cause of fights when the night-clubs turned out their punters. In the mid-seventies, there was, according to locals, some trouble between the blacks and the whites which culminated in white bigots from Camberwell and Deptford attacking the youth club, known as Oakwell, held in the school.

Even though Honor Oak largely escaped the worst upheavals, Ian was raised in a time of racial tension and hostility which left its mark and helped him identify the type of person who would hold him back, harangue him and limit his opportunities because of colour. As a result, Ian's friends were predominantly black kids.

Meanwhile, Nesta had her hands full bringing up the Wright fledglings. There was plenty of brewing testosterone in the home, but precious little wage-earning. 'Though we never actually starved, we never had the normal things most kids have,' Ian once recalled.

Nesta was a formidably maternal figure, running a typical, informal Jamaican household. The food and decor were Jamaican. And there were always aunties and uncles, cousins and friends in the Wright home.

The Jamaican English tongue rattled around the walls of their small flat, cluttered as it was with photos and mementoes. Outside in the mixed environment of the estate and the school, the Wright children quickly learnt the pragmatic art of being bilingual, having one foot in the white world, the other in the black.

It was what you did if you wanted to get on. You could assert your roots in private, with black friends or relatives. But when talking to his teachers or supervisors, Ian was softly spoken, polite, with a mild London accent : 'He never said the things he does now, like "Nuffink", in those days,' claims one.

Still today when Ian's holding court with any of his many black footballing friends, he sounds and looks like he could be standing on any corner in Kingston – Kingston, Jamaica, that is, not Kingston, Surrey.

Back then, Nesta was a firm mother. Ian responded to her demand for good behaviour without fuss. He never crossed anyone he trusted. And as long as they weren't in trouble, Nesta was happy for her children to find what fun they could out of sight. Nesta enjoyed a good party herself, where ska, rhythm and blues and rock steady records would rock the room.

But the overriding lesson Nesta conveyed time and again to her children was the importance of self-respect: 'You're the greatest, don't let nobody put you down'. Hers was a 'can do' credo. Her kids were capable of anything.

Nesta taught them that it was vital to have regard for authority too. Many Jamaicans carried an inordinate faith in the British sense of justice that was to be sorely tested by exposure to inner city actualities. So there was a proviso: she instilled in her kids the need to stand their ground if they felt aggrieved. The Wright kids should always stick up for themselves when justice was on their side: if someone hits you, hit them back.

She also encouraged Ian's budding gift for outspokenness and energetic self-promotion. He was special, and she made sure everyone knew it.

Yet when he was eighteen months old, Nesta had a shock with Ian. One spring day he seemed to have stopped breathing. He was terribly short of breath. His tight little chest wheezed like a punctured concertina and he was obviously very distressed. Nesta was desperate; for once she was powerless to help him. She nursed him through until she could see a doctor, who put the incident down to 'wheezing'.

The attacks persisted though, and eventually Ian was diagnosed as asthmatic. Doctors reassured Nesta that Ian would grow out of it. But as he grew up, he was always especially susceptible to cold weather or moments when he had over-exerted himself. The condition was a major concern.

Sufferers of asthma complain of their chest constricting and of being unable to suck in sufficient air. In bad attacks, you think you're never going to breathe again: in severe cases, this becomes a real possibility. People might wonder how anyone could make it as a footballer with a condition like that: some doctors urge asthmatic children to give up football; others recommend exercise to strengthen the lungs.

Asthma might not have compared with Asa Hartford's condition – the Man. City and West Bromwich Albion midfielder, whom Ian saw on television as a kid, had a hole in his heart, although it didn't stop him from running flat out – but it was a real enough problem for Ian when he was nurturing his career as a sportsman.

After a while, Ian was given an inhaler, and it has remained a feature of his kit bag ever since, even though he hasn't had a serious asthma attack since 1982. But it's not the sort of thing footballers like to be known for – ridiculously, it is reckoned to have an adverse effect on their transfer value. That says a lot about the cynical, superstitious sport in which he has since made his name.

Ian himself has publicly dismissed his asthma as little more than an inconvenience. 'It doesn't really bother me now,' he shrugged a few years ago. 'On the pitch I do special breathing exercises if I become short of breath. But I haven't suffered badly since I was fifteen.'

There are too many myths about the destructive properties of asthma. In most cases, as long as a child is sensible with preventive and corrective treatments and aware of the triggers of their attacks, he or she can lead a perfectly normal, energetic life. Ian should be proud though of the fact that, like Ian Botham amongst others, he is a role model who is living proof of how little asthma can inhibit a professional sports career.

If Nesta felt helpless when Ian was having asthma attacks, her protective personality was a crucial influence on Ian in other ways. 'She taught us to appreciate things, look after what we had and always work hard, try to make the most of yourself. She gave us a sense of real values,' her son once beamed.

Yet as he grew, Ian didn't always feel that special. It was one thing to have your mother cultivate a sense of your abundant virtues, but it was quite another squaring that with real-life experience outside the sanctuary of home, family and friends. Society wasn't kind to ambitious, boisterous young black kids. Nesta's generation was more deferential: England had invited them as guests. Ian was among the first generation to demand more from the relationship with a homeland not of his choosing.

Chief among Ian's expectations is the most basic: respect; not for being one of the country's best footballers, but simply as a person in his own right. It's the Jamaican way: 'Nuff respect' is not just a ritual platitude, it is a statement of unity and an article of faith. On the other hand, to 'dis' is to disrespect.

It's always been so, but especially when black people are considered as a lumpen mass rather than treated as individuals in their own right: Ian has always assessed people on how fairly he thinks they have judged him.

Later, when he was a youth, Ian's sense of worth – and the certainty that he was a child of destiny – was challenged again and again when he felt let down or disrespected. He didn't always feel equipped to deal with the strain, especially when it affected the dreams that shaped his life. He wanted to be liked and was hurt every time his trusting nature was misused. In response, he developed a vociferous, if somewhat fragile, ego.

For the time being, he basked in the warmth his mother extended and was oblivious to all the hindrances waiting outside. He was after all one of the Wright kids, and Nesta's kids were winners.

Neighbours and contemporaries remember Little Ian as playful and smiling, a mischievous little scamp always running around with the other kids. He was always competitive too: 'Beat you to that lamp-post!' Even at that age, sport seemed to be the perfect outlet for his energy and will to win.

'There was no *Space Invaders* or nothing like that – not like kids have now,' says one old friend. 'It was a very poor estate. All we used to do was play football or fight, really.'

Ian himself suggests he was a handful, getting into mischief, but nothing above the scrumping or 'knock down ginger' level. As Buster McLean recalls, there would be the occasional irate neighbour haranguing Nesta for a smashed window caused by one of Ian's shots. But what do you expect? Honor Oak folks were living virtually on top of each other, and from the age of five Ian and his mates were always out playing football.

Either way, to his neighbours and pals he was well-known and extrovert even before he started school. But Ian could be quiet when it was prudent to be so: to adults and figures of authority, he was always respectfully courteous and passive – the perfect Victorian child, just as a properly brought up Jamaican kid should be.

What he resentfully lacked in inches, Ian came to make up for with wit and suss. These qualities earned him status and made him an easy boy to make friends with, even if, as he grew older, there was a cruel tinge to his mickey-taking at times. Ian always had to work the frustration out of his system.

Throughout his formative years, one of Ian Wright's biggest influences was, naturally enough, his older brother Morris. At times, Morris and he were even mistaken for one another, even though eighteen months separated their births.

Not much bigger than Ian, Morris was feisty, vocal, tough and respected – with some trepidation – on the estate. He loved football but was a better cricketer – typical of first generation black British kids at the time. (Later too, Ian showed some promise as a bowler: fast, naturally, and mostly intent on taking the batsman's head off.)

Football, however, reigned supreme. Shortly after Ian started at Turnham School Nesta remembers buying him and Morris West Ham shirts bearing the numbers eight and ten. As far as she was concerned, Nesta was probably thinking more in terms of her favourite team, Brazil, and the attacking heroes Pelé and Tostao who bore those numbers rather than the regulars at Upton Park – funnily enough, to this day, she's a Crystal Palace supporter.

Nevertheless, West Ham was an interesting choice. The Hammers weren't the local team, but in the sixties they had two much more tangible factors going for them: the powerful presence, talismanic for young black soccer fans, of cultured defender John Charles and Bermudan striker Clyde Best.

In a First Division roll-call that was otherwise almost uniformly pink, here were people for the two Wright boys to identify with: Best in particular, even if his flashes of brilliance were often outweighed by a juggernaut clumsiness.

Perhaps there was some sorcery in those shirts too, because Ian went on to wear the number ten shirt at Palace and then make the eight his own at Highbury.

Morris was playing football whenever he could at school. Ian was so keen on the game and so eager to emulate his brother that Nesta, at his insistence rather than any local educational policy, sent Ian to Turnham on half days off. He would shoot and scuff a football around the playground with all the other toughs and softies from the estate.

This was an early demonstration of the fondness for soccer that was to mark out Ian Wright's next 30 years. There was nothing unique about it, though, on a working class estate in south London. But it would come to dominate his entire outlook on life and drive his ambitions. It was his vocation.

The year Ian was born, Olympian heaven descended on the estate in the shape of an after-school play centre set up in the Turnham playground by Bob Mitchell, a balding, stocky fellow from down the road in Blackheath.

Football-lovers among the Honor Oak kids were already lucky to have Turnham nearby. Not only did it stage the Oakwell youth club, possessing an uncommonly large playground that was a decent size for a pitch, but someone had thoughtfully installed floodlights that drenched the players in brilliant light even in winter. (In 1963, such a facility was as rare as it was advanced: the first floodlit football match had only taken place in 1956.)

Outside the school, the Honor Oak estate had little to offer the potential footballer except plenty of willing opposition, dangerous surrounding roads, grey walls and whatever motley ball could be found to kick around. Bob Mitchell's ILEA play centre came as a godsend to parents and children alike.

As soon as Ian finished school, he'd go home, get changed and head straight back for the play centre in the playground at Turnham. There, 'strict Mr Mitchell' and others would organise the boys into teams. Already Ian had developed a taste for hovering in line with the defence, and waiting for the ball to fly over their heads before burying it. He was fast and deadly. He was also what some people might call a goalhanger. In those days, Bob Mitchell never had to caution Ian like later referees would. There was the occasional tantrum, when he blasted a ball over or when someone else wouldn't pass to him, but little to suggest the temper that is such a mark of his performances now. Ian was generally very quiet, very compliant.

In truth, he never felt close to Bob Mitchell like he did to other elders in his football life: there was always a coolness. Bob encouraged that sort of relationship. It was respectful.

'Bob Mitchell really taught us about football,' says one of Ian's playmates. 'He was a nice bloke. He was really good. We used to play football for hours every day.'

Ian spent every holiday with the other boys at Turnham play centre rushing about with a ball or bat from nine till five.

Adolescents would turn up for a game in the evening, to be joined by a growing Ian Wright and, a few years later, David Rocastle: football was banned from his school, Cardinal Vaughan, because of fighting, so Turnham was essential for keeping his eye in.

In an ideal world, every local school would be as much of a local resource as Turnham was and is. Even now, ex-pupils from the estate ask deputy head Denise Dance for a ball to battle over in the playground.

The school also had a reputation for producing great football teams to compete in the school league and the inter-school Invicta Cup. The kindly but resolute Syd Pigden – Lewisham football's 'Mr Chips' – was organiser of the Turnham School team and the borough league from the fifties until his retirement in 1980.

A non-League referee who was once pummelled with an umbrella by an elderly lady after a disputed penalty award, Syd was a triallist at Crystal Palace and retains a reputation for idiosyncratic but effective coaching techniques based on honest, old-fashioned values.

It's said that he used to bestow on his 'man of the match' the honour of cleaning teacher's boots: kids ran their socks off for the right to apply the spit and polish!

Other practices were more widespread. Selection for the school team, for example. Just a stray dog's stroll from the McLean and Wright dwellings is the Honor Oak sports ground which was to play such a crucial part in furthering Ian's sporting endeavours.

'It was at the top of the estate,' Syd recalls. 'We put down a couple of cricket stumps, and I'd line the boys up and roll the ball across from right to left: "Kick it with your right foot." They'd kick away, and I'd mark down those who could actually kick a ball any distance. Some of them couldn't get near it. Then we'd do it from the other side. Ian kicked it with his left foot as well as his right – children kicking with their non-kicking foot is a thing that separates them. From that you got sixteen boys.

'The goalkeeper always picked himself: "You want to try George in goal." I played a boy with one hand in goal once, he was so keen. Nobody said anything when he let a goal in.'

The next part of the Pigden plan was a 50-yard dash. 'The fastest boy, no matter what size, was centre forward. That's how Ian Wright got to be centre forward instead of left wing. And the two biggest who kicked the ball furthest were the right and left back. Obvious really.

'Your second fastest runner was your centre half. Your tiniest boys became your right and left wings (what foot they kicked with was immaterial, because they could always cut in). There was method in my madness.'

The 'Pigden test' wasn't infallible, of course. Former Arsenal and England international midfielder David Rocastle, now with Chelsea, started his career for Turnham when he was eight – in goal.

'He was very brave, and big for his age – but never a bully,' remembers Syd. 'The year he played in goal was when we conceded the fewest ever. The following year he came up to me in his third year and said, "Please sir, can I play on the field?" I agreed, but I tell you I was a bit downcast. He was such a good 'keeper. And of course playing out he was a revelation! Central midfield in front of the centre half. Always capable of bursting through. A natural. And he would always work on his bad foot on that little bit of grass next to the school with the other kids.'

That strip of greenery, no bigger than twenty metres by ten, was also where Ian and the others would labour away at team tactics.

'Ian wasn't the brightest of lads but he would obey orders. The orders were, "You'll stay on the halfway line." And the defence had orders, because he was small and fast, to get it over the opposition's heads, landing in that no man's land between the penalty area and the halfway line.

'And could Ian go! He got so he was able to see his defender's boot drawing back, and would start his run. That's how he perfected the timing you see now. We used to practise it on the little bit of green next to the school. Or else I'd take them there and you'd have the same two boys and go through five different types of corner kicks. Drills are the secret of any success. Ian always listened; he was keen to learn. Somebody was interested in him, you see.'

Syd's eyes water with delight when he thinks back to Little Ian's footballing assets. 'They were the same qualities he's got now,' he enthuses. 'Hunger, electric pace, putting the ball in the net: this business of going up to the goalkeeper, going into the penalty area and putting the ball in.

'It's surprising how few children can actually do that faced by a goalkeeper. You give an average school team a penalty each, I guarantee only three will score. But Ian was the master of it.'

One on one, Ian had nerves of steel that belied his small stature. A cool operator. He modelled himself on the insatiable German poacher Gerd Müller, 'The Bomber', destroyer of the English and shooting star in the World Cups of 1970 and 1974 (which Germany won largely through Müller's contribution).

The kids would call any precocious goal bandit 'a Müller'. Ian admired his surgical precision. The stocky German barely contributed except in the penalty box. He was a 'finisher', and that's how Ian still chooses to describe himself. Young Ian loved the buzz of scoring like nothing else. It was him against another lad, a bigger lad, and Ian would 'mash' him, proving himself every time.

It could be hard work ensuring a good turnout every Saturday morning. Football wasn't always a priority. Rows and squabbles, loud parties and banging of doors formed the night-time soundtrack on the block. 'Knowing the Honor Oak Estate,' says Syd, 'if they'd had a bad night, stopped up to watch a cowboy film or whatever, they wouldn't show in the morning.'

But nothing could divert Syd from his task. Professional managers have to win. As a school master Syd didn't. Even so, he didn't see the point in having a game without an end in sight and his boys were drilled to their maximum potential.

'If that's not sportsmanship,' says Syd, 'I can't help that.' But none of the boys ever complained. And some of them, notably Ian, David Rocastle and Steven Anthrobus, would thank him for their sporting careers.

Turnham may not have had a playing field of their own but they regularly used the Honor Oak sports ground. It's always been the uneasy bedfellow of a neighbouring cemetery, which hogs a little bit more of the green blanket each year: the dead depriving the living. Once one of the boys had a new football boot thrown over the dividing fence; it landed in a grave while a funeral ceremony was being conducted.

But the ground wasn't always available, so Ian and the rest of the team's greatest moments were spread all over the surrounding area: Downham playing fields, Blackheath, nearby parks like Ladywell, Beckenham and Mountsfield. These were Ian's killing fields. And he could destroy a team almost single-handedly.

The striker himself recalls an early episode in his footballing career, when he was playing up a few years for his brother's team. He remembers feeling honoured to be playing at such an exalted level, and also scoring a goal that would have billowed the net, had there been one. There wasn't, and to this day it remains a source of mild regret.

Then there was the occasion in one cup run when Ian's Turnham team were toiling against a powerful wind. It wasn't a particularly strong Turnham side that year, the first year Ian really played, when he was ten.

Turnham were one-down after their centre half skied a clearance and it drifted over his own static goalie's head into the full-sized goal. 'Watching that Zaragoza game and seeing David Seaman's mistake, I can't really blame my keeper,' smiles Syd.

A little later, they were two-down when the ball bobbled over Turnham's disheartened keeper as he stooped to gather a shot. At half time, Syd reminded his troops that the wind was in their favour this half.

'And I told our full backs: "Straight over the centre half's head." I didn't need to say anything to Ian. Ian was so goal-hungry, if half a chance came up, he'd gobble it. I won't say he scored every time, but he'd go for it.

'You couldn't stop him running; but the great thing was to keep him onside. Which was why I specified he stay on the halfway line. If he got a good start he could still outrun most centre halves, much like he can today. And his great facility was finding the net virtually every time. 95 times out of 100.'

And so that day the ball was sent sailing over into no man's land like a World War I missile. Boy 'keepers weren't smart enough to come out and would stay rooted to the line like Subbuteo goalies. Early on, Ian latched on to one.

'Big ball up the middle. Big bounce, off Ian went. Goal,' chuckles Syd.

Next a miscued drop-kick hit the opposing centre back's head and Ian buried the loose ball. It was reminiscent of more recent moments in his professional career, such as his all-time great super-sub appearance for Palace against Manchester United in the 1990 FA Cup Final.

But in extra time back in the early seventies, young Ian Wright finished off the show in a fashion even he was unable to repeat at Wembley all those years later, laying on the winning goal after careering out towards the left-hand corner flag and crossing it over for an easy conversion – just as he did, many years later, for Alan Shearer in England's 4-0 stuffing of Turkey.

Ian was proud to wear the Turnham kit: white shirts with a blue band, royal blue continental shorts, blue and white socks; a classy strip bought from Club Sports on the Old Kent Road when Turnham were in the final of the Invicta Cup. It was pretty washed out by the time Ian wore it, but the club colours were unmistakable: it was a Millwall replica kit.

In fact Ian, in common with most of his friends, supported his local team and set his heart on playing for them. He even went to see them a couple of times, but didn't like the atmosphere, for reasons that will become clear later.

This early experience puts into perspective the more recent run-ins with the belligerent fans from the Den. Later events would bring the feud into even sharper focus. In the meantime, Ian embarked on an uninhibited love affair with football.

Show me the boy, the public schools used to say, and I'll show you the man. In Ian Wright's case, too, there was definitely something in the maxim. Andy Massey, former Millwall player, now with Fisher Athletic, grew up on the same estate as Ian. Though he was two years older and attended a different school, Andy sees little he can't recognise from those early satchel-swinging days, playing football at the after-school club.

'When I see him on the telly,' he says, 'I can picture him 25 years ago, messing about, jumping and running and all that. That is exactly how he used to be when I used to see him, even when he was eight. *Exactly* the same.'

For Syd Pigden, there's nothing surprising about it: 'How would they change? People like him are natural-born players. You hone it but you can't give it to him. You can't take him as a schoolboy and say, "I'm going to make you an England player." Whatever your attributes are as a schoolboy, you carry them through and they get better. But you wouldn't change them.'

Except for one thing.

'This business of discipline now,' Syd shakes his head. 'Back in those days, once he started to get goals doing as he was told, that was the carrot – you didn't need the stick.'

But one important aspect of Ian's character had already emerged: temper. Kids on the estate were already aware of his tough side.

'But when the trouble started, Ian would drift quietly away,' says one of his estate peers. 'See him now and he seems to have lost that. Maybe he's a bit more self-confident. But he was tiny as a kid, and if violence was threatened he knew he'd come off worse; when it appeared aggro was going to start, Ian would melt away.'

Still, with big older brother Morris as an example, Ian put himself about a bit on the estate. When he was an older player at Turnham, Ian and the others would impose their seniority on their younger spars. David Rocastle recounts a typical scene, where, before being chosen for the school team, Ian and other boys would cajole him into playing in goal – or rather to be cannon fodder – while the bigger lads practised their shooting.

Within the school's environs, discipline wasn't really a problem as far as Ian was concerned. He had fights in the playground, lost his cool, like any other boy. No better, no worse.

In the classroom, it was a case of 'No trouble; no interest'. But Ian wasn't the troublemaker, the 'Wright Nutter' he's often made out to be in the tabloid press today. When the teacher was talking, he would sit there and mostly do what he was told apart from the occasional minor tantrum or disruptive jestering.

In fact, teachers and pupils remember Ian as a very happy and positive boy. Yet he always had that will to succeed, and it was that facet of his character that would get him into trouble: 'I *will*, I will!' – sometimes, he'd get angry and frustrated.

Compared to some at Turnham, though, he was an angel. There was one schoolmate of his called Reggie who was always probing the cracks in a teacher, going as far as he was entitled to go and then a little bit further to see how much he could get away with.

Once Reggie attacked a helper in the playground because she took a piece of string away from him that he was slapping girls' legs with. He jumped up, both hands on her throat, feet in her stomach. Later, Reggie became a feature of Ian and Patrick's little gang. It was an early example of how Ian was attracted to danger, would flirt with trouble, court it, but never get involved with it himself.

'My great ethic in life was I realised how little these children and parents had,' Syd says. 'The one thing they did have was their dignity. So under no circumstances would you take that away. I tried not to make clever remarks: "Oh I see you've got your sister's shoes on today, George ..." You'd deal with it more delicately.'

Turnham's intake is still 'poor'. Sixty-five per cent of the children qualify for free school meals. But it's well-resourced and very orderly. Sport and discipline are its fortes. The school ethos has always leaned more towards good behaviour than producing geniuses: 'self-esteem' and 'self-reliance' are keywords.

One of Syd Pigden's responsibilities was the running of 'withdrawal' classes in a hut above the staff room. To the teachers it was the 'sin bin'; to Syd and his boys and girls, it was 'The Sanctuary'. Ian was a very occasional visitor, others like Reggie were regular fixtures.

'The Sanctuary was for any child who couldn't get on. Any child who came to school a bit upset – mum had a new baby, dad had clumped her during the night, sister had stolen a toy; anything that warranted tears, they could come to the Sanctuary. All they had to do was ask if they could go to Mr Pigden's class.'

As well as those cases, there were the hyperactive ones who would disrupt every lesson, who would appear before Syd clasping a note from the teacher, 'Will you look after so-and-so, he's driving me mad.'

Syd's primary activity wasn't to teach his charges facts, but to get them to relate to social life, to be decent citizens. Each class took the assembly once a term, and Syd's Sanctuary kids were no different. Under his resolute but kindly tutelage the biggest thug in the class would quite happily stand up and lead the prayers.

'It's an awful thing,' says Syd, 'but a lot of children are misunderstood and no one bothers to understand them till it's ingrained – I'm not saying I "rescued" a lot of them. I used to say to the mother, "He's on a railway line and it leads straight to crime, and I can't see any way of derailing him." And some of them did end up in prison; there's no point in denying they did.

'You've got to have something in your life. If you're going to trawl the streets in a group attacking people, you're not going to spend a few nights in a prison and retain your dignity.'

There was never any danger of Ian ending up that way. Even if he found it hard to concentrate in class, he was never going to go too far astray. For one thing, he was a sensitive child, and would cry if it was brought home to him how he'd upset teachers or other children. It was clear that much of his toughness and bad temper was bravado, a need to prove himself, and perhaps it still is.

Ironically, given the sort of press Ian receives in football today, the sport had a steadying influence on the young boy, just as the school hoped.

'You have to accept that not all your children are highly academic,' says Ian's former teacher Denise Dance, now Turnham's deputy head. 'And what we try very hard to do is find the thing that the kids are good at, the thing they're interested in – whether it's football or netball or reading or writing or maths – and try and make them reach their potential in that.

'Now if that happens to be football, that's great; if it happens to be science, that's great. We don't make any value judgement. For some children, playing in a team has so many social connotations, it's social education. In an area like this, that is ever so important.'

Denise encountered that view on her very first day at Turnham in the early seventies. She was taking a young class and asked Syd Pigden for some maths equipment. He returned to her holding a crate with milk bottle tops in it. 'Teach them how to count,' he said. 'That's all they'll need.'

'And he was right,' says Denise.

Ian was well-adjusted. No matter how much it pained him, he never moaned because his dad wasn't around, and he never complained when he was kept off and had to miss school to look after one of the other children. As a kid on the estate you accepted these things. It was normal. And Ian always had a supportive family; somewhat extended, but always supportive. Two or three friends of Ian's had similar home circumstances. It was no big thing.

Nevertheless a restlessness was building up in Ian, an ambition that couldn't find expression in the classroom; it had to find a way out somehow. Even from an early age, though he never told anyone outside the family, Ian had set his heart, like thousands, perhaps millions of boys around the country, on making it as a professional footballer. It was the only skill he could conceive of moulding into a career.

Nesta, like many of the hard-pushed mothers around Honor Oak, was happy that Ian was behaving well at school. She had respect for education but little academic ambition for her son. She had tried to instil a work ethic in Ian, or at least a regard for the teacher's position: 'Your teacher told you off, and you needed to be told off.'

She wanted the best for her children. For her, Ian's football was a secondary thing. Like most who knew him, until Ian shot up in his late teens, Nesta didn't realise how good he was at football, or how good he could be. If he wasn't being a problem at school, and if football was responsible for that, then she was delighted.

But it wasn't a proper trade; it was a passing phase. Black men grew up and found a decent trade: plasterer or electrician. And Ian was never smart enough to be a doctor or a lawyer. But for now, let him play. Responsibility would come soon enough – perhaps even sooner than he thought.

These days, Nesta is no longer a prominent figure in the black community of Honor Oak. When Ian had made a success of his football career and money, for the first time in his life, was no longer tight, he offered to buy her a home. She had already moved back to Forest Hill, and Ian bought her house from the council.

Others have stepped into Turnham School to assume the mantle Ian, David Rocastle, Steve Anthrobus and others once wore; retiring head Rick Ridzewcki (an FA coaching badge holder who has the distinction of once refereeing Gary Lineker and David Nish) and his second in command Denise Dance will always provide the means for them to express themselves in sport.

The school is now grant-maintained – a policy designed to keep it as a special asset of the community. It is unique in the area. They are more democratic these days as far as sport is concerned: anyone who wants to play is allowed to join a team, and there's also a girls' football team. The motto is, 'if you bother for the cream, you bother for everyone else'. Ian was part of the crème de la crème during his time at Turnham.

When he left the place, Syd Pigden sent a note to the head at his new school, Samuel Pepys, over the railway line in New Cross. It alerted the teacher to the presence of a special footballing talent: 'Look out for him', it advised.

Syd had written many of these before, and with as much conviction as experience would permit. Once the children left his influence, he felt, anything could happen. Then they'd have to make their own way to training, choose their own crowd to run with, find other (perhaps less worthwhile) pastimes.

That probably says as much about Syd's paternalism, his humanity and concern for 'his boys' as it does about the average child's transition to secondary school. You couldn't lump together all those kids. They were individuals. They all responded differently to their new circumstances. How would Ian get on?

Syd had his doubts. 'I didn't think he had the stamina to stick with it. There was no father to say, "Look, I'll come down with you." With some boys, yes, you were confident. But after they left me, I couldn't control what they did.'

There was a summer holiday to be spent playing soccer, cricket, mucking around in the backstreets of Brockley with Morris and the older kids, Patrick and his peers, and then came the serious business of secondary school.

Needless to say, a bubbly, sporting pupil like Ian soon made an impact at Samuel Pepys Boys Secondary School. However, some of Syd Pigden's fears were about to be vindicated.

3 Waiting in Vain

'I honestly think Ian needed someone to . . . rule him, for want of a better word. He needed someone who would tell him, "You will not do this . . ." or "You will do this . . .", just to keep him on a tight rein here and there. That is what I always found with him. You had to be on top of him. Not nasty, just firm. And I think he respected it, because he acted on it, did what he had to do or what you told him to do.'

Peter McCarthy, Teacher, Samuel Pepys School

ONCE AGAIN, Morris had preceded Ian at school and, as they worked their way through the years, the older brother kept paving the way for Ian in the playground. The boys at Pepys were lively and belligerent, but there was still a sense of order to the place.

Morris was something of a bad boy: small, cool and brooding. He was part of the 'in' crowd of tough kids who would dominate the culture of Samuel Pepys Boys School, the side the teachers rarely saw. To be blunt, he was a hard kid; it was the easiest way to thrive in the roughest school in the area.

Just before Ian joined, Sam Pepys had a reputation as a 'sink' school: the last educational establishment on the list for your child – hardly a tribute to the great Southwark man of letters it was named after. The school tended to pick up the children who hadn't managed to get in anywhere else from the Honor Oak estate, Deptford and Peckham. It was also the school with the highest ratio of black, Turkish and Chinese pupils: around 60% of the intake in Ian's time.

Years ago there were, reportedly, stabbings outside the school gates, and the racial ferment which surrounded Pepys in the seventies was ever-present throughout the decade. But Pepys represented a pocket of calm in the eye of the storm.

In the mid-nineties, since the education authority panicked over its falling roll, Samuel Pepys has become an amalgamated school. Collingwood Girls moved in in 1980 and the new combination was called Hatcham Wood. In Ian's day, Collingwood girls used to like to think they could beat up the boys from Pepys; it was that sort of area. The young ladies the lads really feared, though, were from neighbouring Catford. But that's a different story . . .

Hatcham Wood School still occupies the building Ian Wright once attended. Teachers use the fact to their advantage. It'll silence any room of pubescent teenagers to hear that 'Ian Wright used to sit at that desk'. Ian Wright! *Wow*. There is hope.

The playground where he scuffed his brand new shoes remains. Even a few of those who taught him are still there . . . most, it must be said, remember him fondly. For a so-called 'trouble' school, that says a lot.

Hatcham Wood has a symbiotic relationship with its neighbourhood. In return for their help, it co-operates with police and the local community on schemes to clamp down on truancy, vandalism, drugs and racial discrimination.

On the school notice board, next to information about Hatcham Wood pupils' Crime Prevention panel (which has successfully campaigned to close a pub notorious for drug dealing) is information about a poetry competition. It's an unusual school.

And it's always been that way. Even in Ian's days, the seething seventies, racially-motivated disputes were remarkably rare. Contemporaries recall only one, in the mid-seventies, around the time of the TV series *Roots*: a black kid was told by a snarling white peer to 'Fetch, Kunta Kinte!' when a tennis ball ran astray in the playground. Naturally, other types of skirmishes were commonplace.

As Ian worked his way through the years, Pepys' reputation and the self-image of its pupils steadily improved under the firm hand of its headmaster Richard Cleal. His school was run along traditional lines with pockets of 'progressive' active learning. There was a fairly structured response to the local community in geography and science, for example. And there was also an after-school youth club called Spiral, where classes, meetings, games and discos went on until seven or eight in the evening.

Although it was an all-boys school, Pepys pupils had a busy social life. The lads would meet girls at a youth club by the railway bridge, where the kids would peel off into cliques of black and white, or at dances organised through the school. Ian was still

inseparable from his brother Morris and Patrick Robinson, who
suddenly grew at the age of fifteen into a strapping kid who dwarf-
ed his cousin.

They would hang around in a little gang together around Turnham, or the backstreets of Brockley, playing football or scrumping
apples. Brockley was a place to meet, especially at the top of Pepys
Hill. They used to get into scrapes. 'We never got into any real
bother,' Ian told the *Sunday Mirror*. 'We'd go scrumping, Dennis
the Menace stuff like that, but mostly, we did a lot of running,
didn't we Pat?'

'Yeah, running away!' responded Patrick. 'We were always having to leg it because of Reggie, right?'

Reggie was the Turnham kid who once attacked a teacher. Why
were nice boys like Ian and Patrick hanging around with a troublesome kid like that? Morris could handle it, but Ian, wasn't he the
one who always slunk away from tribulation?

The point is that, with his tendency to get vexed and stroppy,
Ian needed people like Morris and Reggie around to look after
him. One day, though, Reggie took things too far. It was one of
those confrontations around the Honor Oak estate that was always happening, except this time Reggie chose to have a go at one
of the members of the biggest, most dangerous family in the area.
The kind of people you don't want to have a vendetta with. Not
on any account.

Reggie was downright difficult. He kicked up a rumpus with the
lad, started a fight and ended up dealing him a serious butt on the
head, so hard you thought the kid's brains were going to spill out.

Luckily, Ian and the others weren't there to be sucked in, but it
might have been enough that they were guilty by association with
Reggie. Like these things do, though, the whole episode eventually
blew over.

There were, of course, better organised distractions like the
Pepys discos. Eric Summers, head of sports, was sometimes up for
one if they'd all behaved themselves. The boys would have plan-
ned ahead: 'Eric, man, let's have a party', they'd chide, especially
after basketball games. Shooting the hoop had its agreeable spin-
offs.

Come semi-final or finals time each year, local girls would come and eye up the talent while crowding on to the small viewing bench or hanging off the climbing frames that bordered the court. There was often a party afterwards for them to get to know each other better.

The school became well-known in the area for its discos and for bringing in the girls from nearby Collingwood or Edghill. Ian, with his gift of the gab and flamboyant personality, was never backward in coming forward where girls were concerned.

Pepys was a highly unusual, one-off establishment, though it must be said discipline underpinned everything. In the staff room, it was more of a family than a group of colleagues. The headmaster, Richard Cleal, used to work at the Windmill Theatre as a comedian, but there was nothing whimsical about the way he ran his school.

With each new intake, he'd have all the parents and the children in the assembly and really cut it hard on them. The children would emerge long-faced. After that, whenever they saw Mr Cleal, it was, 'Yes, Mr Cleal . . . no, Mr Cleal'. No one considered testing Mr Cleal's resolve.

In those days, teachers could cane – as Ian was to discover to his cost every now and then. For the first couple of weeks, Mr Cleal walked the corridors with the bamboo deterrent. That set the pattern; pupils knew what to expect.

Once, in Richard Cleal's office, a parent was called in to hear the litany of misdemeanours committed by his son. His temper boiled over. He grabbed the cane off Cleal's desk and set about meting out his own punishment to his son, handing the stick back in several pieces to the startled head.

Another time, an ex-pupil paying a visit happened to see his nephew giving a teacher a hard time. He dived into the classroom and began clouting the boy in front of the whole class, demanding he behave himself.

Understandably, then, the boys soon learned that if Eric Summers or his colleague Peter McCarthy said they were going round to their house to have a word with their parents, they'd prefer the teacher to cane them on the spot rather than risk the unpredictable wrath of their parents.

But parental interest in schooling – a prerequisite for success in the eyes of most educationalists – was often impossible to stimulate. At Pepys, you either had that rare species of overprotective parents, who would never stay out of the school – few and far between – or those whom you never saw, even on parents' evenings when they were supposed to come up and talk to the teachers.

No teacher ever saw Nesta at the school. As far as she was concerned, Ian had never been the sharpest tool in the shed; as long as he wasn't being suspended or sent home, as long as he was working hard, doing reasonably well and behaving himself, she was content.

Ian's interest in lessons was sporadic. Nevertheless, in the school streaming system he ranked just inside the top half of his year. He never needed remedial work and he certainly wasn't unintelligent.

In fact, he was useful at English, showed an aptitude for Maths and was pretty good at History as well. But if he'd set his mind to it, he would have been good at almost anything. More recently, Ian has publicly regretted the fact that he was too busy clowning, playing the fool and trying to attract attention to himself to achieve his full potential at school.

Back then he had different priorities. As they seemed for many boys, the lessons were too long and the playtimes were far too short. Ian invested all of his energy in football. He was often bored stiff in class, kicking his heels under the desk. For pastoral purposes, Ian had been placed in Newton House, but there's no doubt if the apple had landed on *his* head, he would have buried it in the top corner rather than analyse the effects of gravity.

The playground at Pepys was small and vociferous: a lot of Ian's ability was picked up on that tarmac battleground. There were fifty games going on in a relatively small area; fifty tennis balls flying round, kids ducking in and out of each other; bang bang, 'Whaaa!' Day in, day out.

You learn fast with a ball that size: agility, balance and how to elude the other person, possibly a careering fifth former with the momentum of a water buffalo. You can't coach things like that on a full-size pitch.

Morris, a decent footballer, though making a name for himself as a cricketer at Pepys, distinguished himself in other ways at playtime. One of the favourite pastimes of his gang (or 'posse') was called 'boots'.

During break, the boys would kick the ball up against a fence, playing 'spot'. If you lobbed the ball over by mistake, Morris and his cronies would encourage the other players to kick you against the wall, until the ball came back. Unfortunately, the jeopardy was doubled by the lowness of the fence.

While Morris was around no one messed with Ian, who quietly latched on to his brother's coat-tails, until he found his feet in the new environment. But there was more to it than that: 'Morris was definitely a bad guy,' reveals a former classmate, 'and Ian possibly suffered because of that.' Nesta's boys were earning reputations, but they weren't academic ones.

Little had changed with the arrival at secondary school, except that Ian was more self-confident. He was still small. 'Ian wasn't small, actually: he was *tiny*,' corrects another of his school friends. The old adage – watch out for mouthy midgets – increasingly applied.

Ian had taken steps to compensate for his stature in several ways. Apart from the verbal dexterity that could reduce a class to fits of giggles or the wit that could burn off an enemy in the playground, Ian decided he needed to learn to look after himself properly. After all, there were two Chinese kids in Ian's year who were noticeably left alone after they claimed mastery of kung-fu.

In pursuit of that goal, for a while he attended a boxing club in Peckham attached to St Thomas The Apostle Church run by Stan Turner, now a newsagent.

According to Stan, Ian never boxed for the club as has been claimed elsewhere, though Ian's other suggestion that he didn't enjoy being hit is confirmed. He used to attend largely for fitness training. However, he's been a fan of the sport for years. And as Nigel Benn is the cousin of his great friend, Manchester United's Paul Ince, Ian has attended plenty of bouts.

Of course, at the time Ian dabbled in it, boxing was considered to provide a boy with moral strength. It was thought that the mental discipline and rigorous physical aspects of the sport were exactly what those 'deprived' lads needed. (A 'proper' career, of course, was out of the question for the likes of them.)

Nowadays, churches have had to move with prevailing medical opinion and ban boxing as being too dangerous. The boxing club closed in 1991. Nevertheless, it helped Ian learn how to look after himself.

'Ian was a bit of a bad boy, to be honest,' opines Stan. 'He was one of those who'd do whatever was necessary. He wasn't particularly bright. He wasn't stupid, make no mistake about it; he was there or there abouts.

'But if he'd wanted to he could have been a lot better, without a shadow of a doubt. He stuck around with the wrong crowd.'

That's not exactly how all the teachers at Pepys remember it. Inside the school, Ian didn't mix with the really nasty guys. The profs knew who the evil ones were. And admittedly Ian knew them – they all knew each other – and he was even slightly attracted to the 'glamour' of badness. But he wasn't going down the wrong road.

'He could be very moody, very sullen. But he was a very funny kid; you could have a laugh and a joke with him,' says Peter McCarthy, sports instructor, then teacher at Samuel Pepys.

There were others who occasionally saw in his aloof, haunted young face, mouth hung in an insolent pout, a malice that wasn't there; however everyone preferred the moments when Ian's eyes would crease with joy into ecstatic slits, and the immense smile dominated his face. He had a hell of a smile, and he used it a lot.

Ian was half cheek, half wit. If he was in the right mood, he'd have everyone laughing with the things he did. He enjoyed mickey-taking and having little pots at people – something his fellow professionals are now very familiar with.

Ian always had plenty of chat; perhaps too much. He would get into trouble for answering back, and as one of the best known lads in the school – he had groups of friends from each of the many sports at which he excelled – Ian was often chastised for leading others on.

'There was just one phase when he was having a great deal of problems,' says Peter McCarthy. 'It was about his third or fourth year. That was a time when he went through a [tricky] period. But there were a couple of times I was asked would I have a word with him. And we'd just go for a little walk and sort it out.

'If we did have a little chat – things weren't going right – he'd listen. I think it meant something to him. It got through to him, because I never had any problems with him. And for a while he would go back to wherever he was and calm down and get on with whatever he was doing.

'The kids looked up to the teachers. They knew how far they could go with you, they knew that the teachers cared for them. They look for someone, I'm sure these boys do.

'Ian needed a father figure. He needed someone to ... well, rule him, for want of a better word. He needed someone who would tell him, "You will *not* do this ..." or "You *will* do this ..." just to keep him on a tight rein here and there.

'That is what I always found with him. You had to be on top of him. Not nasty, just firm. And I think he respected it, because he acted on it, did what he had to do.'

English and Drama master Bob Hubbard remembers a similar child: 'He wasn't what you might call a high-flyer, but he did like school. He was always lively, very keen; he wasn't one of those kids who liked to shirk the issue and not do any work. And we knew Ian was trying, but his first love was football. That showed through in most of what he did.

'As he is now, he was quite witty, though I wouldn't say he was particularly known as a piss-taker. He was never a problem in terms of discipline. There was caning at the school, but I don't think Ian ever got caned – he was too fast! I can't forget him; you never forget someone like that. He was agile of mind and body.'

Nevertheless, other teachers would say he could be a nuisance, that he could be moody and disruptive. Maybe that's because Nesta had constructed self-belief in her boys to such a formidable extent.

With a dismissive stare, Ian could make teachers feel they were a low priority on his list of affairs. They were irrelevant; why didn't they stop bothering him? In his teens, Ian already appeared self-contained, with an air of brashness.

It was a matter of how you handled him. Some of his friends will tell you Ian was lucky, 'one of those people, because he's so small, or whatever, he always used to get away with it,' chuckles one. 'I'm seeing him at school, and I'm thinking, "That little bugger used to get away with it all the time!"'

There weren't many women teachers in the all-boys school. Ian responded better to men who had a strong personality, took a traditional approach to the teacher-pupil relationship and would keep him on a tight rein, just like Syd Pigden had done at Turnham.

All his life, Ian respected people who respected him. And so it remains to this day. One such figure at Samuel Pepys emerged to take his place alongside Peter McCarthy in Ian's personal pantheon.

Eric Summers is one of south London's unsung heroes. A stiff-backed, clip-voiced man with a powerful presence and a no-nonsense, almost military manner, he was the kind of teacher schools like Pepys found indispensable. After a period of working in Germany, he now works at Dulwich Hamlet Sports Centre.

Eric still sees many of the kids who passed through Pepys. For many of them he was a powerful influence. Not only was he a hugely likeable and impressive man, a superb administrator who helped establish Pepys' national reputation for sport despite facilities that were dispiritingly poor, but he was head of the department, and moreover he was black.

Afro-Caribbean boys were in the majority at Pepys. And Eric was such a positive role model for them; living proof that, despite actual or anecdotal evidence to the contrary in the Britain of the seventies, a black man could make a success of himself on his own terms, and without compromising his identity.

Eric is a pragmatist, no purveyor of political correctness – he left Pepys because he felt the school's 'PC' programme was going too far in placing unsuitable women in the sports department. His views on discrimination are honest and matter-of-fact. It exists; you sort it. What's the big deal?

'If you're looking at racism, you find a lot of West Indians have a bad attitude towards Pakistanis,' he suggests. 'Africans and West Indians too; that cuts both ways.

'That's people for you. It's passed straight down through the parents. When the kid goes out, he thinks he can say what his old man says. The difference is these West Indian kids ain't gonna hang around, they're gonna thump him one. That's why people really don't pick on West Indians, because they're immediately far more aggressive, even too aggressive towards each other.

'In those days, most West Indian parents had suffered racism, but they wouldn't say it to their kids. Mine never did. They just treated people the way they liked to be treated. But I know of incidents . . . my wife won't tell me what some people say, because she knows I'm likely to go round and thump them.'

Henry Laville, one contemporary of Ian Wright's who benefited from Eric's nurturing, still marvels at the teacher's significance to Ian and his peers: 'I honestly don't think, even today, Eric realises what an influence he was. A school teacher's a school teacher, but to have your school teacher's number and to be talking to him 25 years later like he's an uncle . . .

'Everybody respected him. He was the man. I've got four brothers ten years apart, and all of us had the same sports teacher: Eric Summers. He's the sort of man who wouldn't realise that there's probably about 2,000 black people out there saying, "Yeah, Eric . . ." ' Henry smiles and nods his head in respect. ' "Eric, man." Ian would echo that too. There's nothing high enough you could say about Eric, because he's brought us all on.'

Eric modestly plays things down. 'I think basically because I was black and they could see I was head of the department, maybe there was a bit of rubbing off and they felt they could do it.'

Eric was at Samuel Pepys for about twelve years, eight of them as head of department. Through a strict regime enforced by five sports teachers, each with specialist areas, he established Pepys as a national force, especially in basketball, his main interest.

'We were fairly well-disciplined,' he says. 'We put ourselves out for them. We put our hands in our pockets when they were short of money for bus fare. We were like a family, my department. Then again, I can say that we weren't short of thumping a few of them when they stepped out of line.

'They knew that we meant what we said. They knew if they ponced around in class they weren't getting out of class to go play football matches.'

Misbehaviour was always firmly dealt with. Eric wasn't scared to use the cane, but he'd give you a fair crack of the whip first. His coaching technique was softly-softly. He'd call you over and quietly tell you what to do. No great bellowing; his sheer presence was enough. And you'd try to carry out what he said.

But Eric made a lot of things happen that weren't strictly according to the rules. For instance, the school gym was out of bounds outside allotted hours, yet Eric would still have them all down there at lunchtime.

There they were: boys buzzing around the forbidden gym, playing basketball with their long trousers on, playing for Eric, sweating up in their shirts and trousers for an hour, and then trooping off to class dripping with perspiration.

Eric gave respect and expected it in return. Ian was one of the boys who best responded to Eric's powerful presence. 'He was a bit frisky,' recalls Eric. 'He was like any kid: if they like you, they work for you. Even the smallest ones. It's so important to them.'

To some of the boys, many of whom were brought up by their mothers alone, Eric was a surrogate father. 'I could have had that effect on a lot of the kids because I was head of the department,' shrugs Eric now, 'and, yeah, I put myself out for them. It was tough – my wife never saw me. I enjoyed myself there. It was a one-off school. I don't think you'd have another one like it.'

Despite the handicap of only having a small basketball court, and against accepted notions of what a rough school from a deprived area can achieve, Eric took his team to four all-England finals, though unfortunately they won none of them.

Two of the best sportsmen at the club stood out in the basketball team of Ian's year: Henry Laville and Keith McPherson, both of whom were knocking six foot at the age of fifteen. 'All of those kids could leap,' recalls Eric. 'I had a kid, 5'8", could dunk. Locksley White – he could fly. When he jumped you thought he was going to stay up there! But that was it; that was the mentality of the kids then.'

Ian played too, as a 'second-sixer' – a sub. He was one of the smallest players at Pepys – just over five foot tall when he left school – but he was a star of the inter-form games, even if he never made it into the more testing matches between schools.

Basketball is an enthusiasm he retains to this day, watching the NBA games whenever he can, sharing his thoughts on the matches with David Rocastle, another devotee of the sport. To this day, it remains Ian's great ambition to be able to slam-dunk.

'He was quick, but he dribbled too much,' summarises Eric.

'Basketball's a bit like football; if you don't dribble, after a while you begin to get the hang of when to let it go rather than hang on to it. Ian's first love was football. Totally. He never really dug deep into his basketball.'

Even as a second-sixer, though, Ian was treated to some inspirational experiences. Any time there was a decent match at Crystal Palace – say against a good team like Maccabi of Tel-Aviv – Eric would take his team.. 'And as soon as they came back all they wanted to do was dunk,' smiles Eric.

Another time Eric took the team – Ian included – to see the famed showbiz stars of the Harlem Globetrotters, with japester Meadowlark Lemon among them. 'Now a lot of people say, "Load of crap",' says Eric. 'Bullshit! Let them go up there and it fires the imagination. They come back and the things they try and do!'

Beyond the sheer glory of taking part, sport provided something more practical for the Pepys boys. 'Sport opened a lot of their eyes up,' believes Eric. 'And it took kids out of a totally black environment, took them elsewhere. We used to travel with the basketball team all the way to Liverpool and places. We went up on the train, and the funny effect we had on people . . . Chap walked up to me and said, "Are you from Samuel Pepys school?" I said, "Yeah". He said, "Oh, I'm really pleased to meet you, I've heard so much about you up here . . ."

'I was thinking, "Bloody hell!" We don't even get this sort of effect in our own school area, or London, but someone in Liverpool knows everything about us and can't wait to watch us play. Mind boggling!'

Eric loved the school, troubled though it was in many ways. He had five people working with him who all gave the same sort of time: Saturday mornings for school matches; Thursdays for the best kids in district games.

'We even had a kid who got a yachting medal for England down at Surrey Docks after it opened up,' Eric marvels. Even before Eric started at the school, they'd had a boy who went on to throw javelin for Britain. For many, sport was the greatest gift Pepys could provide.

Ian's football master at Pepys was Peter McCarthy, an ex-

Thames lighterman with an FA Coaching certificate who had played for Bexleyheath and Welling. He joined the school as a games instructor, then studied at Avery Hill for his formal teaching qualifications.

'The kids were rough, they were naughty and they were villains, but I found it an excellent school,' he avers.

Ian arrived among the initial batch in Peter's first year at Pepys. When the boys turned up for games for the first time, they were asked who played football and who did other sports.

Then Peter asked who wanted to play for the first-year side. A number would confidently step forward. Each, it seemed was the best player – captain even – of their primary school side. But there are primary schools and primary schools. Large secondary schools are quite a bit different.

Through observation, the teachers would gradually sort the wheat from the chaff – a simple matter of eliminating those who couldn't play. Peter wanted willing boys who could play football, and who would reliably turn up every Saturday morning or mid-week evening. Quality was a scarcer commodity.

There was also a distinct lack of sports grounds to accommodate them. The group Ian was in at first had to travel out to one several miles away in Epsom, Surrey, on a double decker bus. Once you'd got there, got them changed and given them a ball, it was time to go home.

Things improved when the school was allowed to use Avery Hill sports ground, but not much – there was still barely an hour in which to do anything. Skill-training under such constraints was impossible.

During the late spring, Pepys was allowed to use Crystal Palace for athletics. One day they arrived to find a Dutch football side were over there training to play a London club in a European competition. Peter McCarthy urged his boys, 'Get changed quickly, and we'll go down and watch them on the five-a-side pitch.'

The Dutch players emerged form the dressing room, and their coach unloaded several bags of balls. Each player took a ball and began flicking it up, controlling it and tightly running around with it. The Pepys kids were mesmerised.

But they had to break off for a games lesson. Peter promised them as soon as it was over, if they were quick, they could watch the Dutchmen again for five or ten minutes at the end when they would be playing five-a-side.

Nearly an hour later, teacher and boys returned. 'But what were they doing?' quizzes Peter, still impressed. 'It was still one ball, one man, kicking it up against the wall of the five-a-side, working on their ball skills. I said to the kids, "You come down here and see Millwall or Crystal Palace out there, all they're doing is seeing who can run the fastest round the track, and who can last the longest."

'All the time we were down there, I don't think I ever saw them [the London clubs] with the ball; last ten minutes for a five-a-side perhaps. Always shuttle runs and that. I often used to remind the kids of what they saw that day.' As one of the best ball-jugglers of his generation, Ian obviously took note.

Spurred on by such lessons, Peter assembled a reasonable team, and Ian was one of them. From the outset, it was clear he was inordinately keen. And as long as he and the others enjoyed – and behaved – themselves, Peter would take them anywhere. Misbehaviour in class also meant suspension from sport, and that was about the worst sanction of all. Ian knew all about that – he always needed someone he respected to keep him in order when he was about to snap.

The boys wore their red and black striped shirts for the school – AC Milan or the Man City away strip, depending on your point of view – with pride. There was no league as such, but lots of friendlies and cup games. As second years, Ian's team won the Blackheath Cup. Then as fourth years, during their final fling together, Peter's protégés reached the final again. It was played miles away in Clapton against an east London school. Pepys lost 2-1, despite Ian's presence.

A settled, successful side played through each year of Ian's schooling, built around a nucleus of Ian himself, Keith McPherson and Henry Laville. Keith was tall and lean, touching six foot like his basketball team-mate Henry Laville, who was built like the proverbial shithouse, but who would always stay out of trouble. Mention Henry's name to Ian, and he would kiss his teeth and say, 'Henry, man, he was one of them boys, he never do nuttin' wrong, man.' Partly because Keith and Henry stayed out of trouble, theirs were the first two names down on Peter's list. Surprisingly, Ian wasn't his number one.

'I always classed Keith as the best player,' confesses Peter. 'Henry was more extrovert on the field. He was a strong defender, but he was everywhere, wanting to be part and parcel of everything. And you noticed him.

'Keith, even as a kid, I classed him like a Beckenbauer. Very quiet, laid it about, just swept up . . . swept up all Henry's mistakes!'

Both big defenders duly made it to the first rung of the professional football ladder. Henry was an associate schoolboy with Charlton, signed professional forms with them and stayed with them for another five fruitless years before drifting out of the game.

Keith was on West Ham's books. He played one first team game, went on loan to Cambridge United – where he played eleven, scoring once – before joining Northampton, for whom he played 182 games. He's now at Reading – he played in the 1995 play-off finals, battling vainly against the victorious Bolton strike force. He has played over 150 games for the Berkshire club.

Ian, though, was the enigma. Henry Laville even feigns surprise that Peter McCarthy counted him in his top three for that year. He's joking, but only slightly. Ian's enduring problem – his size – worked against him when he was still in his teens.

'He wasn't an exceptional player at that time. I've got pictures that if you saw Ian's legs, he's bandy, but bandy in the wrong way – inwards. And because he's built up his top half a bit more these days, and built up his thighs, he doesn't look so bad. But if you saw the pictures I've got of him, well, to be honest, you'd say, "No, he's not a footballer." '

Yet Ian loved football, even if the relationship was not yet fully consummated. He played cricket in the summer, was a decent bowler in a few games. But his heart belonged to soccer. Even if he was played out of position.

Peter McCarthy played Ian on the wing because of his size. 'It was one of the reasons why the others went on to professional clubs, and Ian didn't,' he suggests. 'It was at that time in English football when bigness counted. That's what clubs wanted in those days. If there was a little player, the opposition manager would say, "I want that little fella put into the top row of the stand." And they would do it.'

Strikers weren't 5'2" and slightly built: they were bullish, rock-shinned, bone-headed: Peter Withe, Paul Mariner. You've heard old people use the phrase 'donkeys' years'? Well, that's what the late seventies were . . .

Peter had a job for quite a while getting Ian into the district side. 'He's so small,' was again the refrain. 'Eventually I think I got him into the district side about the third or fourth year,' says Peter. 'He didn't play many times in all honesty.'

The speed and confidence, the willingness to take defenders on, were still there and the mercurial brilliance would occasionally show itself, but the prime asset Syd Pigden had seen in him and cherished at Turnham – the killer instinct in front of goal – was nowhere.

Ian wasn't a great goalscorer for Pepys largely because, in an old-fashioned 2-3-5 formation, he was stuck out as a wide man. But some things hadn't changed since primary school days. 'He used to want to run all over the place,' remembers Peter. 'He was just a busy bee. You used to have to say, "Ian! Ian! Position!"'

'And his temperament; could be surly, or sullen. I would have to stand on the touchline near him: you could tell when he was ready to go. You'd have a word with him, and he'd look. But in those five years I never knew him to get into trouble on the football pitch.'

Ian was already starting to emulate the heroes he and Morris had at the time. Like many black kids, Ian didn't like to go to football grounds. Those who were so obsessed that they went to watch the popular teams in the area at that time – West Ham, Chelsea, Millwall, Palace – were harangued for the company they kept, by the hooting, jeering masses. But this denial of slavish devotion to a single club allowed black kids to be more objective and discerning about their favourites.

Ian was already a keen student and acolyte of certain players. No Afro-Caribbean kid could ignore the dignity and power of Cyrille Regis. And Laurie Cunningham, before he went to Spain, was a hero for his transcendent skills. Nesta would harp on about the 'greatest ever football team', Brazil, but when Ian was in his teens the South American samba kings were going through a bad patch. In 1978, the Argentina side of Kempes, Villa and Ardiles captured schoolkids' imaginations everywhere. The diminutive magician from the Buenos Aires backstreets, Diego Maradona, was yet to make his international mark.

But English football still had its heroes. Even some of its villains were heroes. For Ian Wright, the main man was Stanley 'Stan the man' Bowles, the Manchester City and Queens Park Rangers maverick. Ian admired his ability to play football, his fantastic strikes and his incredible dribbling, but he also had that extra quality, the capacity and willingness to entertain. As Ian was later to do, Stan entered into a dialogue with the fans – not all of it sweet talk. Stan responded to them, and they to him. It was a kind of loving.

Ian also admired Stan's audacity, that impudence bordering on arrogance. Stan always looked as if he knew he was a better player than his adversaries, and he was going to prove it. That is very much Ian's attitude too. There was, obviously, one other major similarity between the two: the temperament.

Stan is now coaching players at Brentford, handing on his exemplary skills to a new generation. He empathises with Ian: 'Somebody said a few weeks ago that I was a big hero of his. I think he's got a similar sort of temperament. They say bad-tempered, but I always say you've got to have that bit of spite in you. It adds something to your game, without a doubt.

'I was naturally bad-tempered; well, you don't like losing, do you? And he's the same. Without my temperament, I don't think I would have been the same player, and I can see the same in him. He's got it in him, hasn't he?'

Naturally, as a veteran flair man from the heyday of Frank Worthington, Peter Osgood, Trevor Brooking *et al*, the off-pitch mythology that shrouded Stan was important to impressionable youngsters. It was said that if he could give as good a body swerve to a boozer or a bookie's as he did to defenders of the time like Terry Mancini, he would've been an even better player. It's said that Stan once missed a kick-off in order to watch a horse he'd backed in the three o'clock come in, running out eight minutes into the game.

Stan had a nasty side, and Ian was fascinated by that in people, especially as he could be hot-headed himself. It was the lure of the bad guy again. Stan had 'edge'; his contemptuous approach would inform the young lad's efforts as he practised those bold Bowles moves and cheeky touches time and again in his street and playground games. Stan's example – proving that the impossible could happen every week – was important to the young striker. Like his idol, Ian was always prepared to shoot the moon.

'He keeps scoring these fantastic goals and they can't all be flukes,' smiles Stan. 'But he's done a couple of curlers like I used to do as well; I've seen him score those little chips that stand out. You can see the similarities there.'

There's a famous *Monty Python* sketch spoofing a TV football show, where the presenter applies pompous philosophical theories, using more long words than a Welsh train journey, to describe a goal by his soccer player guest: 'an almost Proustian display of modern existentialist football'. The footballer's description? 'Well Brian, I hit the ball first time and there it was in the back of the net.' Though obviously a jibe directed at the supposed denseness of footballers, it also said something about the tendency to over-analyse a spontaneous art.

What Ian loved Stan for, his capacity to do something different, has clearly rubbed off on him; that inexplicable, maverick touch. 'Sometimes you'd think, "I want to score a spectacular goal, not just a goal",' says Stan. 'I watched a lot of videos with people working on my new book. And they're saying, "Why did you do that?" And you think, "Cor, that was a good goal", but you can't tell them why you did it.'

Stan had learned his trade in the lower divisions and, like Ian, arrived in the top ranks of the game late, at the age of 23. The Queen's Park Rangers chairman bought him on the strength of one brilliant game for Carlisle as 'the replacement for Rodney [Marsh]'. But when Stan was playing in the Second Division he was always thinking to himself, 'This is easy', just as Ian often told himself in the school team.

'At QPR when I first went,' reveals Stan, 'I felt they were totally inferior to me. I thought it was easy money. So I just went around and did it. By the time I'd got to QPR anyway I wasn't bothered.'

Ian could see physical similarities too. Although Stan was pushing six foot, he never looked like it. His litheness and knack of holding off physically stronger opponents – albeit occasionally with the help of an elbow – gave hope to the slender but spirited everywhere, Ian included.

Just as Ian was dogged by adverse assessments of his stature, so was Stan before him. He gives some idea of the frustration that causes to a lower division player trying to break into the big time: 'Bobby Robson wanted to buy me when he was at Ipswich,' says Stan. 'He told me later the only reason he didn't buy me was because my legs were too thin.'

There were other heroes for the teenage Ian. He admired Cyrille Regis for his power and goalscoring, but also for what he meant to the dreams of youngsters like himself. Laurie Cunningham was another uncompromising black pioneer, closer to the sort of player Ian wanted to become himself. Silkily skilful, fast and lithe as an antelope, Laurie was an attacking midfielder for whom the term 'mercurial' was inadequate. His creative audacity could be breathtaking.

Critics remarked on his slight frame, how a rough opponent could sideline him with a few early, emphatic assaults, and it's true that the leviathans of late-seventies English defences could crock him out of the game. But Laurie's propensity to wind them up in retort was a rare joy in a dullards' era. The fact he was flash, black and – most importantly – an effective demolition man, made him the focus of inane persecution from fans too. They encouraged their gladiators, their hard men, to teach him a lesson.

Lacking the protection referees give to today's skill merchants, Laurie suffered more than his fair share of injuries. That was his greatest weakness, but people in the game nevertheless used his frequent absences to feed the fallacy that black players 'lacked bottle'.

Laurie Cunningham forced his way into the England side at the same time as Viv Anderson – a pioneer who latterly became the Football League's first black club manager at Barnsley.

But Viv was a defender. Little surprise, then, that Laurie became an idol of the teenage Ian Wright. Laurie emerged from Second Division Leyton Orient, the folksiest club in London and the team the whole region has a soft spot for, with their perennial financial imperilment and cultivated football.

His starring roles for the east London side, especially in Orient's brief, sparkling forays in the FA Cup, brought him to the attention of Ron Atkinson at West Bromwich Albion where he established himself as one of the so-called 'Three Degrees' alongside Brendan Batson and, another of Ian Wright's great role models, Cyrille Regis.

Cyrille Regis made his name with West Bromwich Albion and surged into the England reckoning with performances of fluid skill and power. He was acutely aware that on his broad shoulders rested the hopes and fears of any number of young black kids. A few years ago, when Ian was playing against his boyhood hero, during a lull in the match Ian confessed his admiration to the big striker: 'You're my hero,' he gushed. 'I love you.'

'My role models when I started out were people like Brendan Batson and Laurie Cunningham,' says Cyrille. 'In those days, when I first came into the pro game, it was rare to see black players at that level.

'As a young man, I can understand how Ian must have looked at us and thought, "I can do that – be like them." '

Ian would have appreciated the lyrics to one of Jamaican DJ Dennis Alcapone's songs, written as a precursor to England's World Cup Campaign in 1982, and popular in the dancehalls of the day: 'If England want to do some good, gi me no, no gi me no Ron Greenwood/Forget yuh pride and yuh prejudice and carry the man Cyrille Regis/Take out yuh likkle, likkle book, and write down the name Garth Crooks/But if you want to see some skill, then watch the team Brazil.' The song didn't have much success, except in reaffirming the suspicions of black people towards the football hierarchy.

Cyrille is honest enough to suggest that even today racism arrests careers for black footballers. 'But believe me,' he asserts, 'it's nothing compared to what I went through in the seventies. It's different now because most clubs have black players. Some places were worse than others. I used to get some horrendous stick at Leeds. But they've had five or six black players since and it's changed. Of course you had the banana throwing and the chants. I got hate letters through the post too.'

But by far the sickest and most alarming incident happened to Cyrille during what should have been the greatest moment of his life: 'Once,' he recalls, 'I even got sent a bullet before I was due to make my England debut. The note said, "If you step on the Wembley turf the next one will be through your knee."

'It does get better once people think that you can play a bit. But the thing that has really helped is the influx of good young black players over the years. It's dispelled all the myths that they don't like cold weather and all that sort of stuff.

'When all that's happening, you have to love the game to carry on. I had tremendous help from my team-mates at West Brom. Our fans at the Hawthorns were great as well. There was a great camaraderie there, a great spirit in the dressing room, and that definitely helps.'

The achievements of Cunningham and Regis lit the way for black youngsters such as Ian all the way to Europe and the international scene. 'That was a great help to me,' Ian has commented, 'because I would look at their example and say to myself that I could make it as a player as well.'

Cunningham, tragically, was killed in a car crash in Spain. But Cyrille remains an important totem to black footballers of Ian's generation. 'It didn't really take me aback that Ian regarded me as a role model of sorts,' he smiles. 'In fact, it was a great feeling that somebody had come along in my field, and regarded me as some sort of mentor – especially someone of Ian's calibre.'

Even with such icons among his pantheon of stars, in his early days at Pepys, Ian's weekly football ration was down to a minimum. As he strode back home to the estate, he would occasionally pop in to his old school, and often complained that he wasn't playing enough – then he'd join up with the other kids in the Turnham playground in the play centre.

But towards the end of his school years, Ian found another outlet for his soccer skills. Henry Laville played on Sundays for a church side in Deptford called St Paul's.

The instigator of the team was the Reverend Rodney Bomford. It began as an altar boys' side, but, much like the dance hall high up among the church rafters and the licensed bar for adults downstairs, it had been appropriated by the masses, many of whom had never darkened its pews.

'They would always say, "I've got a friend who's much better than little so-and-so who's too young anyway",' relates the Reverend. 'And they'd bring the friend in, and then the friend would know someone even better. So the original ones got edged out.'

By the late-seventies, the club had five teams ranging from under-11s to under-18s. Like the players, not all of the managers were reliable, but one in particular was: a stocky man called Ernie Hutchings, one of many laid-off dockers in this once-thriving maritime area.

For three years from the mid-seventies on, Ernie coached the youngest group to formidable success in the Dominic Savvio league, originally set up by Roman Catholic priests for church teams to play in on Saturdays.

Pragmatism got the better of piety: the organisers saw the light and, by the time Ian Wright had been recommended by friends, matches had moved to Sundays.

He joined an under-13s team in which future Southampton *Wunderkind* Danny Wallace was already something of a star. On the sabbath, Ernie had his hands full trying to round up stragglers in time for the 10.30 kick-off and fend off local scouts drawn to the team like bees to a honey pot; there were other players who seemed just as good as Danny, including Henry. It worked, though. St Paul's were very successful.

'We had a lot of extremely gifted boys,' confirms the Reverend, 'several of whom had professional careers: David Memmett played for Millwall, went to America for £1m with two other players, when that was still quite a high figure for the Second Division, and Andrew Massey got into the Millwall team; he played a few games for us.'

The Revd Rodney allowed Ernie free rein over the young side. He even allowed the coach to retain a 2-3-5 formation, widely considered archaic in the systemic seventies, instead of his preference, the less swashbuckling 4-4-2. The formation meant that Ian was overlooked as a goalscorer once again, watching from the wing as scouts noted down the names of Wallace, Laville and others.

'It was a little black team,' recalls Henry. 'Fourteen brothers, and Ernie was white! What was really good was going to all these small white villages in Kent. Ernie used to deal with all the crap that us black guys used to get. But he didn't care. All he cared was it was his football team.

'We'd arrive by minibus. And I must admit, when we were going somewhere new, for the half an hour after we landed until we got to know a place better, we were quite civilised. But then, once the game was over, we'd beaten their team and that, anything could happen.'

A year after quitting St Paul's, Danny Wallace sealed his reputation by putting the ball past Bruce Grobbelaar in the Liverpool goal for his team Southampton. He was just seventeen. Of course, he later went on to play for Manchester United and England.

That two future England stars both came from one team says a lot about Ernie Hutchings' boys.

'St Paul's were firing on all cylinders,' says Henry Laville. 'We won everything going. We used to take on all comers. We used to go anywhere. What happened was, we were winning 14-0, 18-0, 21-0 and stuff like that, and then we were told we had to go out of our league and go into the next league. Under-12s in an under-16 league! And we kicked their asses as well.'

'Sometimes, you might say, they tended to be selfish with the ball, like I suppose all boys are,' says the Reverend. 'But coming from a place like Deptford, we sometimes noticed playing other teams that individually we were much better, but as a team sometimes not so. However, Ernie's teams always played more football than any of our others.'

Oddly enough, St Paul's' strips, bought as 'a bribe' to encourage dependability after an early cup success, were the same as those of Arsenal Football Club: red shirts with white sleeves and white shorts (bring your own socks).

It was some years before Ian would don that kit for real, but by now he was beginning to make a name for himself on the youth scene.

A feature of the south-east London football scene in the mid-seventies was the number of indoor and outdoor tournaments, mainly five- or six-a-side, played at the likes of Lewisham baths during the winter. (Nowadays the big local competition is organised by the Metropolitan Police at Ladywell Park.)

Ian was much sought-after in his age group for those competitions and could find himself playing two or three nights a week free of charge. He was already a quick thinker, with fast feet, but these were the games where his skills were honed.

It wasn't just the regularity and high standard of the games, it was the dexterity you needed to survive. Ian received loads of touches, he had to wheel on a sixpence, keep the ball low and dispatch it into a small goal, and had to make his mind up quickly with four or five blokes – most with a pathological hatred of 'flash' ball-players – bearing down on him. Ian helped win quite a few trophies from those tournaments. And the benefits of so much intensive playing would resound throughout his professional career.

Of course, such events were 'trawled' by the London's semi-pro managers and the Sunday league sides. When you heard there was a five-a-side for under-16s in West Wycombe, you went and maybe checked the talent out in search of that good centre half your team needed. Ian was coming to the attention of the trawlers. He knew it. And he loved it.

Many people recommended him. Some had great faith in him. But no-one wanted to bite the bullet and sign him up. And yet it was around this time that Ian stumbled into a move that was to have enormous significance for his education, his football and his entire future. Years later, the repercussions would rock professional football.

A smattering of appearances for his district side, the indoor six-a-side tournaments and the recommendation of friends already there brought him to the notice of his local team and childhood favourites: Millwall Football Club.

Ian wasn't with Millwall from the start of the season. It was in the autumn of 1977, after he had played a few games on the wing for the school and had a few district games under his belt.

Scouts from the Den had seen him play but he hadn't made much impression: they queried whether he had the physique or the mettle to make it. Quite separately, a friend of Ian's said he had arranged a trial for him at the club. So he turned up at the allotted time with his kit, but no boots. Instantly, the omens were bad. Ian was disappointed to find out that the youth team organisers knew nothing about him. Still, he was confident and keen, so they gave him a workout and Ian duly worked his heart out.

He was with Millwall for six weeks or so and was hugely excited about it. He told his friends about Millwall's interest: a couple of them were already associate schoolboys with pro clubs, like Henry Laville on Charlton's books and Keith McPherson with West Ham.

Ian would have been the third member of the Pepys's team that year to make it on to pro books. 'When I spoke to him,' says Henry, 'I said to him, "Look, you know what it's going to be like down there; you know exactly what it's going to be like."'

'Bob Pearson was chief scout. He was a good guy. But Millwall was definitely a hotbed as far as blacks were concerned. Even though they had probably the first two black guys in Phil Walker and Trevor Lee. They were some of the first you saw as a young guy.

'I remember looking at them when I was twelve or thirteen, thinking, "Wow, man". But no way could you stand on the terraces and support them. No way.'

Nevertheless, it was the first step in the fulfilment of his dream. Ian didn't have enough confidence or application to make it academically. But he was special at football; it was his best chance of a prestigious career.

On the football field, he could outrun, outwit and outdo others in his peer group, and that was important to him. He would test and prove himself at Millwall. His talent would overcome any problems he encountered. Not for the first or last time in his life, Ian was determined not to let potential discrimination hold him back in life. When Ian began at the club, he was pleased to see a few faces he recognised, including Andy Massey, a couple of years older than him and a trainee professional, whom he used to play football with at Turnham's play centre. (Andy had also played for the same Sunday side, St Paul's, a few years before Ian.)

Andy used to take the under-13s/14s. 'I saw him a couple of times then. I used to talk to him, but there were better players around at the club then. I never thought he would make it, to be truthful. I thought he was too small.' It was the usual view.

Millwall, in fact, were on their way to winning the FA Youth

Cup for the first time in their history, the cue for every father and every school in the country to contact their Youth Development Officer.

'At that time Millwall had a really good youth policy,' says Andy Massey. 'They had some really good players and obviously you couldn't pick everybody. I can't say Ian really stood out. He wasn't as exuberant as he is now. I would say he was quieter because he was in the shadow of the better players. Maybe if he'd made it at Millwall and got an apprenticeship, he might have come out that way.'

As it turned out, Ian wasn't getting in the team, so Millwall obviously didn't 'fancy' him. He got disheartened. He was crestfallen. He thought he'd made it – perhaps that was his biggest mistake. It was embarrassing to be rejected. He had always considered himself the best player in his team.

If others were linking up with pro clubs before him, that was down to his size, and he couldn't do much about that. He thought scouts would judge the quality rather than the stature. But if his own club didn't want him what could he do now? Where could he go? For the first time in his life, the self-belief his mother Nesta had instilled in him was challenged and punctured. It was a dreadful blow; one it took him years to come to terms with.

Ian's departure from Millwall was an acrimonious one. Rumours circulated that he had been bawled out for failing to turn up for training because he wasn't in the side. He was said to have responded as he saw just – as his mother had taught him to – and told the manager where to go. There were some unruly kids around at the club and Ian wasn't the only one who had trouble.

But other kids didn't matter. Nothing else mattered. Ian had been rejected from the team he'd supported all his young life. And lingering at the back of his mind was an awful thought. Maybe it wasn't about size. Maybe he just wasn't good enough. If his local club, languishing in Division 2, wouldn't keep him, who would?

For a while, Ian Wright thought he'd never make it in football. He was inconsolable, but bottled it up inside him. Sport is like that: it'll just as easily break you as make you. There are few experiences more gratifying than spending your time pushing your body to the limit, excelling at something all your peers adore. And you can never score enough goals to lose that surge of adrenaline when the net billows with a ball you've put there.

Equally, though, the introspection of sport and the single-mindedness of performance help a young man or woman uncover certain home truths about themselves – good and bad. Once they've found out, some don't like what they see.

Pushing fourteen, Ian kept it a secret from his games teacher Peter McCarthy that he was training with Millwall. He could be like that about personal things. He was only clamorous about things that didn't matter.

When Millwall kicked him out, Ian's attitude changed. He lost faith in himself and lacked the confidence to do anything except to confront. Lots of things seemed pointless, especially school. He was boiling inside, as if someone had deprived him of something that was his. He became sullen and unco-operative.

He was more spiteful in the playground. He was restless and bored in class; he would muck around and disrupt lessons. This was the 'phase' Peter McCarthy was referring to, the period when he would have to have a walk with Ian and talk him round; the spell when Ian came within an ace of the remedial class and the spiral of decline. But he never mentioned the real root cause once.

Ian never said what he wanted to do with his life. None of the kids were like that. No lad would sit down and say, 'When I leave, Mr McCarthy, I'm going to do this . . .' A lot of them wouldn't talk in personal terms at all. Teachers weren't confidants. To find out what was going on – to do with family and home life – was very hard work and the Pepys teachers wouldn't push it.

In a poor, troubled area like Brockley, it was sensitive information. The last thing you wanted to do was come across like a prying copper.

Ian was typical: in his last year at school, he had no idea what he wanted to do. The more he thought about how silly he was to muck about at school, the more it annoyed him; the more annoyed he was, the more he appeared bored and disruptive. A teacher could offer support and interest, but they couldn't change your destiny. They didn't understand.

But something profound was happening: Ian was growing up. Childhood ended when Millwall slammed the door shut on him. Responsibility began, and it weighed heavy with Ian.

'I can't honestly say what I thought he'd do when he left,' shrugs Peter McCarthy. 'I knew he'd get by, because he was very resourceful, the type of boy you knew he'd take care of himself. He was never top of your list of those you thought would make it, but you knew he wouldn't go the wrong way.

'It's the same as it was with the other two, Henry and Keith. If you could call a young man a gentleman, that was Keith: very quiet, very well spoken. And Ian was their friend. And I thought to myself, "Although you've got a fiery temper, you could be nasty – I'm talking tackle-wise – you'll get by." '

Ian wasn't different to any other kid really: he wore the jeans and T-shirt his mum bought him, had his hair in a mini-Afro and was always out playing or getting into mischief with his siblings, cousins and mates. And just like every other kid at Pepys, Ian was looking towards a future that could appear bleak and uninviting. In 1978, when Ian left Pepys, opportunities for the scions of south-east London were terribly limited.

The Conservatives' 'Labour Isn't Working' posters tapped a well of working class dread of unemployment, rapidly edging towards the three million peak it would reach a few years later under Tory Prime Minister Thatcher. It was hard enough for bread-winners holding onto their jobs; kids were bottom of the pile.

In one way, according to former students of Pepys, the school failed its black pupils. It armed them with certain tools, but not those for professional advancement. It prepared them for life, but what sort of life? 'Sport was pushed like nobody's business,' claims a classmate of Morris's, 'but black kids weren't pushed academically. Look at the school and it was over half black. But the test was the sixth form – it was predominantly white.' There was no one who was able to harness Ian's intellectual potential like Eric Summers and Peter McCarthy had his athleticism. It might have been a practical policy in some boys' cases, but Ian was intelligent enough to have done better.

'I never got an impression that black kids were channelled only into sport,' comments Eric. 'We did turn out quite a lot of kids that went to university.' But in the next breath he qualifies that: 'You'll find there's a lot of black kids out there, qualified up to the eyeballs, who can't get jobs.' There was clearly the sense at Pepys, as there was at Turnham, that personal discipline and excellence at sport (the two were intertwined at Pepys) were as much as could be hoped for from many boys, and virtually as much as they would need.

There was, within that sporting framework, plenty of room for individual specialisations. Pepys offered 22 different sports – an incredible range. One Monday morning in assembly after the usual presentations, Richard Cleal asked 'All those boys who have represented the school to stand up'. And at least 60% of them got to their feet. That was the difference: Pepys gave sport to every one of them. Most schools offered opportunity to an élite. Not Pepys.

Still, despite Ian's sporting prowess – he bubbled at cricket and basketball as well as his beloved football – Nesta kept on at her school-leaving son about what he was going to do with his life. She'd always taught her children to be responsible and she didn't want a layabout for a son. She hadn't travelled thousands of miles to make a new life and a different future for herself in the fifties for him to end up that way. Ian had to take advantage of the opportunities a big economy offered. Men got a trade. It was a matter of self-respect: Jamaican migrants were proud of the skills they imported with them.

Ian decided that he'd have to think seriously about the future. Behind the bombastic brashness, he was a sensible kid, smart too. At that time he wavered between self-doubt and savoir-faire – something he was to experience at various stages in his later life. But what he most wanted was some stability in his life – that was for sure. It was time to be realistic and put childish things behind him.

Reluctantly, Ian temporarily put his life's aspiration on hold. So much so that by the time he left school, Ian Wright's stated ambition was nothing loftier than to work as an assistant in a local sports shop.

4 Time and Chance

'Why not make a plan and be someone. Hold up your head so
eyes can see you're trying. Time is the master, but time can be
disaster if you don't care. You young and gay, you old and
grey.'

John Holt, 'Time is the Master'

WHEN IAN QUIT PEPYS, he found himself for virtually the
first time in a decade without a significant, senior
male figure to watch over him, to make sure he kept
his temper under control and didn't 'go the wrong way'.
Even though he'd put professional football on the back-burner,
Ian began to restore his shattered pride. His schoolmate Henry
Laville, an associate schoolboy at Charlton, and still on the long
road to a pro career that Ian had been nudged off, was strongly
aware of Ian's inner belief.

'Once he left school,' recalls Henry, 'Ian wished us all the best
and we used to speak to each other on a weekly basis but, in his
own mind, it was always a case of him genuinely feeling that he
was better than . . . not so much me, but some of the people I was
playing with. He genuinely felt that. And I think that was what
was really, really driving him all the time. He genuinely felt that
he was better.'

Ian's old 'Mr Chips' at Turnham, Syd Pigden, wasn't surprised
that he had dropped out of the Millwall reckoning – he was re-
signed to his boys' failures. But he was bitterly disappointed.

'I thought it was very bad they let Ian go at that time,' he admits. 'Of course, when Ian was starting, we wanted workers, not
gifted, flair players. You wanted someone who'd run up and down
the pitch.

'Watch that fellow Parlour who plays for the Arsenal first team
now. He's the most hard-working player I've seen for many a year,
but he hasn't got it. There's something missing. That penalty box
to this, but no finesse.

'That was the sort of player they were looking for in those days. The Rodney Marshes, Stan Bowleses were being hounded out of the game. No-one wanted someone who could put their foot on the ball.'

In any case, Ian was in good company. The attrition rate in trainee professional football is huge. Every year, the game is littered with hundreds more broken dreams.

Some of them are patched up at a later date, or at a different club. Every scout has his equivalent of the 'man who didn't sign the Beatles' story.

It's often been said in football circles that the son of Ted Buxton, now England's chief scout, played against Ian Wright at this time and alerted his dad, suggesting he go watch Ian playing in south-east London. Ted, it's said, didn't bother. Another one bites the dust.

In fact, over the next few years Millwall would reject Ian's contemporary Paul Elliott and younger pal David Rocastle, both of whom went on to enjoy exceptional careers with the likes of Arsenal, Leeds and Chelsea. Steve Anthrobus, now with Wimbledon, but brought up on the same Honor Oak estate five years behind Ian, was released from the Den after 21 games.

Newcastle United's new hitman Les Ferdinand, enshrined in 1995 as one of Britain's most expensive strikers, languished in non-League football with Hayes until the age of 22, when QPR took a chance on him. Even then, it took a long time – and spells on loan with Brentford and Turkish team Besiktas – for him to establish himself as a hot Premiership item.

Footballers develop and blossom at different ages. Size can be very important. But in the mid-to-late nineties, as all the women's magazines keep telling us, it's not so much your size as what you do with it. Diminutive players like Tony Cottee, Paul Walsh and John Spencer thrive. Back in the football scene of the late seventies and early eighties, the put-it-about priorities that produced Paul Mariner, Peter Withe and John Fashanu prevailed. But there's more to Ian Wright's story than that.

Many people from the area maintain there may have been an extra factor at Millwall Football Club that militated against black kids, and which Ian could have come up against. 'I think there was a racial element there,' says Syd Pigden. 'Ian wasn't the sort of person to stand there and just take it.

'You've got to remember this was a time of a lot of incidents of racism. Racial discrimination was handed down from generation to generation in families. And remember Ian was a teenager now. Mix that with his mercurial temperament and he was bound to react. Whether it was another lad or a staff member I don't know.'

At the time of Ian's trial – 1978/79 – Millwall's senior team form was the mirror image of the successful youth team. Manager George Petchey was getting flak from all quarters. Their ground had been closed for the fifth time due to crowd disturbances. (The legacy is such that, even in today's New Den, the mesh in the goalnets is narrower than a Spanish trawlerman's, in order to catch missiles.)

Originally, the Den was built on the site of a patchwork of allotments. Some say the vegetables never left, as Millwall constantly topped the crowd violence league tables promoted by Sunday tabloids at the height of hooliganism. Their fighting prowess was permanently mythologised in football folklore after the notorious *Harry The Dog* BBC documentary in the mid-seventies.

It exposed the concept of the soccer 'firm' while examining a close-knit, fervently racist group of young men whose only outlet was frequently well-planned 'trouble' connected with the match.

Opposing fans in the home stand would timorously chant 'Harry the Dog's a poodle!', ever-fearful that the ominous chant of 'Mill . . .' – *boom-boom-boom* – 'wall . . .' – *boom-boom-boom* would unexpectedly emanate from behind the bloke next to them. There was no more bowel-loosening sound in football. And Millwall loved nothing better than to 'take someone's end'. Truly, no-one liked them, and they didn't care!

'Crowd behaviour was always bad,' says Syd, who first frequented the Den just after the war with his brother. 'Any winger who came close to the crowd got a mouthful – "Effing so-and-so!" – no matter whether he'd done anything or what.

'Never been any different. Really and truthfully, when that riot at Luton [in 1985, just weeks before the Heysel tragedy] happened, I remember my brother saying, "I'm not surprised." They are mindless louts. They just attach themselves to Millwall.'

In 1964, David Prole's *Football In London* viewed the club in a similar light: 'Over the years, Millwall have won a reputation for being tough customers. This may not be entirely deserved, but mud always sticks if enough of it is thrown, and Millwall certainly play hard: their supporters will not tolerate anything less than 100% effort.

'The Den is not a place where praises are easily won ... The language may not be that used in more polite circles, but it is far more pungent. They breed powerful lungs down New Cross way, and the derision penetrates.'

If the promenade down narrow Cold Blow Lane was intimidating enough for rival fans, the Den was a terrifying venue for travelling players. In his book *Only A Game?*, published two years before Ian Wright crossed the Millwall threshold, Eamon Dunphy provides a memorable insight into the scene from a player's point of view:

'Teams hate coming to the Den ... I remember thinking, "Where is this?" Then you go and have a look at the pitch, which is bumpy, terrible. The away team dressing-room is a dungeon, no light, no window. The bathrooms are horrible. Then you get out there to face them – the Lions. And they come storming at you and most sides just jack it in.'

In the seventies, the most visiting teams could hope to come away with was their coach intact. Naturally, given the history of new settlement in the area and a virulent local National Front organisation, tension between races was never far from the surface. In common with most English grounds, Millwall's terrace population was largely white and nationalistic. Black supporters weren't rare, but those who consummated their relationship with the club on the terraces were pioneers.

Millwall's reputation for racial intolerance is cemented in football folklore, but when black players first began to emerge through junior ranks, the south London club was foremost amongst them. In truth almost every club was to blame. The game's equal opportunities policy had yet to emerge from the dark ages. Gordon Lee, the Everton manager from 1977 to 1981, was alleged to have promised fans he would have 'no niggers in my team'.

Black fans in the sixties and seventies were frequently subjected to abuse – physical as well as the well-documented verbal kind. 'I don't go to games,' said one black Arsenal fan, 'because I'd look like a pea in a pound of rice.' You never know what will happen from one minute to the next if you look different: anonymous punches, insults (direct and indirect), unpleasant challenges can arise from any quarter. Like pubs, football grounds are tradition-ally the domain and stomping ground of white working class males.

When the vogue for throwing bananas at black footballers be-gan to accompany ritualised monkey chants aimed at an increasing number of those on the pitch, Millwall supporters were foremost amongst the exponents along with kindred spirits from Everton, West Ham, Leeds and Newcastle.

Even as the sons of settlers in south-east London forced their way up through the professional football ranks on to the first team sheet, a new, two-faced discrimination – 'our blacks are better then your niggers' – emerged. Even acceptance was colour-con-scious. When Newcastle United signed their first black player – striker Tony Cunningham – the refrain rang out, 'He's black, he's broon, he's playing for the Toon, Cunning-ham, Cunning-ham.'

On the pitch, white players openly abused their black counter-parts. It was a time-honoured weapon in the wind-up armoury. All the more so since the stereotype had it that black players were 'sensitive' and lacked the necessary mental rigour.

Stylish Albert Johanneson, a black Leeds player, raised under the yoke of apartheid in South Africa, was hounded out of the 1965 FA Cup Final against Liverpool by physical and verbal pressure. At Goodison, he was subjected to an approximation of the 'savage' chants of the Zulus in the then popular film of the same name.

Clyde Best, West Ham's fitfully brilliant striker, set the pattern for the next ten years after making his debut in 1969. He endured torrents of abuse, gallons of spittle and the 'sledging' of defenders with a massive, quiet dignity. It was mute defiance, the same dis-played by Cyrille Regis, Laurie Cunningham, Viv Anderson, Luther Blisset and others over ensuing seasons.

Trevor Lee and Afro-haired Phil Walker both joined Millwall FC in 1975, aged 21, at a time when the club's bigoted fans were at their least tolerant. They at least managed to establish them-selves, which says something in the club's favour.

'There were loads of black players at Millwall,' asserts Andy Massey, a Millwall regular after serving his apprenticeship a few seasons ahead of Ian. 'There was no racial tension. To be quite truthful, in football clubs, once you're in the dressing room, whether you're black, white, yellow, if you're playing together, players are not like that. Every team I've played for, blacks have been accepted just the same as whites. I've got some really good black mates through football.'

Andy rejects the suggestion that racial origin would influence any decision about whether to take on black players at the club, even in 1978. 'The crowd go mental, don't they, but I wouldn't think that would have influenced the Ian Wright situation. If Millwall thought he was a good enough player they would have signed him straight away. I know that for a fact.'

But who would pick players they felt might not handle the instant ire of their own fans? It's a situation white players never have to face. At the time Ian was training with the Cold Blow Lane club, black apprentices were routinely abused at many clubs, subjected to bigoted insults by their own coaches.

At one top London club, the youth team coach would persistently use offensive racial taunts in order, he claimed, to test the toughness of his kids, to 'build character'. If they responded strongly, they were stuck with the stigma of having a chip on their shoulder. The club now has a number of black players in its side, many of whom have graduated from his coaching. Others drifted away long ago. The ones who made it won't hear a bad word about him – at least in public.

But that man was by no means alone in his way of thinking or 'coaching'. Some were calculated in doing it, others were just being themselves.

'It's counter-productive isn't it; it doesn't work that way,' says Paul Elliott, who should know: born a matter of months after Ian and Lewisham-bred, he was rejected by Millwall, Luton, Chelsea and Charlton, before the latter took him on as a trainee. 'I think that was just a very insular attitude that people thought would motivate, make people tick and it was always going to be a very negative way of doing it . . .

'You can't treat people that way. At the end of the day, regardless of race, colour or creed, you've got to treat people the same way: that's the only attitude that was ever going to be the winner in the end.'

Nevertheless youth team coaches frequently considered it a prerequisite to prepare their black juniors for the barrage of abuse they would get at grounds like St James's Park, Goodison or other clubs with a smaller black presence. Again, there was no equivalent test for white trainees.

'I encountered more racism, probably, in the early stages of my career, when I was a 16-year-old playing in Charlton's first team up north: Leeds United, Sheffield, Newcastle,' confessed Paul to Chelsea's official newspaper, *Onside*. 'I felt a level of protection in south London and I think that put me in good stead. I never really experienced it [discrimination] very much as a youth because I wasn't susceptible to those situations. I was a little bit detached from that environment. I just used to go to school, do my sports.

'But at sixteen years of age I had a very rude awakening. That was quite interesting . . .'

Such experiences led directly to his involvement with the Campaign for Racial Equality's 'Let's Kick Racism Out Of Football' project. The question ringing round his head was 'Why should we have to tolerate this?'

'It's hard enough going out there and fulfilling your job description for a club – Leeds, Chelsea, Tottenham, Arsenal – but then you've got an additional problem of personal abuse,' he explains. 'People always used to say, "Well, it's not really meant that way, you know." But I used to say what about "You scouser so-and-so" or "You Scottish so-and-so", not just "You black so-and-so"?

'At the end of the day, it's not your scouser so-and-so or your Scottish so-and-so that people are handing out leaflets about saying they want you to leave the country. It's black people that's been happening to and continually so.'

Nevertheless, Paul Elliott accepts that prejudice among fellow professionals was hardly a problem: 'Not really . . . there were one or two . . . but it wasn't meant as a personal thing, merely to put you off your game.'

Before he started to train with Millwall, school team-mate Henry Laville reminded Ian of their reputation amongst the black community. Henry himself had been alerted to the problems en-countered at professional clubs, discovering some racism at Charlton even before he trained with them.

One evening, Sam Pepys' games instructor Peter McCarthy was watching a district match featuring a couple of his school's players. District games were always buzzing with scouts checking out new talent or simply keeping an eye on the boys they already had, to make sure they weren't poached or spoke to anyone from another club.

But a fellow from Charlton had other things on his mind this particular night. It was a cold night and he decided to hold forth on how genetics affected footballers. He was coming out with all the familiar bigoted nonsense: 'black guys can't play, haven't got the bottle, can't play in the cold . . .'

Peter McCarthy heard all that. Then a week or two later, the same scout rang up from Charlton and said he wanted to try out Peter's boy Henry Laville. 'We were really annoyed at this bloke trying to sign him,' say Eric Summers, head of sport at Pepys. 'When Mr McCarthy heard that he went straight to him, said, "What the hell are you on about? Last week you were giving us all this stuff about black players can't play football, not hard enough etc, and now you're saying you want to sign him up!"'

However, Henry didn't listen and signed up with Charlton. 'I finished up reporting them to the FA,' recalls Peter McCarthy. 'Because Millwall wanted Henry and I knew what was going to happen, and it happened: Charlton wouldn't release him. They kept him there as an apprentice and in the end they got rid of him. And he drifted out of football.'

Henry's story is instructive because it is just the tip of an ice-berg: a generation of black footballers whose potential was never realised were hassled out of the professional game in the seventies. Against their instincts, clubs were signing black players as trainees. But even after they made it through to junior level, man-agement could still all too readily find excuses not to play their black players at senior level.

'I'm not trying to put myself on a pedestal,' says Henry, 'but I was, from school days, one person who everybody automatically thought, "Oh, he's going to make it to the top without a shadow of a doubt."

'But I joined Charlton, which I think was my biggest mistake. I had every other club in England after me. And I joined Charlton because that was the done thing: come from south-east London; join Charlton Athletic.'

From associate schoolboy forms, Henry signed as an apprentice on 1 July 1980. Two years later Henry still wasn't getting any first team football. He decided to put manager Alan Mullery on the spot, to have a showdown. Mullery said, 'Look I could give you the same contract for another two years.' Henry balked. He had yet to make his first team debut. After six loyal years, he wanted something better than that, some guarantee of first-team starts.

No such guarantee was forthcoming. Henry disappeared off to Canada and played for an entertaining outfit called North York Cosmos (not the well-known refuge for crocked celebrities playing in the Big Apple).

'It was fun,' he insists. 'But when I look back, I know why I wanted to go. I basically just wanted to get out of this country. I enjoyed it for eight months and then my contract was up. I had to come home and I still had clubs chasing me. But I sat down and said to myself, "I don't really want to do this." ' Another talent extinguished.

Like Ian Wright, Henry had suppressed his natural reaction to the discrimination he encountered because he wanted professional football so much. 'It's something that's never bothered me,' he contends. 'I appreciate, as a black person, it's always going to be there. But if you keep on looking at it, you could just go mad, basically. You can start picking holes in everything. It's a case of, "Yeah, it's there, but get on with it, mate." '

That's not to say that no black players made it at Charlton. Far from it: there were some highly significant graduates, not least Paul Elliott, who dominated the Addicks' defensive line 63 times before moving on to Luton, Aston Villa, Pisa, Celtic and Chelsea.

Like his Lewisham friend Ian, Paul drew on the unfailing font of family support to help him through his career's ups and downs. 'I never dreamed I'd be doing what I am now,' he revealed in 1995. 'I come from a very humble background. My parents came in the fifties, had it very hard: they were the first generation to arrive in this country.

'Obviously, the racism and all the other problems were clearly prevalent in society then, so I was lucky that they made such a big impact on my life and the person I've turned out to be.

'And my own periods of adversity – I had a double fracture at eighteen which could have ended my career soon after I joined Luton; just on the verge of the World Cup squad I did my left cruciate ligament, after I finished in Italy, and obviously now I've done my right cruciate. You have to take something from those experiences.'

And, with words that might have come from Ian Wright's mouth, Paul explains the value of his mother's devotion. 'The pride I have is that despite such serious setbacks, I always went on to better things. And it was that inner drive, determination and will to win [which] my mother had inbred in me as a young man that I used to overcome that adversity.'

The likes of Paul, Henry, Keith and Ian kept their eyes on the prize. Football dominated and closed off their lives, shut out the rest of the world and its problems. 'I knew Paul Elliott, of course,' says Henry Laville. 'I was one of those guys, I must admit, I did try to stick with the brothers. As you're probably well aware, there weren't many black players around when we were playing, and we did sort of stick together. Ian wasn't around then, but we used to go and watch him playing for 10-Em-Bee or whoever.'

Weekends, there would be a game in the morning, whether it was Charlton for Paul and Henry, West Ham for Keith or 10-Em-Bee for Ian. The brothers would meet up later on, probably play a five-a-side, or a bit of tennis. Evenings were for pure raving: clubs, blues dances, music, women, beer . . .

Sunday, as the Lord bade it (but for different reasons), was just a case of rest – or rather just a little kickaround . . .

Of course, there were certain environments where you were less likely to encounter discrimination than others, where either the issue was irrelevant or displays of prejudice were fervently opposed. These included schools and council offices, where active anti-racist policies operated, and where black people could progress.

Moreover, athleticism – along with musicianship and brawn – was one of the few qualities colonial wisdom attributed to black people without ambiguity. It's no surprise that one of the early fields of achievement for migrants in this country was sport: athletics, boxing, soccer and cricket. Sport was another of those rare 'safe' areas. Both Ian's schools had promoted sport as social conditioning, a way to interest potential problem kids and produce socialised, co-operative dole fodder.

Those who took the baton and ran with it all the way to the top were lucky. Sporting prowess elevates people 'above' their background. Athletes – boxers apart – are perceived to have risen above their background and all its inherent problems: villainy, poverty, aimlessness. On another level, dedication is an honourable resource, and implies co-operation with accepted mores. Training and playing also occupy so many hours of the week that they effectively withdraw the junior pros from the buffeting and bigotry they would experience in more orthodox employment. It's an escape of sorts, but not without its own costs, as Ian Wright, more than most, has discovered. Sports people shouldn't pick on differences: it's one on one. Real winners are the most selfish people in the world. It's all about individuals and teams, not tribes. That's where supporters are different; wrong even.

In football dressing rooms, the banter is robust, but light. Mostly all young players talk about, in common with their seniors, is football, women and beer. It's the dressing room culture: everyone's fair game for jokes – such as shaving foam in their suits, their car being 'stolen', their soap 'disappearing'. It's all incredibly puerile, an extension of the levity of childhood.

What footballers don't like talking about is serious business: racism and politics are just like pension plans – boring! Race is often just a difference, these days, an opportunity for taking the piss. Things used to be bad back in the seventies when there were maybe one or two black lads in a squad of 30-odd, and when the prejudices of the mass could be imposed on a grimacing victim. If the youth team coach called him 'nigger', the least other players could do once he'd graduated to the first team was treat him in a fashion he was familiar with.

Once black kids emerged in numbers to take their place in youth teams, it wasn't so much of an issue. If you wanted to get on, you didn't kick up a rumpus: no-one likes a troublemaker.

Once the Millwall option was removed from his horizon and school was history, Ian had no such refuge. But as his friend Paul Elliott alluded earlier, south London had its compensations. You could still be a big man in the Afro-Caribbean community, in its counterculture, a world parallel to the white mainstream. Once he left school, Ian found himself a job in the white world by day, and otherwise immersed himself in the Caribbean firmament.

Most of his friends were black, even at school, where the environment was obviously mixed. Now Ian naturally graduated to a different world. And in its own way, it was a withdrawal from the broader realms of society.

An American Indian chief once bemoaned the fact that while his people knew everything about American culture, the white American was utterly ignorant of their culture, and strove to keep it that way. In this country, there are still white people who say they 'have no idea what a black household looks like', as if it will have mud on the walls, *Coronation Street* dubbed in a different language on the telly and shrunken heads in the fridge. It was attitudes like that – ignorant, whether well-intentioned or not – that wound up kids like Ian Wright. People couldn't understand why he could be surly. Chip on his shoulder, just like the others!

In the south London of the late seventies, an air of mutual suspicion pertained that was to have an indelible effect on Afro-Caribbean residents and their relations with the white residents in the area.

The rise of anti-immigrant groups in south and east London is well-documented. Working class areas close to docks, where settlers of every nationality have made their homes for centuries, are traditional recruiting grounds for those who are seeking out scapegoats for poor employment prospects and social conditions. Huguenots, Jews, Afro-Caribbeans and Bangladeshis have all made their homes in London over the last 200 years. Blacks mostly gravitated to places like Brixton and Lewisham, particularly Brockley. In 1993, the Isle of Dogs, a rude bulge of the East End looped by the Thames, returned British National Party candidate Derek Beacon, a self-proclaimed racist, in its Millwall council ward. The massive capital investment in the toytown architecture of this hi-tech business Utopia in London's Docklands wasn't able to stop the simmering xenophobia of the region, a short bus ride from Ian's home in Brockley.

But the only surprising thing about this far-right triumph was the fact that it had taken so long to happen. Those who didn't live through the seventies might find it hard to appreciate what things were like at the time Ian was growing up. Racially-motivated attacks were common in Lewisham; it was not unusual for whites to scream 'Immigrant!' at black passers-by; graffiti everywhere related the ritual battle: 'Black power', 'NF', 'Repatriate now'.

In a society where possibilities were already restricted in the fields of employment and housing, black people's lives were qualitatively worsened by the indifference and active antipathy of the indigenous people.

Those who look for a clue to Ian's fiery temper as a player could do worse than examine the background to his developing years, his first years outside the protection of school, for clues.

Ian's teenage years were marked by the sudden emergence of ancient laws adapted to modern police requirements. Section four of the Vagrancy Act 1824, or the 'stop under suspicion' – SUS – law, to give it its more celebrated name, meant that if two policemen 'suspected a person of loitering with intent to commit a felony', they could apprehend and charge the suspect, whom magistrates could then fine or imprison.

Originally, the law had been designed to deal with demobbed vagrants after the Napoleonic wars, but was now largely employed as a harassment of persons the police disliked or were suspicious of. The burden of proof was very low and the police did not need to produce a victim or a crime. Commander Len Adams of Lambeth Police Force famously claimed it was 'necessary for me in my attempts to prevent crime. Although it is an old Act, it's still very relevant to the needs of today.'

Norwood MP John Fraser was one of many critics who slammed the trend as summary justice inimical to the English tradition. 'It is one of the few laws where the defendant does not have to do anything apart from being suspect,' he pointed out. 'The prevention of crime should never be a vehicle for the infringement of civil liberty. The SUS law itself is suspect.'

The policy had already peaked in 1976, the year of the worst battle between law enforcement officers and black youths at the now emasculated Notting Hill Carnival. It was denounced as 'the main reason for bad relations between the black community and the police'.

According to figures supplied by the Runnymede Trust, of those arrested under SUS in 1977 in Lambeth, 75% were black; in Southwark and Lewisham the figure was 50%. In 1978, 197 out of 256 people apprehended in Lambeth were black; it was 125 from 170 a year later. There was an extraordinary 91% conviction rate.

Ian's school Samuel Pepys wasn't immune to such policing. Teachers recall that their pupils were stopped all the time; they'd have to go and testify as to their good character. Black kids had to get white people to vouch for them – what kind of effect can that have had? It was commonplace for Ian and his gang of friends to be routinely apprehended around Lewisham and Brockley, even though Ian still had those legendary elusive qualities when it came to trouble. In Brixton especially, police began to 'stop-and-search' people under another resurrected law; anecdotal evidence suggested that strip searching, in broad daylight, was relatively common. Today's figures still point to enormous discrepancies, concerning those people the police elect to apply the 'stop-and-search' law to . . . in favour of whites.

Community lawyer Paul Boateng, now a Labour member of Parliament, demonstrated the gift for a soundbite that has seen him rise to the shadow cabinet, in describing SUS as 'Conveyor belt justice. Its effect on relations between the police and black community has been disastrous. Many of our youths are having their whole lives ruined by a finding of guilty on this charge and the frequency with which it is used.'

Mavis Clark, community worker with North Lewisham Project believed 'the SUS law is making criminals of black youths. All the police need to do is to say they saw them looking in a shop window or standing at a bus stop acting suspicious and the youths get convicted.'

Lewisham Labour councillor Russell Profitt suggested that 'many coppers on the beat see young blacks as an easy target for arrest.'

But the likes of Independent Lewisham councillor Alan Humble fuelled the anger and disillusionment of young black citizens: 'The SUS law,' he claimed, 'has been instrumental in removing from society in this borough some of the people who have terrorised people from the north to the south.' Police added that 'policing problems vary from place to place' and that any tool which reduced crime was worth a try – they had the paramilitary Special Patrol Group waiting in the wings as back-up, and their heavily armoured vehicles could often be seen cruising Ian's manor.

In its annual report published in August 1979, the Commission for Racial Equality warned that 'race relations progress is too slow. Unless the momentum of progress can be increased, there is a real risk of relapse into racial turmoil.'

Despite warnings from Police Commissioner Sir Patrick Mac-Nee that scrapping SUS would increase street crime, the SUS law was revoked in 1980. But relations between black south London youths like Ian Wright and police who had little or no interest or faith in a multi-cultural society had become desperately poor.

Months later, the mistrust was to reach an all-time low in Ian's neighbourhood. In January 1981, around 150 friends and relatives arrived throughout the night for the joint birthday party of Angela Jackson and Yvonne Ruddock at 439 New Cross Road, the Ruddocks' three-storey home. Some time around 5.40 a.m. the following morning, a fire started in the downstairs front room, the best in the house and off limits to guests for the duration.

Mrs Ruddock discovered the room ablaze, but failed to stifle it by closing the door. Partygoers were alerted, but smoke began to fill the hallway and creep upstairs. The staircase formed a chimney and within minutes the fire was licking its way to the top. The ravers on the upper floors, most of whom were between fifteen and nineteen, didn't stand a chance. Young sound system DJ Gerry Francis died after returning to the house to salvage his amplifier during the conflagration. Thirteen black youngsters perished in what came to be known as the New Cross Fire.

The catastrophe sent shock waves through the local community. *West Indian World* in offering a £5,000 reward wrote that 'the Lewisham mass murders must rank on a par with the atrocities committed in South Africa and the Deep South of America against black people.'

For the most part, black people felt resigned. There had been racial attacks and other incidents – from graffiti to firebombings – in the area for years. Immediately the schism between police and black residents widened. Officers were said to have suggested to survivors that a firebomb had been used. Eye-witnesses testified that they had seen a white man throwing something at the house shortly before the windows blew out upstairs.

But police were quick to stifle the rumour mill. 'I do not believe the motive for this fire was race,' commented Commander Graham Stockwell. 'We are keeping an open mind about arson.' His remarks were insensitive to say the very least. Attacks on black and Asian households were rarely conceded to be motivated by race; and then he turned the spotlight of culpability back on the community that had suffered the loss. Typical.

For Ian, there was something very close to home about the fire: one of his best friends, 17-year-old Mike Polack, was very badly burned – around 40% of his body – but managed to cheat death. Angry locals organised a 'Deptford Disaster Fund' and there were meetings at the Moonshot Club, a regular venue for community activism. But Ian and his friends, hassled by the same police who were supposed to be investigating the inferno, were resigned to what had happened. They had no faith in 'John Bull' after the way they'd been treated. They shrugged their shoulders. It wasn't the first incident – it may have been the worst – but it wouldn't be the last.

'New Cross was literally just up the road,' says Henry Laville. 'And that's one thing that to this day really got me: that you could have such a huge issue as that, thirteen burned to death. And it wasn't national news until two days later. And there was no letter from the Queen. Couple of people die and the Queen sends a letter of condolence, but nothing like that. Again, it just brings it all back home.' The virtual silence of the rest of the country spoke volumes.

Relatives of the deceased even received hate letters. One dispatched from Catford read: 'What a great day it was last Sunday when I heard about all those niggers going up in flames. I hope the black bastard that mugged me was there.' The NF wanted permission to take in the charred shell on New Cross Road along the route of a proposed march.

Nevertheless, the constabulary launched the biggest investigation for years, involving fifty officers based in Brockley station up the road from the Turnham estate where Ian lived. Years later, recriminations about the case still resonated. Police were accused of intimidating witnesses into providing a story about a fight that suited them; vital witnesses themselves, including Mrs Ruddock, were reproached for withholding evidence.

By the time of the inquest, the area was split down the middle: with black residents wondering why the racial motive hadn't been followed up and police believing that the tragedy was the result of a 'lovers' tiff'.

The time of the inquest marked the nadir of race relations in Lewisham. It was quite appallingly handled. Coroner Dr Davies was extraordinarily insensitive and was seen not even to be taking notes. He summed up using police evidence alone. The impotent rage of an entire community found mournful expression.

At one point Davies said to Orville Gooding, whose 14-year-old son Andrew perished in the flames, 'Mr Gooding, I understand your grief.'

'I don't think you do,' responded Mr Gooding.

Others were more plaintive. Davies's call for one bereaved father to come to order was met with the pitiful cry, 'We must have some outlet – this is killing us, man.'

The dreadful reputation of police in south London amongst black people reached its low point at this time. The Brixton 'uprising', triggered by the arrest of a local cab driver for alleged drugs offences, lit the blue touch paper, but the situation had been smouldering for years.

It is a measure of the appalling state of police affairs in the area that it took years for the investigating officers to earn the trust of black witnesses in the New Cross Fire case. A chance discovery pointed to a new suspect – the 'throwing man' turned out to be someone trying to raise the alarm. It is now widely accepted that the man who started the fire, after a row with his lover, fled abroad. There is insufficient evidence to bring him to justice; the case is now closed.

When the New Cross investigation team honoured themselves with tasteless commemorative ties – a laurel 13 in Roman numerals to represent the deaths and a 50 denoting the number of officers investigating the incident – it irresistibly recalled the unofficial Brixton police 'spade' tie which depicted a hand of cards, all spades and was issued to the station's robbery squad, and supposedly banned in 1979. After two decades of 'community awareness' little had changed, except, as one of Ian's schoolmates avers, 'kids today are more integrated, they've grown up together more. Black kids can get away with saying more things before they get their balls cut off.'

Such was the world that Ian Wright grew up in: hateful, suspicious, black versus white. Such experiences hardened him. Natural cockiness doesn't endear a youth to the police. Ian learned to keep his head down, to withdraw from situations where there might be confrontation – he knew from what had happened to his friends how easily 'they' could twist things and stitch you up.

As 'dub poet' Linton Kwesi Johnson was notifying, no white organisation 'can do it fe we . . . we must stand up fe we self'. Like so many before him, Ian had already decided to immerse himself in the escapist black underbelly of London and just get on with it. If people are looking for an explanation of the pent-up frustrations that burst out of Ian Wright on the football pitch, they should examine the backdrop to his adolescence.

Jamaicans, who are proud to think of themselves as the most rebellious of the Caribbean islanders, more than most carry in them what has been called a 'rage without retaliation'.

In those days, sixteen marked a watershed for black and white youths alike. At that age, the rite of passage was the pub for white kids, the 'blues' for black kids. Ian was a blues dance boy. New Cross was relatively quiet. Brockley was blacker, the place to meet, especially at the top of Pepys Hill.

The blues was a distinctly Caribbean accomplishment. A response, in fact, to the difficulties many black kids had experienced trying to gain entry to white-owned clubs, and the harassment and sexual tension inside them. By their very crepuscular nature, blues dances were shady dens. In the seventies, they were like nightclubs in someone's house, professional all-day-all-night parties that took over a house and took a weekend or more to close.

Many were well established – on the map. Neighbours were ignored. Beer – West Indian imports or the sweet, extra strong zombie lagers that Jamaicans prefer – was bought in and sold in a corner. In another room, a pinball machine or *Space Invaders* arcade games might flicker.

Rooms were dark, sparkling with spliffs glowing like moving fireflies. Basements were stacked with speakers the size of wardrobes pumping music out at foundation-shaking level, where couples hugged up to the stock-in-trade of the Jamaican music maestro: reggae for the dreadlocks crowd, Lovers Rock for the youths to grind a 'gyal' close – wallpaper-stripping music, they called it. And there was soul providing a breather from the more intense Jamaican stuff, perhaps James Brown to get the dance jumping up in a different style: 'Say it loud. I'm black and I'm proud!'

The blues created its own topsy-turvy, reverse world which black people populated, where they bought, sold, loved, fought, dealt and danced, for the most part, uninhibited by 'John Bull' – the police.

'Late night blues,' sang reggae crooner Al Campbell, 'I've got to find me a spot/I wanna kick off my shoes and rock it in a late night blues.' They could be rough, full of 'sticksmen' – rogues – dangerous, but the rules were set out on black man's terms. Few white kids would penetrate this bastion of blackness. You could cool out. It was a place a young man could feel good. Ian loved the blues dances.

But they often had their flashpoints, which were electrifyingly exciting if you could duck and dive to avoid them (that had always been one of Ian's skills): a broken glass, the glint of a blade and the crumple of one body, the rush of others; blood, a frisson of fear ... Violent, dangerous frustration channelled back into the community. What Linton Kwesi Johnson dubbed 'rebellion running down the wrong road'.

There were plenty of local sound systems around in those days playing the music Ian loved. They'd 'string up' at youth clubs, blues dances, night-clubs or Notting Hill Carnival. It says quite a lot that the people that dominated in Ian's day still 'carry the swing': Coxsone, Saxon and, soon, Jah Shaka, who went to Ian's school, Turnham. Fatman and other crews from north of the river would play out in Lewisham regularly.

Saxon is one of the most productive sound systems of all. Not only have its MCs Tippa Irie and Smiley Culture graduated to pop crossover, but it was the launchpad for Maxi Priest, a Lewisham boy who used to run through his early singing paces above Deptford's Sound City on New Cross Road.

Ian loved to check the sound systems: the spontaneous explosions of rhythmic microphone chat, the trouser-shaking claxon horns, the familiar seismic basslines, the swaying crowd baying for the sound crew to stop a killer record and start it again: 'Hitch it! Haul and pull mi operatah!' It was bedlam, it was on the edge, it was hugely exciting. It was a black thing.

Ian was always a reggae man as a kid – 'Coxsone' Dodd's Studio One sound and the root of reggae. He preferred the cultural side of the music, the songs with a message, the ones that never made the charts. That's why his heroes as a teenager were not so much the crossover stars such as Bob Marley, but reality singers like Gregory Isaacs and Dennis Brown. 'Dennis Brown: melt you down, man. Gregory Isaacs too. Studio One music, article!'

They had it all. Dennis's biblical gravity: 'Here I come, with love and not hate/My head is anointed, and my cup runneth over/ Surely goodness and mercy shall follow I, all the days of I life.' 'Cool Ruler' Gregory's poignant romanticism: 'Financially I'm a pauper/But when it comes to loving, I'm all right.' Gregory was a romantic brute. There was a certain attractiveness in that for Ian.

It was the fashion among ravers at the time to have gold caps put in their teeth: the reggae star Big Youth went one better and had an emerald, a ruby and a yellow sapphire put in his front teeth to represent the red, gold and green of the Rasta colours. In Ian's case, the gold tooth was in homage to his brother Morris, who had three of them, though it gave him a roguish, ragamuffin look that he liked and that fitted with the Jamaican 'massive' he moved with.

Reggae was faraway fantasy music. It spoke of deliverance from humdrum lives. One of Dennis's popular refrains would have a particular resonance in Ian's case. Adapted from Ecclesiastes 9:11, it warned that 'the race is not for the swift to the swift, but those who endure . . .' Time and chance come to us all, with forbearance.

At the beginning of the eighties, the blues dances became more violent, macho places. Women were less likely to attend, and Ian was always keen to meet girls, even though he was a man's man. The more formalised night-club scene became alluring.

One of the first Afro-Caribbean clubs to open in Ian's area was the legendary Bouncing Ball. It was at 43 Peckham High Road, but you won't have seen Del or Rodney Trotter quaffing a lager top there. Like the blues parties, this licensed establishment, owned by Ken Edwards, who ran his own sound system called Admiral Ken, was almost exclusively a black venue. It was one that Ian and his friends would often frequent.

It was a small venue, shabby and gaudy inside. On the low excuse for a stage, underground greats of the day performed with regular backing band the Cimarons: the Equators would play there; Prince Jazzbo, Cornell Campbell, I-Roy and Sugar Minott – the 'Good Thing Going' man always seemed to be on the bill. Behind the stage were the posters advertising upcoming attractions. The music was the usual Jamaican mix: reggae, some rock steady, and a soulful bowlful from the southern States. It was full of rogues but it was a great little venue.

Alongside those who empathised with reggae's militant image, the 'stepping razors', the Natty rebels, Ian would chide those who preferred soul music. Like his brother Morris, who had introduced him to music, Ian wasn't really into soul until later, and the likes of Henry Laville, a 'soul head' who listened to stuff like the Jones Girls and Johnny Bristol, used to get teased and laughed at endlessly for their soft taste.

Back in the late seventies, there was no house, garage, urban, underground, hip-hop and swingbeat. You either liked soul or you liked reggae, that was it. Roots reggae represented an uncompromising Caribbean root and expression, spiritual Afrocentricity and musical evolution within a rigid tradition. It was heavy, dread, often macho. 'Music like dirt', Jamaicans said. Few white people were into it.

For outsiders it could sound threatening. The impenetrable bass wasn't the only thing that formed a wall. Reggae emphasised black-white differences like a musical segregation – a little like jungle music became in the mid-nineties.

The Jamaican language itself turned 'them' off; you could use that to your advantage to exclude them like they excluded you from so many things. It was loud, black and proud. That was part of the attraction to those who felt alienated from white society like

Ian. There was a resonant truth in its dark words of awesome prophecy and deliverance.

Soul was the opposite. It wasn't Jamaican or Caribbean except through the tortured cultural lineage of some of its exponents, though it boasted an ultimate African root. But the modern incarnation was pretty, soft, American ... aspirational, conformist. White people liked soul music, they danced to it in discos: soul venues were always more racially mixed than reggae sessions. It was something Ian grew into as he began checking out the clubs on London's heaving night circuit.

Ian used to hang on the coat-tails of his brother Morris. When he was older, he'd check out Crackers, All Nations, Bouncing Ball, Four Aces and the 100 Club among other venues. But even at an early age, Ian was showing himself to be intrepid enough on his own.

Gradually Ian turned towards soul and funk music on his nights out. Nowadays, he lists among his heroes Michael Jackson and James Brown, who epitomise black success and the highest expressions of African-American culture. Unfortunately, they have both also come to symbolise the flawed black male: Jackson, cosmetically blanched and Caucasianised, haunted by unproven stories of alleged child molestation; Brown, ripped off throughout his career, hooked on drugs and wielding a pistol, was released from jail after attempting to shoot his wife and certain police officers during the early nineties.

How representative it is of Ian to mention those artists as idols, even after their tainting media exposure. Ian's like that. He knows what it's like to be a black superstar. He recognises the harassment, the misrepresentation. He understands the pressures, which can make a man crack like that, and he's seen people, friends, go the same way. That's all part of the tension of poverty and alienation.

He's heard what Jackson and Brown are supposed to have done, according to the press. But they've never let him down. To Ian, they're still the same brilliant artists; great black men, he's adored for years. And he'll stick by them, keep saluting their name and their achievements.

But in the early eighties, after attending an all-boys school, Ian was discovering the joys of female company. He wasn't the sort to sleep around. In fact, Ian was inclined to get very serious, very soon.

In 1981, when Ian was eighteen, he fell head over heels for the girl who was to be his lover and confidante for the next eight years. Sharon Phillips was a quietly confident and charming girl, very down-to-earth. Born just a few months before Ian, she was already showing her capacity to cope with life by bringing up a baby boy on her own. But Ian was very taken with her. He tumbled fast and heavy, and was into Sharon in a big way; the baby too.

Shaun Phillips, born in October 1981, a week before Ian's 18th birthday, proved the apple of Ian's eye. Soon after Ian and Sharon met, the two of them set up home together on the Honor Oak estate. Moving in was a huge commitment for a young lad like Ian, especially in the light of the attitude of so many youths towards their 'baby mother'. And it was a struggle for the young couple in their council home, but Shaun and Sharon now meant everything to Ian. Nesta had moulded a young man willing to shoulder responsibilities beyond what was expected of him. Family stability was all-important to him, all the more so since his own father, Buster, had hardly been around when he was young. Ian's mum Nesta had tried her best to bring up her four children, and she'd done a good job, but she wasn't the sort of mother who would rush down to the school pitch to watch her son score goals, or show him how to play conkers, or listen to his endless stories about his 'wicked' bowling, or any number of other boys' things.

Ian was determined from the outset that Sharon's baby Shaun was going to have support from him as long as he needed it. It was something he had to do. Ian had always craved paternal indulgence when he was young; now here was the chance to lay something to rest in his own past.

It's part of Ian's character to compensate for adverse situations when he can. Again it was part of what his mother Nesta had always taught him: do the right thing. It's an aspect of Ian's character that never receives exposure today, when he's caricatured as an immature, hot-tempered hedonist.

What the newspapers and gossip-mongers of football don't know is the honourable, selfless side of Ian Wright, and it showed itself at this early age. Ian's determination to give Shaun a good start in life was so strong that after just a year of living with Sharon he discussed things with her and decided to adopt the one-year-old child. It was an extraordinary decision. Ian didn't have to do it. He might have stuck around for a few months and then run off with someone, as so many 18-year-olds would. He might have lived with Sharon and left Shaun at a loose end. It showed how much affection he had, and still retains, for the child.

Ian's a sticker. A serious monogamist, if you like. He has claimed only to have had five girlfriends. While the jury's verdict on that may rest on legal definitions, Ian was someone who liked to have certainties in a life that was all too often liable to let you down or spring surprises. It might not have stopped him from going out at night raving, but Ian didn't shirk his obligations towards anyone, and still doesn't.

He decided to settle down, sort out his life and work out what he wanted from it: his young family was very important to him. From now on, Shaun would be known as a Shaun Phillips-Wright.

It was one thing to have a family; it was quite another to be able to provide for its members. Times were tough, and it was hard to find work. But someone as determined and stoked up with self-belief as Ian will always find something. He would do whatever was required to make ends meet as long as he was keeping the dream of professional football alive.

Ian's first job in the sports shop – all he'd wanted when he left school – had not worked out. Now he had a family the most important thing was to get something reliable. The obvious answer, and one his mum Nesta approved of, was to find a trade: panel beater, builder, plasterer – the latter not a great occupation for an asthmatic – or electrician like his father. The next five years brought a succession of ups and downs in employment.

One of his early positions was at Tunnel Refineries in Greenwich, working for the on-site contractors, Millcroft. On his first day there, his boss saw this small, wiry, enthusiastic lad and wondered whether he could cope with the jackhammer he was supposed to wield. It was a tough, damp and disgusting work environment. The supervisor needn't have worried. Ian applied himself to the task as if he could work out all his frustrations through the rigorous machinery. He worked hard and stuck with it; the story of Ian's life.

Later Ian was a trainee plasterer for Lewisham Council, working out of one of the local depots. But there were frequent bouts of idleness. And the asthma which had dogged him since he was a baby would re-emerge every now and then until 1982, the year of his last debilitating attack.

Ian had a number of escapes from the daily grind. First, there was his family; second, the nightlife; third, there was football.

As far as the latter was concerned, Ian was as busy as he'd ever been. There were still five-a-side tournaments to be played. Ian continued to hone his ball skills, enhance his reflexes and, after his brief appearances for the all-conquering St Paul's Sunday side, he moved on to senior local football. He had an insatiable appetite for the game. Lee Lang, the manager of one of the black teams in the area, Carib, would call his type, 'have boots, will travel'. Ian was a gun for hire.

The team that most frequently benefited from Ian's presence was 10-Em-Bee, a team formed through the amalgamation of two pub teams in 1974. They were one of the few black sides in London, part of a response to popular demand by young Afro-Caribbean men who either couldn't get into other sides for whatever reason, or preferred to play with their friends. They are also one of the most ambitious and dynamic teams at their level, a reputation that was rewarded by the Greater London Council when it was being abolished. The team were handed the administration of a sports ground off Old Bromley Road in Downham, where they frequently played.

The gift was well deserved, no-one would dispute that, but a fortunate windfall all the same. As councils come under pressure to sell off their open spaces to balance the town hall budget, cheaper pitches are increasingly in short supply. Private pitches can cost around £80 to hire – nearly £4 per man. Downham was a happy break for a club that had its share of ups and downs.

Since 1989, 10-Em has been one of only two black teams in the Nuclear Electric Kent County League, the other being lowly Moonshot, the struggling side affiliated to New Cross's community centre. Over the years, 10-Em have passed through the Metropolitan Sunday, South East London Amateur, South London Federation, Beckenham League and London and Kent Border leagues with games on Sundays and Saturdays.

Throughout their existence, 10-Em have been the sort of side who would slaughter the opposition week after week, then lose their best players and struggle for ages. They have always prided themselves on being able to give semi-pro teams a run for their money. In 1994, for example, they took Sheppey to a replay in the Kent Cup.

Wherever they've been, they've always been a strong, spirited side. And they've always been very successful. Promoted to the Kent County Premier in 1994, they just survived relegation after a fitful campaign the following season by beating second-placed Lordswood 6-2. They were as delighted as Lordswood were depressed, but the partying went on all afternoon. They'd been a bit worried beforehand and kicked off late because they only had eight players at first.

It's been like that throughout their history. There have been several incidents that the local press has made too much of, but clubs like 10-Em are used to others accentuating the negative. They know it's individual players who have been the problem rather than the team itself. In 1994, their goalkeeper was very volatile, and was banned after a violent tantrum. 10-Em expelled him from the club.

10-Em are a very friendly, popular side, but they're also seen as the ones who will troop half an hour late into the League's annual general meeting to the good-natured jeering of the other clubs. But 10-Em still look to be respected.

They've produced some very good players over the years. Not all of them have progressed like they might have. The ones that have are celebrated in the photo display on the wall of their changing room and offices at the Downham ground. Ian is there in his Palace kit, the one he wore after he laid down the yellow of 10-Em for the last time.

Formed from the union of two bar teams, 10-Em was always as much a social club as anything else. In the old days, the team would meet before each game in the pub. Conrad Marquis, Freddy Chambers and others were Ian's spars. He'd never enjoyed football so much as with 10-Em.

Each game was an event. 10-Em are a well-supported side, about fifty people turn up for their more important games. In the old days there'd be a portable stereo the size of a small family car pumping out music while the team dispatched another set of rattled opponents. These days, the only music you hear at their games is the trilling of several mobile phones and the sing-song chat of their owners.

Ian had an outstanding period at the club, his goals powering them to cup finals year after year and several title successes during their mid-eighties peak. But he wasn't being paid for it: this was a labour of love. And he could still turn out for Carib or other sides on days when 10-Em weren't playing.

Danny Fairman, 10-Em's manager, was to emerge as an important figure in Ian's life. Along with secretary George Davis one of the motivators behind the club, Danny became a driving force behind Ian Wright in a quite literal sense. He could see the quality as well as the hunger in Ian's performances.

All players used to get kicked, but Ian used to be kicked around more than most. Centre halves hated Ian because of his size and speed. He'd wiggle his way through and he was like lightning chasing after a through ball. His control was good. And relatively small as he was, he would be able to hit it from wherever he was on the pitch with enough power and accuracy to scare the man between the sticks.

That's the sort of player he was at seventeen: lissom, spontaneous, unpredictable and direct. The same qualities he shows now. Why did it take another four years for Ian to make it? Everyone knew he was good. Danny was one of those guys who was prepared to work at it to see a friend succeed. Ten years older than Ian, he made it his business to see that Ian's talent didn't go to waste.

Too many young black men who should have made it at League clubs had failed to make the grade, and Ian was too special to go the same way. Although 10-Em were recognised as the best team in the area at their standard, every black club had their tales of rejection, of kids whose talent counted for less than the colour of their skin.

By popular account, Ian wasn't the best of his time, but he had two important things going for him. For a start, there was that edge to his play, which later was characterised as the 'fire in his belly'. Also, Ian was so determined to succeed he put the prejudice he encountered to one side, because he loved his football.

Others would simply avoid situations where discrimination would arise. Why go to a club to be abused, to have your blackness thrown back at you as a weakness, when you spend the rest of your life trying to get away from that attitude? Generations were lost to the game who weren't prepared to stand the abuse.

And all the players knew about abuse from their own bitter experiences. Danny was a West Ham fan. Others followed Chelsea, or Tottenham. But they followed from afar. The lads would give them stick about the racialists that went to the games. In the non-League arena, black clubs like 10-Em used to get it all the time from players and fans when they played in the national cup or against teams from the sticks. 'You get out on the park, don't you,' says one stalwart of the London non-League scene, in the curious understatement of the sympathetic white man, 'and there's people playing against you saying a lot things they shouldn't.'

'The teams down in Kent, the one that 10-Em's in now, were the worst,' claims Lee Lang, team manager of Carib, who himself was tried out by Palace twenty years ago, but couldn't handle the discrimination. 'All the racist abuse. It's still within sport all round. I don't care what anyone says, racism will always be there. They are trying to change things, but you're not going to get it.'

Still, more black players were being signed at this time. Danny tried Ian at Terry Venables' Palace, Orient, Charlton and Luton. He would take him or ring up places and say, 'We've got a player here we think will be a good pro.'

'Everywhere they went – midweek, Sundays – Danny and others were on the phone all the time, recommending him to teams. They'd say, "No, no, mate",' says an old team-mate of Ian's. 'I think as soon as they realised he was black they didn't even bother looking at him.

'Palace said no at first. A lot of clubs he went to, and after Palace *did* sign him, they were saying, "is that the same player we could have got?" Racism. You'd get no end of grief. With Ian we couldn't believe he wasn't taken on. And half of the trial was about that.

'We could see the potential then. But none of the pro clubs

wanted him. They'd say, "Too small", "Not good enough", those sorts of things. You can't watch a player once and decide the man's not good enough. Everyone thought Ian would never make it.'

'No disrespect,' a black veteran of the south London soccer scene pointed out to me, 'but it took a white man to put him where he is.'

At seventeen, eighteen and nineteen, with Danny working his ass off to get him started, you couldn't give Ian away. The crunch came in 1982, when he was nineteen. Time was running out if he was to get his foot on the ladder. Danny had arranged a trial through George Petchey, the Millwall manager, when Ian was a schoolboy training with them four years earlier.

'When I was manager at Millwall,' recalls George, 'he was one of the kids that was knocking about there. I can't remember him particularly. We had a tremendous group of kids and they had all sorts of kids in there that escaped. There was a great load of local boys there: the Wallace boys, Ruddock, McCleery, Stevens, O'Callahan.

'When I saw him play for Millwall, though, I thought he would have stayed there and done ever so well. But unfortunately he got into a bit of trouble with one or two others – they were all bloody stupid there at the time, there was a lot of indiscipline. So I rang Brighton and said there's a young kid that ain't too bad, that I could recommend. He must have been around eighteen. I asked the manager if he'd like to give him a game. He said, "Well, what standard is he?" I said, "Well he'll play in the Combination." So I got in touch with Ian and he came down. He turned up without his boots, so we had to find a pair.

'He didn't say much to me. We just talked generally, and he seemed excited about it, and wanted to do well. I think he fancied it down here, because it's a helluva place, Brighton, and I think he fancied it a little bit.'

Ian did indeed fancy it at Brighton, but not for the scenery and the ozone. Danny drove him down there and all he could think was that this was the one. He was confident, but determined not to blow it. Sometimes in trials he'd wanted to succeed too much, thought that the important part was actually *getting* the trial. Not this time. He was going to keep his head and show what he could do. After all, realistically it could be his last chance.

According to George, Ian applied himself to the task at Brighton and was most impressive. The manager gave him a run out against Swindon reserves and he scored a good goal: typically, he outpaced everybody down the left-hand side and cracked it in.

'I thought that was sufficient,' comments George. 'He was slightly built but he was like greased lightning. And he was always going to be some sort of a player. I could never see him not being a player, even when I looked at him when he first came into my sight at Millwall.

'But apparently the staff there at Brighton at the time had too many strikers and they couldn't afford to take another one, so I'm told.

'He just came at the wrong time. Six months later when I was here, we'd have kept him. It was just unlucky. At that time they'd just signed Dean Saunders, they had Terry Connor, Ferguson, Fashanu . . . they had so many strikers it was untrue. And he was just too old. If he'd been a year younger I think they'd have taken him, but he was over junior age.'

'When you have a trial and do as well as you can, and the response is a no, you do get downhearted,' Ian commented. 'When Brighton said they didn't have anything for me after I'd played so well down there, I gave up hope a bit.'

'I scored goals, I worked hard,' he added, 'and after six weeks commuting they said no – for no apparent reason. That was one of my biggest disappointments, because I knew I'd done enough.'

By taking time off work, Ian also lost his job. It was another little tester, a further dig in the ribs. But the almighty blow was that Brighton trial. All Ian was looking at now was playing out his career with 10-Em and the boys. Not that he wouldn't have enjoyed that: it's just that he knew he could have made it as a professional, and still no one would give him a chance to prove it.

Meanwhile the clock kept ticking away.

When Ian returned home, he told Sharon he was close to giving in. No job, no contract, no prospects. It was back to the drawing board. Even his close friends were beginning to doubt he could make the grade after the Brighton heartache.

David Rocastle, Ian's old spar from the Honor Oak estate, used to travel north of the river every day for his youth team training at Arsenal's training ground. He would occasionally bump into Wrighty on the bridge at Brockley station and berate him for not making it, for not converting his talent into a career, even though he knew Ian was trying. Time was just slipping by in Rocky's eyes.

But, like Shakespeare's Henry V – if you please – Ian Wright was about to redeem time when men thought it least likely he would.

5 An Appointment at the Palace

'With Ian, it wasn't a case of knowing he could make it as soon as I saw him. But you could see he had ability, he was two-footed and could go past players on either side. He wasn't a big lad – very slight in fact – but he got involved: he didn't take any prisoners. The more I saw of him, the more I was sure he would make it.'

Billy Smith, ex-manager of Dulwich Hamlet

10-EM-BEE WERE STILL STORMING as the season closed in May 1985. Ian, in particular, was firing on all cylinders. Word was getting out to all the London clubs pro and semi-pro; those who'd seen him before, those who'd previously rejected him and those who'd never even had a sniff of his talent. But the word wasn't always about Ian, now 21; it was more often about his small striking partner at 10-Em.

Nevertheless, the pace of Ian's life was about to accelerate beyond his wildest dreams. He and Sharon had just had a new baby, Bradley, and life was sweet. Sharon was a wonderful mother, the sort of stable, homely type that Ian needed, and he knew it. These things were important. Even if football was stagnating, on a family level, things were moving along nicely.

Soon after Bradley's birth, towards the end of that season, Greenwich Borough's manager, looking to complete a team that was emerging under his guidance as one of the most useful in non-League soccer's upper echelons, was one of those who followed up the tip-off about Ian Wright. Mick Wakefield had a mind that needed opening up as far as black footballers were concerned. He wasn't racist exactly; he just needed a little convincing that what was to become the main tenet of the Crystal Palace Chairman's philosophy – 'Noades' Law of Black Players' assumed that black players lacked 'bottle' – was a fallacy. Nevertheless, he found himself on the sidelines watching the local black side over at Downham one evening. 'I knew straight away he had it,' says Mick, without a hint of retrospection, 'I'd actually gone to see the little fella playing alongside him. But I forgot all about him immediately I saw Ian.

'The first you noticed about him was his fight. He had pace and ability like a lot of coloured players, but it was the aggression that stood out.

'I'd never seen that hunger in a coloured player before. Barnesy is a classic example: John Barnes never played for England like he really wanted it.'

Mick's admiration for Ian is sincere, and his views represent the feelings around at that time, handed down over the years. It doesn't make them all right, but it does make them understandable. There were some levels of prejudice in football Mick couldn't stomach, as Ian was to discover, but in the context of performance, Mick still had much to take on board.

'I already had one coloured guy, Mark Gall,' he says, 'who was a much better player than Ian. I had him four or five years and he scored 150-odd goals, but he didn't have the aggression Ian did. He had the potential to be even more successful than Ian, and there were always people after him, but when I said people were interested in signing him he didn't want to know.

'Like a lot of lads – I had six in my team who could have made it – he preferred to enjoy his football on a Saturday and stay around his friends.' Sadly, well-intentioned Mick couldn't see that his own crude views may have limited his player's ambitions.

Whether that's true or not, Ian was so hungry – 'have boots, will travel' – that such reservations didn't apply. Mick asked Ian to play a few games with Greenwich at the tail-end of that season. Even though he retained his link with 10-Em, it was clear Borough were a very good side.

Above all, it was a step-up. After all Danny Fairman's vain attempts to have his protégé signed professionally, at least this had broken the logjam. The 10-Em-Bee manager and the rest of Ian's team knew there was nothing more to offer him. He'd done as much as he could with the team, and they with him. And if a black player could make it as a professional, he owed it to himself to go for the big time.

Ian took his new opportunity very seriously. He felt a huge sense of responsibility. A lot of friends, people he respected, had invested time, energy and faith in him. Everyone expected him to acquit himself well. He had to repay their faith soon.

It was time to get serious. Exit the japester; re-enter the respectful lad who had charmed his way into every side since he was four. Ian was nervous, but not like he had been at Orient and Brighton. No-one performs well when they're anxious, and Ian was better hardened to rejection by now.

'He was quite quiet,' says Mick Wakefield. 'He conducted himself very well: always enthusiastic at training. There was none of this tantrum stuff you see these days.

'He was exceptionally talented. I didn't need to tell him anything: there was nothing I could teach him because he already had it all. What can you teach a lad like that?'

The only misgivings again concerned his stature. 'He was so thin; like a rake,' remembers Mick. 'And I reckon he must have grown three inches since I first knew him.'

Ian's first awayday with Greenwich Borough was a revelation to him. It involved a trip to the Kent coast, to Deal, and the club hired an executive coach with a video, bar, curtains – the works. 'You could see he just couldn't believe it!,' smiles Mick. 'He said, "It's like a living room!" Funnily enough, the very next week, the same coach crashed with that pop group Bucks Fizz in it.'

It was immediately obvious to Mick that Ian was far too good for local football. He had pace, vision, a good shot, and he worked hard off the ball: 'He'd be back at our box helping win the ball, then he'd charge upfield when we had it and kicked it forward, then if we lost it again, he'd be straight back to our box again. There was none of this standing around on the halfway line waiting for it in those days. He used to come and get it.'

Ian didn't travel alone, though. A team of spars, a posse of old mates would always turn out to watch him. Ian had the sort of character to attract people – with his magnetism, wit, feistiness – and the personality to retain their loyalty; he was inordinately dependable as far as friends were concerned and he expected the same treatment back.

A gaggle of Lewisham lads – some from 10-Em – would gather on the touchline, loudly commenting on the game, urging, scolding, laughing – and often to the accompaniment of a loud ghetto blaster playing whatever tunes were the current favourites: soul, hip-hop, dancehall reggae.

'I don't know how many there were,' recalls Mick. 'But they didn't half make a fucking racket. I don't know what that music was, but it certainly wasn't Elton John. The team always liked it, though, and I think that sort of thing is always good for building up spirit in a side; like Wimbledon have their music in the dressing rooms. I think more teams should do it.'

Greenwich were a class side with the emphasis on youth – the oldest player was 24. Mick liked the kids to be eighteen or nineteen, and so hungry, you'd get immense enthusiasm out of them. They liked their beer and their raving, but at that age, their body could take it: they'd always turn up and always crave success.

'The scouts came swarming,' Mick marvels. 'But then, we always had scouts around us because over an eighteen-month period I hand-picked a very successful team. I'd hardly be at home in the evenings. I used to go to all types of games, everything from League reserve games, to people kicking a ball in the park.

'We had some great players by the end of it: David Roberts, Paul Kelly, Murray Jones, Mark Gall. It was a great all-round team.' Mick left Greenwich Borough at the end of the 1986/87 season. In five terms in charge, he had won the club seven trophies. He's now with Docklands giant-killers Fisher '93.

Amongst the all-rounders in Mick's best team, though, Ian was pre-eminent. Although the striker was one of the older players there, Mick was canny enough to spot his potential. It was probably too late to put him on a contract; he'd surprisingly never signed one with 10-Em-Bee, which shows either naiveté or that old uncertainty. But Mick felt sure Ian was destined for the big league.

'I didn't normally pay the players,' Mick points out, 'but I knew he was a very exceptional talent and I thought he had a chance of making it as a pro, so I paid him wages: £30 a game. He was pretty shocked.'

This was the first proper money that Ian had ever earned from football. The magical effect of that paltry sum shouldn't be under-estimated. It was like a finding a nugget after fifteen fruitless years in the goldmine.

Ian went straight back to his mother. Nesta looked at his beaming face and knew there was finally some good news on the work front. But not what she imagined. 'Look, mum,' he said ecstatically, 'look what I got paid just for playing football.'

Not that the experience was all joy. Ian had been used to abuse from what crowds there were at 10-Em's away matches, and the lads had been used to dealing with it in their own way. But Mick Wakefield was appalled by the treatment meted out to his two black strikers by some supporters in their league.

'You've got to go to some of these grounds to see how bad their supporters are,' says Mick, still disgusted. 'When they were giving Mark Gall and Ian stick I used to say, "The way to answer these people is to stick the ball in the back of the net." And that's what they'd do.'

But that wouldn't always stem the disgusting vitriol heaped on the heads of his twin black strike force. At one ground on the coast, Mark and Ian once jumped into the crowd to sort out a particularly nasty individual. Mick couldn't condone it, but he smiles about it now. That supporter got no less than he deserved and, at this level, a player could let himself go like that and get away with it. But it made the manager wonder how Ian would cope in the beckoning professional game.

Mindful that the player would have a chance to find out sooner rather than later, Micky Wakefield looked to the future. By the end of the 1984/85 campaign, Ian had played six times for his red-and-white braves and scored eight goals.

'I sat down with him after that,' says Micky, 'and we spoke about the following season. He promised to sign for me. I wanted to get his signature, because I was certain he was going to be signed by a big club soon. But it never happened.'

New horizons were opening out in Ian's life. Danny Fairman was still badgering away at anyone who would listen about Ian being League material and finally scouts were starting to take notice.

At the dog-end of the season, while he was still splitting his playing duties between 10-Em and Greenwich, Ian was watched by the youth development officer at Crystal Palace, Peter Prentice. It followed a call from 10-Em's Danny Fairman. Or two, or three.

'The night Ian was spotted,' enthuses Greenwich boss Mick Wakefield, 'I think I counted seven scouts there from Sutton, Charlton and other clubs apart from Palace. I think they'd come to see Mark Gall, but he was injured early on. Wrighty stole the show that night anyway. We beat Deal Town 7-2 and Ian scored four of them.'

As only seems to happen in football, movies and pantomime, one person's injury led inexorably to another's opportunity. Peter Prentice approached Ian after the game and offered him the opportunity of a week's trial with the Selhurst club the following pre-season. Ian was cool: he'd been along this route before. It was one thing to be casually invited for a trial. It was another to get a contract with a League club. Nothing was ever quite cut and dried for Ian Wright.

But suddenly all Danny Fairman's boats were coming in at once. Billy Smith, now manager of Kingstonian, was in charge of Isthmian League club Dulwich Hamlet back in 1985, as well as performing the odd scouting function for Palace.

As it happened, in the summer of 1985, 10-Em had played in a cup final at Dulwich's Champion Hill ground. One of Billy Smith's friends was there and was enormously impressed with Ian's contribution to the game. He passed on his observations to the Dulwich boss, who had already been contacted by Danny Fairman some time before.

It was probably a good job that he hadn't added a question mark about Ian's discipline – off the field of play. When 10-Em had contacted Dulwich to check the details of the fixture, they had been warned in no uncertain terms that no alcohol was to be allowed before or after the game. This was something of a shock to the system for the 10-Em regulars – after all, they owed their existence to the two public houses that had joined forces to create the team. They even met in the pub before a game, for god's sake.

When they arrived at the ground for this important tie, the prohibition rule was repeated. It didn't go down well – unlike the prospect of a lager or two. But boys will be boys, and a number of the 10-Em side decided to ignore the consequences and slunk off unseen for a jar in a local watering hole – Ian Wright amongst them. Happily, this 'beer hunter' subterfuge was overlooked in the report to Billy Smith.

'So I went to watch 10-Em-Bee,' relates Billy. 'Ian did well and I invited him to come down to Dulwich for pre-season training. I remember it was a nightmare trying to contact him. He seemed to be coming from all directions.'

Suddenly everyone wanted a slice of Ian: Greenwich, Dulwich, Palace ... Only 10-Em were willing to let go, wish Ian well and, fingers crossed, hope for the best. Bloody hell he deserved it!

Ian didn't need to think twice about the offer from Palace, the erstwhile 'team of the eighties', languishing though they were in the lower foothills of the Second Division midway through a decade that was supposed to belong to them. He was still single-minded in wanting to dump the plastering, the unemployment, the drudgery and make it as a pro. But after his previous experiences with big clubs, Ian wasn't prepared to burn all his boats in case they rejected him. Again, it says something about his confidence at the time. For once he was staying cool, preparing himself for a let-down.

Ian was smart. He went for the best of both worlds: he didn't say no to Micky Wakefield's Greenwich, preferring to keep that door open, and while he awaited the real test – his trial with Palace in pre-season – he would also train for Dulwich with a view to a place there – Billy Smith always kept his boys going over the summer, even if it was just to meet and loosen up once or twice a week. It would also serve as an easing-in for what he might expect at Palace's Mitcham training ground.

'Eventually I got hold of him,' says Billy, 'and he came down to join us. He was with us for about three or four training sessions. I was scouting for Palace at the time, and I could see there was something about him. I told Steve we had a boy who was worth a look.'

Peter Prentice, brought in by Steve Coppell to handle the renovation of Palace's youth policy and who'd already made his offer to Ian, was starting to worry about Billy Smith's excitement. Billy would pop in to see Steve Coppell, Palace's manager of one year's standing, have a cup of tea, and keep the Palace staff up to date on the non-League scene. In his time, he had made some decent discoveries for the Selhurst club: Andy Gray had just joined, still to come were Alan Pardew, Tony Finnigan, Ian Cox, Murray Jones (a Greenwich Borough lad) and, ironically, Keith McPherson, Ian's old school team-mate.

One day Billy came in to see Steve and, amid the usual banter, enthused, 'I've got this black kid who's come to train, and he's too good for us, so send somebody down to look at him, he's a bit special.'

'Ian had started training with Dulwich to get fit for his trial with us and with a view to playing for them if he failed to make it with us,' says Peter. 'The two clubs have always had close ties, and I was talking to their manager Bill Smith who kept going on about this lad Wright and I'm thinking, "Oh gawd, I hope they haven't put him on a contract!" '

As it was, it hadn't yet crossed Billy's mind to sign Ian on pro forms – he had an amateur Isthmian contract. From now on, things would move too fast for him to make good that omission. Persisting with Ian's case, he saw Steve Coppell directly, suggesting he come and watch a Dulwich Hamlet 'Possible vs. Probables' just before the season started.

The manager couldn't make it. In truth, he took the whole 'boy's a bit special' thing with the usual pinch of salt. But YDO Peter Prentice went along to see how the lad he'd seen last season was shaping up. Playing for the 'seconds', Ian scored four goals before half-time against the senior team.

Peter was now understandably anxious to confirm the loose appointment he had with Ian. 'I spoke to him as he came off the pitch to remind him that he was going to train with us,' remembers Peter, 'and everything followed on from that.'

Ian didn't get to play a first team game for Dulwich. Instead, he turned up at Mitcham to try his luck with Palace – another potential do or die session, but one which Ian handled more diffidently than before. He didn't rush to answer Peter's inquiry. He was just cool.

'By that time in my life I was prepared to trudge out a living for the rest of my life,' Ian revealed. 'I told my boss about it then told him I didn't want to go at first. The business at Brighton played on my mind. I couldn't stop thinking that that was as good as I could play, that I couldn't possibly do as well again. I didn't see the point in turning up if they were just going to show me the door. I went to that trial thinking, "I'm going to do this how *I* want." '

Steve Coppell treated him no differently to any other kid straight off the street: 'I just gave him my standard spiel at the start of a week's training at the beginning of pre-season,' he recalls. 'I said to him, "It's an opportunity. Try to feel at home with us and do your best." '

Ian was offered a week's training, 'just to see what he could do'. At the time, Palace were pretty strapped for cash and were quite keen to bring lads in to train. There had been quite a high turnover already that season.

'Sometimes after one training session you know they're dummies and you want to kick them out,' says Steve. 'But with Ian it was obvious after just three days that he was a fair player. We made a commitment to sign him straight away and that's when we offered him a three-month contract.'

'We had a few friendlies and it was because so many regulars were out with strains and blisters,' recalls Peter Prentice, 'that we had to put in whoever we could get.

'I clearly remember Ian's first game for the club was a Palace XI against Kingstonian. We had a very depleted side, full of kids and triallists like Ian, but we beat them and he scored a magnificent goal in the first half.

'It was enough to convince Steve Coppell to offer him a contract there and then and he was in the first team soon afterwards.' If you examine the official records, you will see that Ian Wright was signed from Greenwich Borough. No mention of 10-Em-Bee or Dulwich. It's been the subject of anguish for certain of the parties involved. Why didn't Ian sign with 10-Em just before so that Palace had to pay an impecunious club a transfer fee? Or Dulwich – they could have done with the cash. Did he think a signing fee would be an encumbrance that might tip the balance out of his favour? Did he simply want to be free of any ties?

Much has been made of a what is really a non-starter of a story. 'There's a lot of speculation about this,' says Steve Coppell. 'Ian informed me at the time that he never played with Greenwich Borough. He trained with them and may have had a couple of games at the end of the previous season. And when he came to us we didn't have to pay any fee to anybody, he was free.'

That didn't deter the Sunday tabloid the *People* from printing a spurious piece, seemingly based on the angry grievances of Greenwich Borough, which appeared in October 1990 to coincide with Ian's call-up for international duty and which suggested Palace had ripped off the non-League club and stolen its players.

'I was absolutely furious when I read the story,' spits Micky Wakefield, on whose supposed comments the piece was alleged to have been based. 'It was rubbish. Palace didn't need to pay Greenwich a fee because he hadn't signed anything with us at that time.'

So a future England striker, 'golden boot' winner and great servant of two London clubs, was acquired for nothing. Once he was earning decent money, friends believe that Ian made a small donation to 10-Em's depleted coffers as a friend and out of respect for what they'd done for him. As it was, Ian was initially put on £100 a week – and now look at how much he has earned from just playing football, mum!

Steve Coppell was surprised at the quality of his acquisition. 'Everything appeared to be an asset,' he says. 'He was really raw, and his rawness was magnified by his enthusiasm. He wanted to do everything, take everything. He was buzzing. He was respectful to the senior pros, but at the same time, his ability put him on a par with them. Even after three days it was obvious he was something different.'

His fellow players recognised Ian's quality instantly. Genial George Wood, Palace's veteran goalkeeper, was typical. 'I couldn't believe he'd never played pro football,' he reminisced to the Palace fanzine *Eagle Eye*. 'As soon as I saw him in a practice match I thought, "Hmm, put him in the side Saturday."

'He was a chirpy, cocky lad and the other players couldn't believe he'd never played at any club before. It just shows: how many people are playing park football like him?'

By now, Ian was trying to cram everything in quickly simply because he had arrived so late, like a tardy guest at a banquet. The first couple of weeks pre-season, he just lapped it up. He loved the training, never got tired: left foot, right foot, heading, pace – the one thing Steve Coppell always looks for in a forward – he had a little bit of everything.

Reports emerged from the training ground of how the irrepressible young debutant made mincemeat out of the pedestrian centre back Mickey Droy, who had been signed on a free the previous

March and who looked more like one of James Bond's adversaries than a footballer. However, Ian knew when enough was enough; when not to push it too far. But inside he was boiling with joy. He acted like a pro. Like everybody who wants to do well in football, he learned about the game as he was talking it. It was just like the 10-Em dressing room, except at a higher level. He could handle it. 'I thought it was quite easy,' Ian said later. 'I didn't realise that you can come in at a certain time of the morning and be finished a few hours later. It made me think, "If this is what you've got to do, I don't mind doing it".' He couldn't contain himself. This is what he felt he was born for. The first people he told were his family and his friends from 10-Em. It was the least he could do: he owed it all to them, more or less.

Very gradually – and not soon enough from his point of view – Ian was able to spend some of his hard-earned dosh: buy some of the clothes he wanted, look after Sharon and the kids, buy some things for his mum, see a few friends right for cash. When he went back to break the good news to his old teachers at Samuel Pepys, he was already sporting the big pimple cap, jauntily pulled to one side, that remains his trademark.

Amongst those he saw was Peter McCarthy. 'The first I heard he was doing reasonably well was when he was at Greenwich Borough. I thought, "That's not a bad league, he must be doing okay."

'And then he came up to the school to see me and the other teachers. I said to him, "How's it going, where are you now?" And he said, "I'm at Crystal Palace." He was the first to tell me he was up there. I thought, "Oh good".

'I wasn't quite sure how long he'd been there, but straight away I said, "How's things going? Are you behaving yourself?" "Oh yeah, yeah, course I am." I thought, "Good. You've made it. It's up to you now." '

Few of the Pepys champs returned to their old school, and some of the teachers from Ian's era, most notably Eric Summers, had gone by 1985. But it was a moving moment for Peter, his old football coach. 'I like to think – although he's been through a lot better people than I am – that when he did go into football, that he remembered a lot of what he learnt at Pepys.

'I was very surprised that he went into professional football, to be honest, much as he liked it. Once the boys left, I must admit, I would try to say to them, "Do you belong to a club?" If they didn't I would say, "There's a local one where you live, do you want me to phone someone?", to see they were all right. Ian was all right then.'

Ian was more than all right. Amongst Palace's most faithful – those impatient wretches who feel the compulsion to attend all the pre-season matches – Ian was becoming an instant crowd hero. The next time he paid a visit to Pepys, Ian would have to stay in his car outside, and abandon his visit after the kids mobbed him.

'That summer we went on a pre-season tour to Exeter,' says Steve Coppell. 'We stayed at the University and we played a couple of games down there, Exeter and Torquay, maybe Plymouth. Even after just a couple of weeks training he came with us on that tour of the first team, and he played a game or two as well.'

He'd quickly established himself in the dressing room culture too. Ian can be very quiet when he's not sure of his environment or the people in it. Among friends, though, he's ebullient and expansive. Ian had never struggled to make friends. There were few funnier, more attractive personalities than his on top form. Ian was used to the banter from 10-Em, and he was always one for being with the lads, talking football, football, football. It was heaven.

'He always got on well with his team-mates,' remembers Peter Prentice. 'And he had an awareness of people around him, which you tend to find with players who come from non-League football. They are more appreciative and have a bit more perspective on what life is all about, whereas kids who sign on with clubs at sixteen don't know anything else.'

It helped Ian that Palace were one of few clubs with a decent quota of 'brothers': even if there was an obvious divide between black and white, there were never really any cliques as such. Nevertheless, Andy Gray, signed the previous autumn, and his friend Tony Finnigan, a former England under-21, were two that Ian gravitated towards.

From a professional point of view, Ian could have perhaps

chosen better but he had been drawn towards irascible individuals all his life, people who were a bit spicy. Outside football, or if there was no axe to grind between the two of you, Andy Gray was brilliant company, a nice guy to be with; good fun on an evening out. But he could be a sulker – like Ian to some extent – a mixer and a headstrong character who upset some of the senior pros soon after his arrival. He also had a weight problem. In short, Andy wasn't always fit enough in mind and body to do himself justice. On his day, though, he was one of the best players in his position.

Andy had entered the game late, just like Ian, but whereas Wrighty's attempt to cheat time meant working at his trade, trying to stick to what the boss said and learning from the older players, Andy Gray was less compliant. He earned an unfair reputation for having a chip on his shoulder – always the routine when a surly player happens to be black. And as Gray was someone, like Ian, who wouldn't take stick from anyone, it's likely that the perception of him amongst others in the game was dictated to some extent by his colour.

He had two spells at Palace, the first ending in curious circumstances in late 1987 after speculation over his attitude towards an inquiry from Graham Taylor's Aston Villa that Palace had rebutted. Andy initially expressed his resolve to stay put – he was their best player that season – but then suddenly slapped in a transfer request making public his unhappiness, over some time, at the club.

Andy wasn't one to hide his feelings. His brooding mood and lack of motivation filled the dressing room like a noxious brume. When Steve Coppell eventually responded, it was surgically: he simply cut the promising midfielder out, selling him to Villa Park for £150,000, a third of the price he might have expected.

At a press conference, the manager cited the player's intolerably bad influence: he was unsettling the rest of the players with his call to arms – and Ian Wright in particular. (This explanation was rendered all the more quaint when Palace re-signed the player in August 1989.)

Tony Finnigan, a strong and skilful midfielder released by Fulham, had been recognised early in his career as a great prospect but was, like Andy Gray, dogged by questions about his attitude;

he was 'the type you loved to have on the park, but not the sort of guy you wanted in your dressing room', according to one Palace insider.

Even though he made over a hundred appearances for Palace and often looked a class above some of his team-mates, he also had a chequered history at the club. Tony quit Palace in 1988 for Blackburn, one of Don Mackay's acquisitions, but he left the Lancashire club after a tormented twelve months in which he was subjected to racial abuse from his own fans and had his car repeatedly vandalised. (In 1994/95, the Premiership-winning club contained not one single black player in their first team squad.)

From then on, it was a sad downward spiral for a stylish player who'd promised so much. In 1993, Tony found himself back at Fulham, training as a non-contract player. 'I really will go anywhere and try anything,' he said. 'I know I've had my problems in the past, but I'm ready to get my head down and work hard now. All I want is the chance to show what I can do.'

Ian Wright is an honourable man. He isn't the sort of guy who will drop an old friend, even if it goes against professional advice. He's a believer in the basic goodness of people – unless they've crossed him. Tony and he had good times together at Selhurst, and kept in touch over the years. Now, Tony needed his friends even more. Ian refused to drop his former Palace pal even if it meant being dragged into an area that would endanger his image as a media star.

But it all went horribly wrong for Tony in November 1994, and there was nothing even Ian could do to stop it. Fulham manager Ian Branfoot noted that Tony hadn't turned up for training one morning, but there was nothing extraordinary in that. However, police staging an undercover narcotics operation in central London's Covent Garden swooped to arrest Tony, then still with Fulham, and a Manchester woman, Susan Ellis, found with a kilo of heroin on them. Both were charged with possessing the drug with intent to supply.

It is to Ian's eternal credit that he ignored the obvious possibility of 'guilt by association' and quietly supported Tony. Obviously, Ian had no knowledge of Tony's socially destructive habit, but like a true friend he still keeps in touch with his troubled mate.

Back in the early days of Palace, though, Andy and Tony were Ian's new raving partners and, from the first days at Palace, with money burning his pocket, he enjoyed the night life of London. Palace, a young side being constructed by a relatively glamorous manager, would make a name for themselves over the next few years: both on and off the pitch. Thankfully, Ian's adrenaline and enthusiasm made up for any sleep that he lost nightclubbing.

'When he was at Palace we used to see more of him than now he's at Arsenal,' says Lee Lang from Carib. 'Even used to play with us occasionally. Sunday morning he'd come for a kick about. Which he wasn't supposed to. When he was at Palace he was still one of the boys.

'That was it with Ian: football, football, football. If he wasn't playing for 10-Em or whoever, he'd find a game elsewhere.'

'When he was at Palace,' says another old acquaintance, 'he was always caught out. There were nights when he should have been home in bed because they were playing someone important the next day, and he was caught out.'

Ian had always loved to rave. Now he had the status and the cash to go to town. Shaun was five and starting school at Turnham, and Sharon was stuck at home nursing Bradley through his first years. Luckily, the soccer player's lifestyle is conducive to raising a family: training in the morning, afternoons free.

But Ian enjoyed his nights. With Andy Gray and Tony Finnigan, and in later years, Wimbledon's John Fashanu, Mitchell Thomas and Garth Crooks of Spurs and the Arsenal boys Michael Thomas and Kevin Campbell, a few boxers and the like, this was the dawning of the network of young, gifted and black sportsmen who found themselves on the same wavelength and at the same nightclubs. They came to be dubbed the 'Black Pack' after the hard-drinking scoundrel gang of Frank Sinatra, Dean Martin, Sammy Davis Jr. *et al*, known as the 'Rat Pack'. They also represented a new generation of successful black men: wealthy, assertive, glamorous. And there was a certain kudos and self-assurance in the 'Black Pack' thang: they quickly established themselves on the London society map.

Three of the Palace 'Black Packers' were Billy Smith 'discoveries'. 'The Ian Wright experience was very similar to the way I found

Andy Gray,' he says. 'He had been let go by Palace and Brentford and came to me at Corinthian Casuals. He did well, and then got another chance at Palace. In a way, seeing him do so well in his career gave me even more pleasure because I knew Andy longer.

'They were very similar people, though whereas Andy to an extent thought the world owed him a living, Ian was never like that.'

Billy was drawn to the black players, though not through altruism or any liberal instincts. In fact, it was the adverse social conditions that made them what they were in his book. 'I found them the hungrier ones,' he says. 'Most of them are unemployed and they really want to make it. It's still their escape route.'

Billy likes to recall the devotion to association football of a bunch of black kids, who used to hang around when he was at non-League Carshalton – they would habitually turn up for reserve team games. 'We didn't pay them, so it must have cost them a bit, but they turned up week in, week out – because they wanted it, they were dedicated.

'You don't get that with the lads that have lived a comfortable life in the suburbs, where they can play their tennis or their golf. If you are from East London, or Brixton, you've got a different attitude.

'Ian was like that. He had that desire, that hunger. Those players are winners for you. He hasn't changed in that respect.'

It was soon obvious that this particular winner, unpolished as he was, was ready to be unleashed on the League. After a brief spell in the reserve team, Ian made his debut against Huddersfield, coming on as sub for another Coppell new boy, stocky Andy Higginbottom, and joining Barber and Gray upfront. Ian was so nervous, he remembers running around, aimlessly chasing the ball and making little impact on his debut. His chief memory is of ending the game completely breathless.

'He wasn't like a starry-eyed kid, though,' declares Peter Prentice. 'He'd been rejected by Millwall and Brighton and others and had drifted into the non-League scene while working as a plasterer with Lewisham council.

'He stood out a mile at that level, and though he had to adapt to the rigours of training full-time, he was very, very quick and had good vision even then.'

By the first week of October, Ian had launched himself four times from the Palace bench and made his first abortive start – ignominiously subbed in a League Cup draw at home to Charlton. It wasn't the same auspicious start that Chris Armstrong was later to make; more like Bruce Dyer's in fact.

'Ian served a long apprenticeship as a super-sub,' remarks Steve Coppell. 'It was a deep learning curve for a 21-year-old to go from not being involved with professionals, to getting a more professional attitude.

'And sometimes he did do stupid things. He lost the ball in situations where he should have just laid it off and yet occasionally he'd do something that was just outstanding.'

The reaction of the Palace faithful to Ian's early cameos was mixed. 'Who's that bloody whippet up front?'; 'He may be a headless chicken but at least he's trying'; or 'Jesus, isn't that a footballer?' Those were routine terrace refrains. The crowd empathised with this gangly lad who could hardly keep his feet, because everyone knew he'd come into the game late; like Bambi on the ice, perhaps, they sensed one day he would be their king. They needed to believe in a hero.

More down-to-earth qualities were there if you looked. Ian was everywhere. Was he fast? Was he? He was like shit off a stick, that's how fast he was. Steaming around in that tippy-toed run of his, like a gazelle playing pig-in-the-middle. He was completely unprocessed, utterly enthusiastic, palpably desperate to prove himself, wanting to play everywhere, wanting it all.

He would beat three players then launch one into the stand. He would run box to box and slip on his arse. And he would twist, feint and glide with an urgency unlike any previous Palace player before him – even the much-fêted Vince Hilaire. And he'd shoot from anywhere – the old trademark is still potent. Sometimes his enthusiasm got the better of him. Steve Coppell, like many a manager before him, would remind Ian, as gently as a football coach can, where he was supposed to be playing. He was like a rampant stallion.

What was clear, after a soul-destroying period for the club, was that Coppell's Palace might have a player on their hands at last. It had been a long time. 'It was a miserable Second Division team,' says John Ellis of Palace's now defunct fanzine *Eagle Eye*. 'Nobody could score, and suddenly we had someone who seemed to be able to play football.'

Managers often create a team that is the antithesis of their own style as a player: George Graham used to throw caution to the wind playing for Arsenal; Kenny Dalglish was a subtle, cultured performer. Neither created teams after their own image, and so it was with Steve Coppell. Although work rate was always one of the Manchester United winger's strong points, he also had flair, especially when Ron Atkinson's team sported him on one flank and chirpy Gordon Hill on the other. United were cocky, flash and fitfully brilliant.

As a team manager, Steve Coppell was less flamboyant. His purchases for Palace had pragmatism stamped all over them, both in terms of outlay and type. Cash was tight – Ian was told he was only given a three-month deal originally because it was all the club could afford.

Steve was prepared to work within Ron Noades' strict financial parameters, even though the youth team that had recently produced Hilaire and Billy Gilbert amongst others was virtually extinct: it had withdrawn from the South-East Counties League during Alan Mullery's reign because Palace couldn't afford to take on enough apprentices to field a side, and wouldn't recover for a few more years, due to the efforts of future manager Alan Smith and Peter Prentice. Palace were living up to Enfield manager Eddie McCluskey's description of them as the 'smallest big time club I've ever seen'.

After the torrid first half of the decade, in which managers passed through Selhurst as if it was a revolving door, Steve Coppell, the league's youngest gaffer, introduced a stable, consolidating regime that was just what the club needed. (Palace had had seven managers in four years: Terry Venables, Ernie Walley, Malcolm 'fedora' Allison, Dario Gradi, Steve Kember, Dave Bassett – for all of two days – and Mullery.)

Steve Coppell's pithiest early recruits all had a physical presence that the wily winger had patently lacked himself: the combative Gray (just three months younger than Ian and also getting his first pro runout) and tempestuous Finnigan, garguantuan Droy, Glaswegian winger Alan Irvine and Derby's Kevin Taylor. It wasn't as if there was much that had gone out the other way: Vince Hilaire and Billy Gilbert had left after Mullery, then Peter Nicholas, Jerry Murphy, Kevin Mabbutt (brother of Gary) . . .

Peter Nicholas sounded one of several premature death-knells when he left in the spring before Ian arrived: 'I've wanted to go since the summer when Billy Gilbert and Vince Hilaire left,' he said. 'Once they went, I felt the club didn't want to go places.'

It had been that sort of spell. Cash-strapped Palace had to take in the Valley-less Charlton as lodgers. And their ranks were stocked with several of the ageing players that their 'team of the eighties' used to put five past at other clubs. As they say, be nice on the way up, because you might need someone on the way down.

At least Steve Coppell had arrested Palace's fall, even if scoring was still a problem. Before Ian had settled in, Gray and Finnigan were both tried up front alongside the lumbering Trevor Aylott, Tony later dropping back to defence, and Andy to attacking midfield.

Once Ian Wright was a feature, it would have been tempting to put such an obvious goalscoring talent straight into the team that was having trouble finding the net: only Kevin Mabbutt and Andy Gray notched double figures in the six campaigns up to 1986/87. It says something about how unco-ordinated the Brockley boy appeared that Steve Coppell chose to employ him as a late sub, a greyhound to harry opposition defences.

But midway through October, the Palace boss sent Ian on in exchange for the pedestrian Aylott against Oldham at home. With minutes to go, Palace were trailing 2-1. Then, in a late red-and-blue frenzy, Kevin Taylor made the scores level. Incredibly, in the last minute, Ian Wright latched on to a hopeful cross from Alan Irvine at the near post, glancing a header in from an impossible angle – oh my god: GOAL! Ian hurt himself in the process – the process of celebrating his first professional goal, that is, as he ran and ran and ran.

The crowd sang his name for the first time: '. . . *Ian Wright, Ian Wright, Ian Wright* . . .' So began a love affair that was to last six years.

Palace fans at last began to believe that it was definitely worth persisting with him. After another goalscoring super-sub appearance against Blackburn, Ian was given a run out from the start for the first time in the League away to Bradford. But Ian was over-eager, and he was relegated to the bench for the next eight games.

It's a cliché often trotted out that such and such a player 'treats every game as if it's his last'. Ian Wright's problem was that he played each match as if it were his first. He was obviously gifted, but positionally inept. Ian wasn't yet the super-confident man he came to be later. He had yet to prove anything – one goal was nothing. He thought the manager should have persisted with him.

'Ninety per cent of the time he was good fun to be around,' recalls Steve Coppell. 'But he did tend to get very morose occasionally if things didn't go right. His chin would be on the floor, and that also was exaggerated.'

People who didn't know Ian saw him as a typical goalscorer. Poachers are all the same; they're not happy unless they're in the goalmouth smacking the ball in. 'The only one I've seen smile on TV is Gary Lineker,' claims George Petchey, 'and that's only cos he's got a good set of teeth.'

For the most part, though, Ian was a livewire, absolutely determined to learn his trade, with a voracious appetite for professional knowledge, which he would coax from or observe in other players. One incident is typical. In his second year at Palace, the young striker attended a Professional Footballers' Association function and got talking to Chris Waddle, who had already noted the impact Ian had made. This was great: a hero of Ian's who actually thought he had what it took.

Ian often needed reassurance in those early years. He spoke with Chris for some time that night, working through his thoughts, testing his interpretation of the game, and pleased when Chris Waddle concurred with his views. It meant that all the time he'd been playing at being a pro for school, St Paul's, 10-Em, he'd been on the right track, thinking the right things. There was no great mystery kept from him, just a lot of tricks, disciplines and ideas to take on board.

Much has been made of Ian's late entry into the game – not least by the persistent references of the man himself. But in truth he was in a better situation than many of his contemporaries who'd been at a League club since they were kids. Many of them, like his old school team-mate Henry Laville, had never made a first team appearance. A large proportion of footballers don't make their debuts until they are twenty or so.

Others don't make so much of their tardy entrance. Ian's big hero Cyrille Regis came into the game at around the same age; Les Ferdinand likewise; Ian's later colleague at Arsenal, Alan Smith, entered the professional game at nineteen. John Barnes didn't actually start playing *football* until his teens. The biological fact is that players develop at different ages. Ian's frustration stems from the simple matter that he wasn't able to do what he adored from an even earlier age.

It's disingenuous of Ian to protest as if he's the only one: perhaps it was the success of those he considered himself on a par with – Paul Elliott, Danny Wallace, Steve Anthrobus, Paul Walsh and Keith McPherson, for example – that grated with him. He felt he was being left behind, which is an ungracious approach to say the least.

There was almost desperation in his longing to fulfil a dream. 'I may have come into the game late,' he told a reporter soon after signing, 'but I'm determined to make up for lost time.'

It was that old clock ticking again.

'He was just wonderfully naive,' says Steve. 'Sometimes I had to think twice about whether he was just asking me stupid questions as a wind-up. He wanted it desperately. I've never seen a player who wanted to be a professional more than Ian Wright.'

The manager was hugely impressed with his non-League acquisition from an early stage. 'There were so many standout performances,' he says, 'even as a super-sub. I couldn't think of a better sub to have at that stage, and when he established himself, he was so good.' However, it was also becoming clear that someone was needed to chaperone Ian. He was a quick learner with huge potential, but he needed someone to look after him, keep him heading in the right direction. Gray and Finnigan were good mates, but they weren't model pros. They could possibly lead him astray. Coppell began his search for the man who would look after Ian and bring out his full potential. Whatever it was Ian had could easily slip out of its harness. He needed breaking in.

'It was obvious he had something,' Steve said later. 'What we had to do was channel it in the right direction. He has only one flaw: he's a hothead.'

Ian stuck at it, began to unlearn some of the bad habits that had made him such an asset at non-League level, but which made him a liability amongst the big boys. He worked on his positional awareness, his reaction to other players and closed the season sweetly: ten starts on the spin. He enjoyed the pre-season, went a bit mad and returned for the next campaign rampant.

By now, news was beginning to spread about Ian's success, but he was still 'one of the lads'. Early on in his Palace career, Ian actually went even further in maintaining his links with his past. If Palace had used him as a non-playing sub or brought him on for one of those-blink-and-you-miss-it cameos on the Saturday, he might turn out for some local team the next day for a kickaround if they were playing in some vital cup match – he has the medals to prove it.

Ian never did that for 10-Em. They recognised that it was no good for their 'graduates'. So many had failed to break through, so many had the odds stacked against them, that the last thing they wanted was to add to the obstacles in his way. They knew that plenty of lads would feel they owed something to the club and its members, but it was the club's policy not to invite a player who'd made it back to play, just in case he got into trouble with his League club – it was totally unprofessional risking injury in some meaningless match against a team of cloggers just to 'keep your eye in'.

Friends at 10-Em and the other football clubs were kept informed of developments at Palace in Ian's entertaining progress reports, enlivened by wicked impressions of his team-mates and other significant figures, and funny anecdotes, all related in his usual frenetic style by the man himself. Ian would turn up at 10-Em training sessions and keep the dressing room in stitches with his stories of life as a football pro, or he'd give them the low-down in a bar or a night club over a few drinks.

His former team-mates were made up for Ian: he was obviously loving every second of his new life, and he deserved it. But he was still playing at being a pro, not acting professionally. It was all very well acting the part with his friends, it was another doing it consistently on – and off – the pitch.

It was still a surprise to some of Ian's old acquaintances that when the new season started, and Palace began to show some form, a character called Wright was one of their stars. Eric Summers, Ian's old head of sport, had left Pepys and gone to work in Germany for a year and a half. Soon after he returned, he was mooching around in his house with the football on the television, more as background than anything else, though the local heroes, Palace, were playing.

Then he looked at the TV screen and saw a familiar sight. 'I saw this figure running across the pitch,' he says. 'Ian's got a very distinctive run. Like, quick movement, up on his toes. My eyes just picked it up and I thought, "Funny, I know that run." And the bloke went, "Wright . . ." And I went, "What?" "Ian Wright . . ." And I was shocked. I turned it up.'

Eric hadn't had any contact with his former pupil since he'd left school. He was quite surprised Ian had made it: Henry Laville, yes; Keith McPherson, sure; but little Ian?

'I didn't really think Ian had that hunger in those days that would make him a top sportsman – it's something they all have,' confesses Eric. 'For him, luckily, it grew up a little bit later. Whoever took him in at 10-Em-Bee, there must have been someone there who helped him develop. I remembered Ian as a highly active sort of guy with a lot of pent-up energy. Like now, he's "whaaa!" Frustration. He wanted it so much he was making mistakes. He tried so damn hard to get there.'

Ian had finished his first season on a roll, but there was no guarantee that situation would carry through into next season. Steve Coppell liked him; Ian knew that because the boss would spend a lot of time answering his questions, working on his game. But Steve could be aloof at times, and when you want something as much as Ian wanted a career in football, you wanted to fill those silences, plug the void. He needed to score goals to prove himself to Steve and all the others. It was the only way he knew.

As it happened, Steve Coppell was running out of attacking options. Andy Gray had been the club's top scorer the previous season with a mediocre ten goals. He and Barber were paired upfront with Ian Wright in the opening weeks. Ian, who had finished with nine in his last term, scored in the first game of 1986/87 in the 3-2 home defeat of Barnsley, but failed to repeat the feat until mid-October. Prolific wasn't the word that sprang to mind, and Steve Coppell managed to convince Ron Noades to open the club coffers for a recognised striker.

Mark Bright was languishing in Leicester's reserves during Bryan Hamilton's brief tenure at the club, though he had been groomed as a replacement for Gary Lineker (who had moved on to Everton). Mark was a shrewd selection by Steve Coppell. Just a few weeks younger than Ian's influential older brother Morris, he had been fostered out with his brother to a family living on a miners' estate in Stoke, where there were few other kids of Afro-Caribbean descent: an entirely different upbringing to Ian's.

Also in contrast to Ian, Mark had done well for himself financially, working as a hydraulic engineer while battling away in non-League football. In fact, when he was invited to join Port Vale, his first League club, he took a drop in salary.

Despite the fact that things weren't working out for him at Leicester and that, under Hamilton, Leicester were about to lose their five-year grip on top-flight football, Mark still needed some convincing that a move to London was in his interests. When they met, Steve Coppell emphasised the fact that he would be guaranteed a regular first-team place, and that he would be occupying a fundamental role in a promising young side. He also mentioned that he had a green striker who would benefit from playing alongside a man like him.

It's been suggested that Mark Bright was also keen to get away from the bigots in the Filbert Street crowd who habitually harangued black players. But Palace, even with a side that under Steve Coppell's tutelage was emboldened in every department by Afro-Caribbean players (who, at one stage represented the majority), wasn't without its unreconstructed white supremacists. The bigots in the crowd may have been reduced to a rump by the new nature of the club, but they could be vocal enough.

Standing at Selhurst, near some of those New Addington nutters, soon after Ian Wright had established himself in the Palace side, was informative. It was a small but certainly not select crowd. When Ian was being cautioned near the touchline for a needless foul, some of Palace's own fans were amusing each other by shouting out, 'Oi, ref, watch out or he'll mug you!' and 'Don't do it ref, he's got a knife!' I heard it. Ian must have too. One of the first songs sung to honour Ian Wright betrayed the tug of loyalties going on in the minds of those who sang it: '*He may be black, he may be white/We don't care, he's Ian Wright!*' The devil can always cite scripture for his own purposes.

For Steve Coppell, race was never an issue in the dressing room. After his upbringing and experiences in south London, Ian was no shrinking violet on the subject.

'He wasn't sensitive,' says the manager. 'He was very bold about his colour, not reticent at all. It was never a problem. We always used to keep the colour thing as a jokey environment. We never had any offence within the club.'

Nevertheless Ian couldn't avoid the issues. 'The first time we went down Millwall and watched Ian for Palace,' says one old football friend, 'we couldn't believe it: the noise and the things that were coming out down there, the bananas that were thrown. Out of this world. I'm not knocking the clubs who gave black people a chance. It's the supporters.' And Millwall were Ian's team, who he'd once dreamed of playing for.

Ian did manage to get his own back on the Den fans in small ways. Once when they came to Selhurst, Ian reacted to a tackle and fell over, apparently in paralysing agony, on the line near the away fans. They seethed and screamed all sorts of obscenities at him as he lay motionless, hurled abuse at him. Then he suddenly jumped to his feet, clearly completely unharmed, and posed in front of them Eubank-style. The Millwall fans were silenced. The wind-up had worked.

Mark Bright is an intelligent man, and a calculating one too. He could see the possibilities at Palace and he longed for a slice of the glamorous London life. He came down on loan to Selhurst in November, made his debut in a 3-3 draw at home with Ipswich Town, and scored the first goal. Auspiciously, Ian scored the third.

Steve Coppell's swoop was motivated by psychology as much as anything else. He recognised that although Ian was a big personality, he was very impressionable too, especially in a world he was new to, like soccer. Gray and Finnigan weren't ideal soulmates for Ian.

Mark was a strong character, motivated, the sort who could dominate people. His influence was more to Steve's liking. In January, Mark Bright signed for £75,000 – one of the first acquisitions after the introduction of the 'Lifeline' prize draw, instigated to underwrite transfers at an impecunious club. It was the move that was the making of Ian Wright.

Steve Coppell had also bought Bright, a belligerent six-footer, for tactical reasons. Mark could take some of the heat off a young man still learning his trade, and in the process show him the ropes. Their styles would complement each other. Palace would convert to a more direct approach to suit them. From now on, the team would exploit the pace of Ian, the muscular presence of Mark, and provide the speediest service to the twin strikers. The rest was up to them.

Mark Bright could be a difficult player to work alongside. He was used to working hard for his living in the real world. He had been struck at how comparatively easy it was to earn a good whack kicking a bag of air around before an admiring crowd, and he never let his team-mates forget that. Throughout a game, he would verbally strafe them with a mixture of encouragement and condemnation. Often when Ian spooned a good opportunity wide, Mark would clench his fists and growl, 'C'mon Wrighty, keep it going, something's going to come.' In the early days, he was the eyes and ears of the partnership. But Ian wasn't immune to Mark's vituperation. There were plenty of times over the four years they were together when, after a chance had been squandered, Mark could be seen shouting at Ian, presumably, in his own inimitable fashion, gently pointing out the error of his ways.

As the relationship matured and Ian had proved himself to the extent that he had eclipsed his senior partner, Ian would shake his head and dismiss Mark's flak with a nonchalant wave. But in the early days it hit home and Ian had to toughen up quickly.

Mark performed another important function for his junior partner. From the outset, Ian was inclined to be too loose with his tackles and with his tongue. Referees would punish him for childish conduct, tantrum stuff. It was another example of Ian's immaturity. He was sent off against Bournemouth during the 1987/88 offensive for the only time in his career for a second pointless tackle, and too frequently played on his nerves.

Mark suppressed that tendency, or rather channelled it. He wasn't averse to using his physical presence – something lithe Ian wasn't able to do – and was accused of following through on 'keepers or dishing it out to defenders on the sly. Ian, though, didn't have the professional subterfuge.

'Temperament is a bit like a muscle,' Steve Coppell has said. 'It can be controlled. Ian is an intelligent footballer and he can control it.'

Aggression was still an important aspect of Ian's game; it helped him focus on the job at hand. It was part of his winner's mentality. Steve didn't want him to lose that much-publicised 'fire in the belly'. He recognised it helped give Ian his edge: 'Of all the players I've dealt with, Ian is the one who most wanted to succeed. I think his excess of commitment has something to do with the fact that he knows what the alternatives are.

'He gets angry, really angry; you can see it in his face. He collected a lot of bookings at first, but calmed down and realised there was no point tackling a full back in a meaningless position.'

Palace and Arsenal cohort Eddie McGoldrick can testify to Ian's unrivalled personality. 'He's desperate to win all the time,' he confesses. 'I'm determined when I play and when I train; I always want to succeed and to do my best. But Ian is extremely competitive. Any professional has got that will to win; you have to or you would never make it. But I think Ian has it that little bit more.

'Whether it's a game of five-a-side in training or the FA Cup Final he's the same. We had a game of head tennis after training one time and I was beating him, really hammering him, at half time. We changed ends and he was getting psyched up. He turned round and started shouting at himself: "Come on Ian, you can do this." And he came back and beat me.

'Other players would just give it up at six or seven points down – it was only a training exercise after all. But not Ian. He had to be at his best and try his hardest. I imagine he'd be exactly the same if he was playing Subbuteo or something like that. He just can't settle for anything else.'

But that rare combative nature had to be harnessed. Happily,

Steve Coppell's hunch about Mark Bright's leverage on Ian's susceptible nature was proving correct. 'Mark's influence was the work ethic,' he says. 'When Ian came in he was haphazard, he was bombing all over the place, and he'd do finishing, he'd do a little bit of everything, but there was no real thought behind what he did.

'Mark Bright came along, knew what he wanted, worked hard in training, and worked hard individually after training.'

Ian swiftly recognised a potential role model. The rookie who had asked embarrassingly innocent questions saw something in Mark Bright that he could emulate. Mark was very organised, knew what he wanted from life, and knew how to get it. Palace was a means to an end, of course, but he was professional enough to commit himself to the club wholeheartedly in a footballing sense.

Perhaps Ian saw a little of Eric Summers in his new team-mate's unceremonious dedication, motivation and strength of character. (There's even a passing physical resemblance.) His presence provoked a similar effect from a young man who in many ways still had a lot of growing up to do – maybe retaining that adolescent air was another way of cheating time.

'Ian didn't have time on his side,' comments Steve Coppell. 'He was 21 the August he joined us. It didn't really give him a great deal of time to have an apprenticeship and settle in slowly. He wanted to get there quick and he's bright enough to realise that somebody with the work ethics of a Mark Bright would help him along. Ian picked up a lot from Mark.'

In fact, for the next two or three years, the two of them got into the habit of staying behind after training, waiting for George Wood to finish his cup of tea, then practising with him for a while, always finishing together.

In other ways, too, Mark was having the effect Steve had hoped for. 'Certainly on the football field he steadied Ian down,' says his old boss. 'He made him realise that if you get booked for tackling the centre half when the ball's just outside the penalty box, they've lost a big advantage; that just wasn't sensible. In things like that, on the pitch, Mark was a big help to the coaching staff teaching him the right thing to do.

'I think without doubt he was a steadying influence off the field

Ian Wright (front row, second from left) with Greenwich Borough team-mates at the end of the 1984/85 season. The team won both the Kent Senior Trophy and the Winstonehead League Cup. Ian never signed for the club, but played – and scored – regularly for them

Born only streets apart,
Ian and his cousin
Patrick Robinson (star
of BBC's *Casualty*) grew
up together (*Syndication
International*)

A professional at last:
Ian in Crystal Palace kit

He'd scored for Palace in the first game, but could do little to prevent the replay of the 1990 FA Cup Final being won by Manchester United

On holiday with senior striking partner at Palace, Mark Bright: Mark taught the raw Ian a lot about the professional game (*Syndication International*)

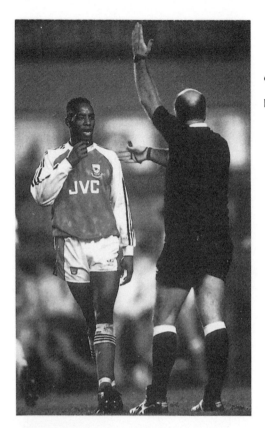

Wright's determination to win means that he is 'fully committed' to games. Referees and Ian Wright don't always get on: here he has words with the man in black during a game against Norwich (11 February 1992), which ended 1–1

Nottingham Forest defender Brian Laws prevents Ian saying something they might both regret during an FA Cup fifth round game (13 February 1993). Ian scored the only two goals

The ref advises Ian on conduct against Sheffield Wednesday
(21 August 1992). Arsenal won 2–1

A quick word in
Ian's ear from the
ref as Arsenal thrash
soon-to-be-relegated
Ipswich 4–1 on 15
April 1995

Five years earlier, Ian Wright was playing Sunday football with his mates. In September 1993 he contributed to England's 3–0 win over Poland, who found him a hard man to stop

As part of the England set-up, Ian consolidated friendships with many players, notably Paul Ince, formerly of Manchester United, now with Inter Milan
(*Syndication International*)

Always a one-girl guy, Ian wed Debbie on the tropical island of Necker in July 1993 (*Syndication International*)

Ian celebrates with typical ebullience after scoring against old club Palace
(1 October 1994). This goal was extra-special: it was his hundredth for Arsenal

too. They became good friends for a few years and, again, Mark looks after himself, and those kind of things helped Ian.'

What Steve means is that Mark would moderate Ian's tendency to excess. Everyone sensed that the combination of the cool-headed target man and the quicksilver firebrand was a winning one, though they had barely established themselves by the end of the first season: seventeen strikes between them.

Nevertheless Palace had again finished in the top six, and Ian had begun to covet the trappings of a professional footballer's life: better deal, big car. Mark Bright it was who tempered his cravings and convinced him not to push the issue too far with the likes of Coppell and Noades: all good things come to those who wait.

It was a subtle shift in Ian's attitude, but in keeping with his character: before he had proved himself he was always more anxious to achieve than acquire; once he had served his 'apprenticeship' and felt he belonged, he relaxed and his confidence knew no bounds. Then he was ready to claim what was due to him.

It was all very well for Mark Bright to tell him to cool it: his partner lived a bachelor's lifestyle in trendy Knightsbridge, with a Mercedes parked in his garage and Egon Ronay as a neighbour – not bad for a foster kid from Stoke. He could do what he wanted, when he wanted, without recrimination.

Ian, on the other hand, had two children and a partner at home in a small house on the Honor Oak estate. His life had been transformed by football and its benefits, but in some ways it hadn't changed a bit. Football is a pressure profession, like acting. Relationships are put under incredible strain by enforced absences, sudden, immense fluctuations in fortune, ever-present temptations and the glamorous lifestyle for one partner, while the other is playing the sheet anchor role, struggling to bring up a family under trying circumstances.

It's the side of football few see, and perhaps indicates another advantage of progressing from the junior ranks: there's no sudden career change to split the family.

Ironically, in some ways, Mark Bright was a more demanding partner than Sharon. He commanded dedication to the job at hand and was a hard taskmaster. He wanted Ian to keep ploughing everything into their professional relationship, and, with Ian's hunger for success, there was little room for anything else.

Gary O'Reilly, like Mark a 'Lifeline' purchase, and an instrumental figure in Palace's rise under Steve Coppell, joined a team that was psychologically and tactically dominated by those two powerful presences upfront, geared to serving the Wright-Bright axis.

'Our game was functional,' he later told *Eagle Eye*. 'Ian and Mark had an almost telepathic understanding and they were very focused. Why play a lot of football that doesn't bring out the best in them? Steve was shrewd enough to come up with a system to suit the players he'd got.'

If 'direct football' evangelist Charles Hughes approved, it didn't mean that Palace were an attractive side to watch. Ian was establishing himself as one of the flair players of the Second Division, if not the League, but it was Mark Bright's more mundane effectiveness and physical approach that established itself as the team's identity.

From 1987, as the Wright-Bright partnership began to establish itself as a strike force in the terrace psyche, Ian's personality grew accordingly. He would dominate the team banter on and off the field.

'He was superb,' eulogises Steve Coppell. 'A wonderful mimic. Great singer, great dancer, good fun to be around ninety per cent of the time. And you missed him when he wasn't there.'

His confidence in games could be imperious. He and Mark Bright scored twenty and 24 League goals respectively in the 1987/88 season; the next season the tallies were reversed. Even though Mark was a close friend, that meant a lot to Ian; he was still the more competitive man.

Ian was the darling of the fans too. The hero had arrived. They sang his name – something that always means so much to a player. He lapped up the adulation. He was made for it.

It seemed the student had surpassed the tutor, and things were never to be the same again. From now on, Mark was to be regarded – unfairly – as Ian's stooge. Mark was the one who won the headers, held the ball up and laid things on for his partner. Ian was more mercurial, inventive, lived on his own wits. He had found to his surprise and delight that in one-on-ones the sprightly dance, first left, then right, then left again and shoot, still flummoxed defenders. And he scored the 35-yarders when, in the standard argot of the game, he had no business even trying a shot.

Ian's charisma was the crucial factor. He seared past players, scored the spectacular goals, and wore his heart on his sleeve. He engaged the crowd, shared his great adventure with them. He missed goals aplenty, but it didn't matter anymore, because there were always other opportunities.

The first signs that Ian was bound for glory were there if you looked beyond the raw material to the finished product. Nike, the hip American boot manufacturers, were amongst the first to spot the potential. Jim Pearson is one of those deputed to look after the various sponsorships the footwear firm hands out to sportsmen and women, the established and the unfledged.

'A large part of my job is to pick out up-and-coming young players,' he says. 'And although Ian came into the game late, he was still new on the scene as a professional.'

There was an extra dimension in Ian's approach that attracted Jim. But to begin with their investment in him in 1986 was just one of many seed investments they make each year. 'To be honest,' adds Jim, 'we pick out new players all the time, but there was something special about Wrighty. You normally pick out a player, give them some boots and hope they'll do well.

'But Ian was different. For a start, he can play – and play very well – and added to that he has a lot of other qualities, too. In fact, he's a typical Nike person, if you like.'

The makers of 'Air Jordan' tend to go for athletes with an edge. They're fond of the feisty ones. Nike people are Cantona, McEnroe, Agassi, Botham. All stars, the best at what they do, but with an extra dimension: they are always in the news for one reason or another. Or, as Jim Pearson puts it, 'in amongst it'. Jim saw that facet of Ian's sporting personality long before the tabloids latched onto it.

The Nike approach was a flattering move as far as Ian was concerned; another piece in the jigsaw of the top footballer's career progression. As long as he kept scoring, making the news at Palace, Nike informed him his relationship with them could prove very lucrative in the long run.

Ian isn't one to scoff at people placing their faith in him: it hadn't happened too often in his life, and he'd always laboured hard to repay those who had. And Ian always repays respect with loyalty: it's fundamental to the personality moulded in the rough world of London SE24.

He'd done so with some teachers, some employers, plenty of friends, the likes of Danny Fairman, Billy Smith, and now Steve Coppell. He's still the same man now. Despite attempts by other boot manufacturers to acquire his endorsement, especially once he'd signed for Arsenal and made his England debut, Ian has remained solidly behind Jim Pearson and Nike. Ian puts loyalty over personal gain every time.

The Nike deal and other organisations beginning to claim a slice of the local boy's blossoming fame put a pressure on Ian that he was now able to deal with. In the early days, his barometer of success was all about scoring goals, and he was now hugely confident in his abilities.

It hadn't always been like that, especially during the super-sub period. 'It affected him a lot more missing chances then,' says Steve Coppell. 'Again, the sands of time running out weighed more heavily on him then than when he actually started achieving things. When he got the self-confidence of achievement then he settled down a bit more. At first, if he missed a chance, it was bad for him.' His striking partner again played a crucial part in building up that reservoir of self-assurance.

'Mark Bright's got a great mentality for chances. If he misses them, no problem, you just get on with it, score the next one. I think he passed that on to Ian.'

Mark Bright, in turn, was conveying to Ian some wise words from the mind of Leicester senior Lineker. Lineker's recognition of mental blocks was useful: his advice to Mark was 'never say you're struggling to score. Just keep going, they'll come.'

It's a pity, perhaps, that Ian and Mark weren't always so supportive to the rest of the Palace squad. Once the pair were ripping apart frightened Second Division defences, Finnigan, Gray, Salako and McGoldrick were expected to supply a constant stream of bullets for Wright and Bright to fire.

Mark Bright's verbal approach soon rubbed off on Ian. A good talker since his 10-Em days, he adopted his striking partner's policy of dishing it out to ensure he got the best service. It didn't always help those charged with supplying the duo's crosses.

'Ian always had amazing self-belief; without being big-headed, without having a big mouth about it,' reckons Steve Coppell. 'When you spoke to him about doing things it was, "Well I can do that, I can do this, I can score you goals, I can cross it." Which explains why he is so demanding of the players round him. He can verbally be a big problem to those people. If someone's weak enough to be effected by it, then Ian can affect them.'

Mark and Ian could destroy a player's confidence, squawking upfront like hungry cuckoo chicks.

'They were both World Class moaners; moan, moan, moan, moan,' says Gary O'Reilly. 'They used to rip John Salako to shreds because he would turn in, turn out, stand on it, fall over, get up, go for an ice cream and come back and they'd still be waiting for the cross.

'You can imagine the conversation. But I didn't mind because I understood them. They made runs and they wanted the ball.'

(In fact, the season after Ian and Mark had flown the nest, Eddie McGoldrick, another victim of the duo's heckling, notched ten goals. While they were doing the business, there was no way he would have achieved that.)

Mark Bright had another important influence on Ian Wright. A single-minded footballer, he often gave the impression that he was doing things for himself as much as for Palace – nothing unusual about that in a footballer. Although they knew they were part of the team, he and Ian made it clear that they were top guns.

Palace were a strange team at the time, as leaky at the back – before the arrival of Nigel Martyn, 'the first million pound goalkeeper', in November 1989 and sentinel Andy Thorn from Wimbledon – as they were irresistible up front. They were a side that could seemingly go to sleep for periods of a game, when even the Wright'n'Bright team was lacklustre. Then they'd score and lay siege to the opposition's goalmouth for twenty minutes at a go.

'Steve Coppell had a system and every player knew exactly what he had to do,' reveals winger Eddie McGoldrick. 'The full backs got it and put the ball into the channels for the wide men – either myself or John Salako, or Phil Barber on the other side – one striker would pick it up and then lay it back for us to cross into the box, where the other forward and the spare midfielder would hope to get on the end of it.

'It proved very successful and Mark and Ian enjoyed stacks and stacks of goals over that period.'

In the drive towards promotion in 1988/89, a different slant began to emerge in response to the 'balance of power' in the team. The Bright'n'Wright legend was a useful promotional tool for both players, and they used it to their advantage. Both had come to the attention of the First Division's big guns, and Kenny Dalglish's Liverpool were being touted as wooers for the Wright hand. Moreover, England spies were checking out Ian's progress for Bobby Robson.

In the meantime, Mark and Ian still had plenty to offer Palace and their commitment would be central to Steve Coppell's plans – not least because newspapers were speculating about who would snatch the valuable commodities from the impoverished south Londoners, and it would sound the death knell to his and the club's ambitions, should they offload their stars. Ian could have accepted an offer from anyone when his contract was up for renewal in 1988.

'The promotion year was important,' confides Steve Coppell, 'because in the October of that year, when we were 12th in what was then the Second Division, things were looking a bit dicey. But Ian made a commitment to sign a new contract with us, and from there we never looked back.

'And I do feel that him publicly showing faith in me and the club at that stage was a vital ingredient in us being promoted that year.'

Not for the first time, Ian showed loyalty at a time when it might have been shrewder to show a little more certitude and selfishness: more money, better players alongside him, bigger crowds, the prospect of silverware. It says something about Ian's sense of values that he invested his stock in the man who had brought him from non-League soccer to the brink of the national squad.

Even though he was acutely aware, at 25 and counting, that his remaining years at the top of his profession were diminishing with every match at Walsall, Hull and Bournemouth, Ian returned Steve Coppell's investment in him personally, by committing himself to the club for the foreseeable future. In many ways, it was an unselfish act, but typical of the man.

There was much that Ian adored about Palace. It was his local side, one that many of his friends and family – Nesta, who often went to Ian's games, the Rocastles, the likes of Arthur, Sefton, Charlie – supported. It was home, even if he had outgrown it.

There was a calculated side to the new deal though, which showed how Ian was becoming more competent and professional in his approach to his career. For the first two or so years of his time at Palace, Ian was simply enjoying playing the game at a high level and being paid for the privilege. But the more time Ian spent out and about with the more premeditated Mark Bright, discussing the game, their ambitions, their potential, the more he began to think about planning his future beyond Palace.

His imperatives in football were slowly changing. His heart belonged to playing football. But Mark Bright's hard-headedness also served to emphasis the relative transience of his career. He had to maximise his financial gain while he could.

The new covenants that Ian and Mark signed, on the strength of Palace's capacity to gain promotion, had 'release' clauses written into their agreements should one of the big five clubs come in for them. They knew that if a bigger fish did bite, it was unlikely that it would take both bits of bait. For the time being, the Wright–Bright duet was working for both of them: the two players scoring fifty goals a season between them was forcing the domestic game to pay attention. It was the best possible showcase.

Mark Bright, with typical arch humour, even left an outgoing message on his answering machine requesting that callers keep their message brief, 'just in case Liverpool are trying to get through.'

Even though they accepted they were very much part of the team, a different agenda had begun to emerge. They needed each other, and they would benefit from the exposure that promotion, the First Division and maybe a cup or two would bring.

By the end of a season in which Mark began poorly and Ian was the chief tormentor of opposition defences, Palace found themselves in third place behind runaway leaders Chelsea and Manchester City. They were in the play-offs. The top flight beckoned. Ian and Mark threw themselves into this brilliant opening.

Three-one down to Blackburn after the first leg of the play-off final (the FA had yet to settle on Wembley as a one-match venue), few people gave Palace much hope of winning through. Even the 30,000 who packed into Selhurst to create what was the best atmosphere for years had arrived more in hope and duty than faith.

In a remarkable display against a team that admittedly bore little resemblance to the Championship team of 1994/95 (save for Hendry, marking Bright), but which came to shut the Eagles out until it was intimidated into stagnation by a hostile crowd, Ian Wright was pre-eminent. As he said, he was built for moments like this.

After a quarter of an hour, his first enterprising scramble of a goal sent Palace hopes soaring up there with the balloons the fans had freed before the game. 'Suddenly an afternoon of real possibilities here . . .' revved Brian Moore.

A penalty given for Hendry's chainsaw tackle on Bright, or Reid's clattering of McGoldrick – take your pick – produced the leveller: Palace were up on away goals, and Blackburn were up and away with the fairies. Ripped apart by Eddie McGoldrick's direct offensives and Ian Wright's pace, persistence and ingenuity, it was only fitting that the Lancashire club's hopes should be fatally wounded by a combination of the two: Ian nodding in a teasing cross from the winger.

Brian Moore announced the certainty of the outcome, and at the final whistle Wright'n'Bright raced into each other's arms. Mission accomplished. There was a brief realisation of what they'd achieved, and then the crowd swamped them like stones in the surf. Ian was taken aback. He likes to be in control of situations. Even after his years as a Palace player, it was a little unsettling to be surrounded by hundreds of fans, no matter how adoring. Then he recognised faces from the old days – Sefton, Charlie – in the throng, and submitted to being carried shoulder high to the tunnel.

It was a weird feeling, like being in some vortex, out of control, and having familiar, friendly faces from your past flashed in front of your eyes, as if to reassure you: 'no matter where you go, we'll still be with you'.

Steve Coppell was relieved. 'Play-offs are cruelty to animals,' he reasoned. 'But there was justice in that result. We were the third best team in the league and we've proved it.'

Newspapers preferred to tap into the fact that the play-off concept was the brainchild of Palace's robust chairman Ron Noades, and condemned the matches as 'an exercise in greed'. 'Never mind the quality, feel the wad', said Joe Lovejoy in the *Independent*.

Well, it was payday all right. The whole club needed it: the supporters, the team, Steve Coppell, Noades and Wright'n'Bright. The close season rest was all the sweeter for the beckoning big time.

Speculation had it that maybe even a European club would come in for Ian, who was fast becoming an advanced student of the football craft, obsessed with the superior quality of players on the continent, the technical brilliance of the Italian defenders, the flair of the likes of Gullit, Van Basten and Platini. For a soccer gourmet raised on the paltry British diet, Europe was the banquet.

'He desperately wanted to play in European football,' commented Mark Bright. 'He's got a satellite dish and he watches all of it.' Mark himself considered Ian one of the few English players who could make it in Italy. Ian's old friends fuelled his interest. Long ago, Ian lost count of the number who counselled him to go abroad and grab the money while he could.

If the opportunity had presented itself, Ian would probably have jumped at it. After all, it was the chance to emulate another of Ian's childhood icons, Laurie Cunningham, who had been snapped up by the mighty Real Madrid in 1980.

It would have been hugely interesting to see how Ian's career would have developed had he moved on to a European club. He could have developed his individual flair in the more relaxed, expressive atmosphere of the French league and worked on the passing that is perhaps the weakest part of his game. Similarly his distribution would have benefited from a lucrative sojourn in Spain or Italy, where the close attention of man markers and the challenge of coping with sweepers as fast and smart as Ian himself – particularly in Serie A – could have been the making or breaking of him.

Such a departure would have benefited a still young man eager to learn whatever he could about the game and the true extent of his own ability. There was a confidence gap, however. Although Ian had achieved something at the first professional level, he felt that he wasn't ready for the third phase – Europe – until he'd had the chance to prove himself against world class defenders – and he hadn't even tested the top defenders in England yet. Furthermore, no foreign club was really showing any interest in him.

So the career progression mapped out like this: promotion (done), silverware, Europe . . . or England. The latter was an increasingly valid prospect as he and Mark Bright powered their side to the limelight and the First Division. In fact, on 12 December 1989, Ian made his international debut, unremarkably, against Yugoslavia for England 'B'. The venue for the match was fitting: Millwall's Den.

Incredibly, even after a season in which he had genuinely broken through to a higher grade as a striker, notched 34 goals and won Palace's Player of the Year award, Ian was nervous about the prospect of facing First Division adversaries the following season. It was new territory again. Until he'd made his mark, come to terms with it, achieved something, he was concerned. It was just as well that he stayed at Palace, with its adoring supporters, club and manager who needed no proof of his prowess. A move then might have proved too much to deal with.

Naturally, it was Arsenal's David Rocastle, clutching a brand new Championship medal and a bunch of full England caps, who Ian turned to for advice about what to expect. Rocky, of course, knew Ian from way back, knew what he'd been through. It was a curious position for him, five years younger but asked to reassure the guy who used to push him around and make him go in goal in the Turnham playground. No worries, he told Ian, you're good enough to play anywhere. David knew that with the hunger he was showing now, Wrighty could be a star at any level.

The main thing was to keep control of himself, keep working at his game. One thing was certain. Goalscoring and success are like drugs. Once you've tasted a little, you want them again and again. And Ian was hooked. He wanted them, freebase.

6 Top Gun

'As a person Ian is quite disciplined. It's just that once the whistle goes, he still plays football the way he has played it since his non-League days: bursting to win. If you were to take away that edge, you'd lose the exciting player that was. I don't think Ian can play in control. He's intuitive and instinctive. If you make him think, the intuition is lost.'

George Graham

N CAREER TERMS, things had never been happier. But on the home front, something was dying. The very virtues that Ian had earlier adored in Sharon – her reliability, common sense and maternal skills – were incompatible with the new glamour entering Ian's life. He was still a stop-out too.

Ian was moving away from Honor Oak and consigning the problems associated with it – challenges he and Sharon had overcome throughout the years of struggle – to the past. With them, he was consigning Sharon to the past too. It often happens: one partner changes, the other stays the same.

Just before Christmas 1989, shortly after both Shaun and his father's birthdays, Ian and Sharon split up. They'd stayed together nine years and been through a hell of a lot: the thrill of young love, setting up home together at eighteen, coping with the stresses of young parenthood, estate life, scarcity and quarrels. Ironically, it was affluence and success that finally pulled them apart.

The break-up wasn't very pretty, and Ian has a tendency to cut people out when they are no longer part of his plans. But he and Sharon were sensible about it, and kept the communication channels open for their beloved children. Shaun was coming towards the end of his time at Turnham School, following in his father's footsteps in the school team. It can only be guessed what effect the separation had on him, just as his father was beginning to make a name for himself amongst the children at Turnham. Bradley was approaching five years old and ready to start at the junior school.

For the Wright family, history was repeating itself. Just as Buster had quit Nesta, Ian left Sharon. It hurt Ian like hell to leave

the children, especially after his own experience. So he made sure
he saw them whenever he could. He would see them some weekends, especially when Shaun was playing football.

Ian has since been quoted as saying that Sharon and his relationship was 'irrelevant to his success' and that 'I moved in with
a girl when I was too young', which seems churlish to say the
least. And, to be honest, it doesn't show him in a good light. Nine
years of childrearing and living together have to influence every
aspect of life. But Ian doesn't like this period of his life to be
examined: for him, it seems to represent an obsolete phase.

But when he complains that he's misrepresented in the media,
he should understand that if he suggests that one of his most mature and creditable acts – adopting Shaun Phillips – happened
during an affair he now dismisses in the press as inconsequential,
he is doing himself no favours.

Naturally Ian considers the children a separate case. They are
different because they are part of his future, not just his past, and
he can be proud of that.

Sharon doesn't follow Ian's career with the closeness she used
to. She's a busy working mum: a supervisor and administrator for
a catering company. But she still respects Ian's success and recognises his sensitivity about his past.

She has brought up both her kids to acknowledge Ian Wright as
their father, and she is more involved in their schooling than Ian's
mother ever was. They still live locally, overlooking the school Ian
and both the children attended. In fact, Bradley is still there. A
lean, confident but quietly spoken boy, he is a charming tribute to
the parents who brought him up. You can see by the shy grin on
his face that he clearly burns with pride for his father, but in a
sensible, unextravagant way.

Both lads support Arsenal, and, says Sharon, 'want to be professional footballers like their dad'. They go to home games to
watch their father play; he happily returns the compliment.

'He's been over and watched our kids play,' explains Turnham
head Rick Ridzewcki. 'The first time I met him was when I was
refereeing a 'B' team match at Honor Oak. There are two adjacent
pitches and it's easier to take two teams out to play opposition as
opposed to just taking one out. At half-time I asked Glenn

Snashall from the other school, Kender, to take over from me because I was trying to encourage my 'A' team, give them a shout.

'I was there on the touchline and there was a guy standing with a hat on with a man with two dogs, and the kids were all going, "That's Ian Wright!" I was thinking, "Who's this Ian Wright?" – I'd heard the name from a friend of mine who was a keen Crystal Palace fan, who'd said, "There's a guy at Palace that's going to be good: Ian Wright." So I went over to him and he had a hat on, he was inconspicuous.

'Shaun was playing on the other pitch for the 'B' team, but he wasn't watching Shaun's match so much, he was watching the other kids. And at no time did he even say anything about Shaun, but he was talking about the other children on the pitch, what they were doing, how great it was to see so many kids playing football: complimenting everybody else, not actually saying, "That's my boy over there."

'He was so nice. But it is very difficult for him now.' Fame has its costs, and it's not a sacrifice Ian has always found easy.

Even if celebrity has limited the opportunities for Ian to watch his children perform, the signs are that Bradley has inherited the genetic legacy of father and grandfather, and Shaun, the elder of the two, has already made his mark in the junior leagues – and not just because some footage of his devastating dribbling skill was used in the video of his father's single, 'Do The Right Thing'.

Glenn Snashall, who ran the Lewisham Schools League for ten years after Syd Pigden, runs the Kender school team. He was more delighted than most when Shaun Wright 'retired' – or rather moved on to secondary school. But now that Bradley is in the Turnham 'A' side (no mean feat for a 9-year-old, a premature elevation his father never managed), a Wright boy is the subject of his covetousness once again.

'Shaun is the more individual of the two lads,' he explains, 'more of a loner. He's got a great eye, good control and thinks about the game. He plays just behind the frontmen, an old-fashioned inside forward. He's just like his father in another respect too: that poacher's instinct. I remember he crucified Kender once when Turnham beat us 8-1. Shaun scored four or five.

'In Bradley's time, the games have been a bit closer; we've had four super, low-scoring matches. Again, he's got a good eye, excellent control, but I would say he's more of a team player, and his distribution of the ball is perhaps better than Shaun's ... swine!'

Gradually, Ian's old friends are beginning to catch the breeze about his talented progenies. Just a few weeks ago, Eric Summers was working as usual one evening at the Dulwich Hamlet sports centre when an under-15s team, Honor Oak, were playing. One lad stuck out head and shoulders above the rest. Impressed, Eric asked who he was. He shrugged when he was told it was Ian's boy Shaun: 'His distribution was excellent,' laughs Eric. 'Ian could never have done that!'

In a cute piece of symmetry, Shaun's side, Honor Oak, have now all graduated to the 10-Em-Bee reckoning. It's a good level for Shaun to be playing at. He also attends the Tottenham Hotspur School of Excellence, which is also quaint, seeing as how Spurs's assistant manager Roger Cross was one of those who gave Ian the push from Millwall.

Bradley plays for a club called Melwood and, tender of age as he is, has already trained as a schoolboy with West Ham. Would Ian be happy if they pursued the same dream as he has?

It's interesting that although acting and sport are similarly perilous occupations, whereas thespians habitually try to deter their children from following them into the profession, footballers typically avow the opposite. Ian is no different, even though his career has been shorter and riskier than the majority.

'I would like one of them to be a footballer,' he told 442 magazine, when reminded of Shaun's cameo in his video. 'Bradley as well, he's nine and he's showing some good stuff and playing well, and I'm really proud of him and Shaun. But I don't ram it down their throats, you know. They love their football anyway.'

He's also pledged himself to providing them with as much support as they need. 'Hopefully, when the time comes for them to do something,' he says, 'I am there to help them and they won't go far wrong with that. I know enough people and I know enough myself to make sure that they go on the right road. It's very hard.'

And, in a little dig at those who made schoolboy forms but never turned pro, or maybe in a modest tribute to his own tenacity, he adds, 'You know, it's easy to show promise at that age and it just fizzles out by the time you get to fifteen, sixteen.'

Back in 1990, Ian's brilliance was still incandescent. He was, in the words of commentator Martin Tyler, 'Direct, dangerous and deadly'. He scored a typically opportunist goal against Manchester United in Palace's first home game of the season – perhaps precipitated by Selhurst's pre-match firework display – escaping the clutches of the Reds' centre backs in the final minute. The last-gasp strike was becoming his trademark: his first goal for Palace had come just before the last bus home, and now he'd opened his account in the top flight in similar fashion. But whereas the goals used to come late because Ian was only on for a few minutes, this one gave warning of a player metamorphosing into a top-class front runner.

Ian had learned to conserve himself, to use his energy more economically and explosively. In some ways it meant he was a more patient performer. One of the lessons he had quickly taken on board about Division One football was that the attentions of the back four were a lot tighter than in the lower league; the likes of Steve Coppell and David Rocastle impressed upon him that the game at this level was all about having one chance in a game and converting it.

Ian warmed to the new challenge. If it meant he and Mark Bright weren't cutting through defences like hot knives through butter anymore, in some ways the new agenda suited his style even better. It was gladiatorial, one-on-one, all about bursts of speed, efficient execution. A serious test, but nothing Ian couldn't handle given the chance.

It was also closer to the more technical, cat-and-mouse style he was becoming such an enthusiast for in the Italian game. Like the patient assassins, Bruno 'Toto' Scillacci, Roberto Baggio and one of his heroes since 1988, Marco Van Basten, Ian would prowl along the defensive line, testing the offside trap and chipping away at his opponents all match – he was quite prepared to keep his powder dry until the final moment if need be. Give him an inch, though, and he'd steal a yard and strike in deadly fashion. Again and again.

There were still lessons to be learned though, not least from an early visit to Anfield. After the game, Steve Coppell suggested 'this will live for us for the rest of our lives'. The manager sat the team down in the dressing room and told them they'd made their way into the record books and that they'd established Palace in the minds of the football public. Tight-lipped Kenny Dalglish poked his head around the door and told the Londoners how impressed he was that they'd fought so hard for 90 minutes. The score hadn't been a fair reflection of Palace's prowess: they should have had four goals.

The trouble is, even if they had scored twice Dalglish's figure, Palace would still have lost: this was the night of the Eagles' 9-0 defeat, the night Liverpool's scorers occupied a whole page of Ceefax. Ian, who had run himself into the ground chasing air, wasn't so much devastated as hugely embarrassed, like the rest of the Palace team. 'It was like a *Rocky* film,' he said afterwards, 'except we lost. We did well to recover from that.'

Despite such setbacks, the great temples of English football – Anfield, Old Trafford, Goodison, Highbury – had fired Ian's imagination. Like his hero Stan Bowles, Ian came alive in front of 40,000 people: it was his stage. And Wembley was the biggest stage of them all.

It was another big twist in Ian's fairy tale that Palace should reach Wembley in their first season among the big boys. That they also reached the twin towers by producing one of the most famous results in their history, a 4-3 victory over the team who had demolished them at the beginning of the season, Liverpool, was in keeping with their spasmodic progress.

A Cup Final against Manchester United should have been the zenith of Ian's career to date. There was just one problem, and it appeared an insurmountable one. Earlier, before the fourth round clash with Huddersfield, Ian had fractured his leg – against Liverpool, of course – in a collision with Barry Venison.

Given Ian's still-flimsy lower legs and the stick routinely dished out by enervating centre halves, it was a wonder the striker hadn't missed more games. This was the first serious injury of his career. Often given to melodrama, Ian believed it might prove to be his last appearance of the season. Whether it was his over-enterprising metabolism, or a break that wasn't as bad as first thought, amazingly Ian was back a matter of weeks later to help bundle out Fourth Division Cambridge in the FA quarter-final.

Incredibly, in his third game back, a touchline tackle by Derby's Paul Blades, which appeared little more than ponderous, ruled a tearful Ian out again: his other leg was fractured. This time Ian was convinced that that was that. But time, for so long his ruler, was to prove the great healer, and a fast one at that.

Still sidelined through injury, Ian drove up independently with a friend in his new £68,000 Mercedes for the semi against Liverpool. When he pulled up outside the stadium, some jobsworth who refused to accept he was a player refused Ian entry. He remonstrated, but the stupid sentinel remained resolute.

It was only when a supporter approached the Palace star for an autograph that the steward relented and let Ian through. Palace were on fire in a sensational game – it could have had something to do with the fact that a Liverpool old boy and Mouth Almighty Tommy Smith had pronounced the Scousers' opponents 'the worst team ever in the First Division'. On the other hand, it could just have been revenge for the 9-0.

Whichever, Palace ran out winners with the odd goal in seven. In a final whistle moment that really should be as much celebrated as David Pleat's rapturous, trying-to-do-me-jacket-up gallop across Maine Road, Ian Wright forgot his cracked bone and surged on to the pitch like a gazelle to celebrate with his triumphant team-mates.

But it was also an indication to those who wanted to look beyond the hype that Ian was near enough fit to play. He made it perfectly clear to David West, the Palace physio, that he was motivated enough to do so. He badgered him to impress that fact upon Steve Coppell. He wasn't going to miss the Final if he could possibly help it.

As it was, the Palace manager was going to pass over Ian for the big game at Wembley, and not just because his explosive striker – so dependant on his own sharpness – had spent most of the previous four months on crutches. 'He was always chasing being fit for the final,' says Steve. 'He and Mark Bright had without doubt given the club almost everything, as regards promotion, finishing so high up in the league and what have you. It was a big decision for me to leave him out, but in many ways it was a tactical decision because of the way we played.'

Ian is never the best at taking bad news like that. Naturally, being the way he is, Ian thought he was worth a gamble because of precedent: how much he'd already achieved for Palace. Surely, he was worth a shout.

But, for the Final, Steve Coppell wanted a more defensive structure to the Palace team. His intention was to stifle United's creativity, master them in a physical manner and sneak a goal. Mark Bright got the nod as the lone striker over Ian because of his muscular presence and far superior holding play – vital for getting a breather. And with super-sub Ian on the bench, he had the option of shuffling the pack if things weren't going to plan.

Whoever it was in football who first patented the great adage 'If you get to play in a final, always do something people will remember' must have smiled on Ian Wright that day. With 69 minutes gone, and United leading 2-1, the Palace hand looked played out. Steve turned to the man on the bench.

'Are you ready?' he asked his striker, who appeared mesmerised by the greatness of the occasion and gripped by a sense of destiny.

'I was born ready,' strutted Ian; he was actually extremely nervous, but always good at hiding it. Ian stripped for action to the cheers of the Palace faithful and came on for Phil Barber. A dreary, over-tenacious battle was immediately transformed, and Ian Wright's reputation was instantly imprinted in the psyche of football supporters in one flash of brilliance still remembered to this day.

Ian received the ball on the left, cut inside one United player, faced Pallister and, with the same glacial fixation he displayed as a youth in Syd Pigden's team, scampered one way, then the other, wrong-footing the England defender and unleashing a killer shot across Jim Leighton into the net. 2-2.

Ian ran amok in celebration, stopped when he realised what he'd just done and fell to the floor. It almost meant too much. He'd scored a goal at Wembley, the thing every schoolboy dreams about when they're kicking a ball around the playground. Ian had been no different. And now he'd done something people will always remember.

'It was a great buzz,' enthuses Eddie McGoldrick, kept off the bench that day by a torn cartilage. 'I still enjoy watching it on the telly now. I think if Steve had started Ian, he may not have lasted, but bringing him on as a sub proved a masterstroke.'

Watching at home, Peter McCarthy punched the air when he saw his former charge score. 'That Cup Final,' he still marvels, 'when Ian came on and straight away, *bosh!* He was there, he was the guvnor, wasn't he. And I suppose that sums Ian up, really: he's been let loose, in he goes.'

Incredibly, two minutes into injury time, a side-footed Wright finish put Palace in front. Ian believed he'd fired his team to glory. But it was not to be. Mark Hughes, another of the League's chief purveyors (and shatterers) of dreams, powered a shot through Gary O'Reilly's legs with an agonising six minutes to go. The game went to a replay at Wembley.

'We set our stall out to play a certain way and we got a 3-3 result, obviously helped by Ian's goals,' says Steve Coppell. 'Again the huge decision of the second game was to know what to do for the best.'

Ian was quite clear about what he felt: he was telling anyone who would listen that he thought he'd done enough to secure a place in the starting line-up. Steve Coppell had different ideas, though. The problem was breaking the news to Ian after the acclaim of the first game. Steve, never one to socialise with the lads, shot from the hip. 'I just spoke with him rationally,' he says. 'Had a chat between the two games, said that I had half a mind to keep the same team, and he just said to me, "Whatever you want to do. You'll get no problems from me, no stick. I'll just get on with my job." '

Second time around, not even Ian Wright – again brought on as a sub – could revive another bland, physical encounter. United walked off 1-0 winners, and tears stained Palace's bizarre yellow-and black striped kit (the only time they wore it).

'I'm ambitious,' Ian said after the Wembley final. 'I've scored goals in a Cup Final and I liked it. But the mark of a true champion in sport, someone exceptional in their field, is that they're not content with that. They want to do that again and again. They have that inner drive to keep on going.'

The following season, 1990/91, was Palace's best ever:

Wright'n'Bright were still a potent strikeforce though Ian went further in eclipsing his partner against superior defenders, scoring nineteen in all competitions. The team managed to lay a few ghosts to rest at Wembley, beating Everton 4-1 in the final of the ill-regarded Zenith Data Systems Trophy, like the play-offs, a product of their chairman Ron Noades' fertile imagination.

The Eagles were never lower than fifth throughout the campaign, ultimately clinching third place behind Liverpool and Champions Arsenal. With the UEFA ban on the Merseyside club still in place after the Heysel tragedy in 1985, such a position held the promise of European qualification for Palace for the first time in their history. Most of the team were thrilled at the prospect of testing themselves against the best from the continent in the UEFA Cup, such as holders Roma, Ajax and Torino. And none more so than Ian.

On 19 April, though, just weeks before the close season, UEFA rescinded their ban on the Anfield club. The prospect of Europe's best coming to Selhurst vaporised in the heat of that spring, and with it Palace's chances of holding on to Ian Wright for another year.

Though Ian began the new campaign under Steve Coppell's tutelage, there was a tension between the two that had not been present before. Ian was struggling with the decision of whether to remain loyal to the club that had made him or to pitch himself closer to fulfilling his remaining ambitions in football. At the age of 28, it would be crucial either way.

This was a pivotal time for the boy who was the pride of south London. His full England call-up had been expedited by the election of Graham Taylor, an admirer since the clashes between his old club Villa and Palace in Division 2, and Ian was included in his early national squads seeking a World Cup berth at USA '94.

No less a figure than Gary Lineker had begun to promote Ian's chances of getting a run in the team, albeit sometimes disdainfully, damning him with faint praise and allusions to his rival's ever more renowned combustibility: 'He does the unexpected, he's lively and excitable . . . he sets games alight.'

In February 1991, the national side had been about to face a Cameroon team fresh from a starring role at Italia '90 but nonetheless perturbed by the freezing conditions at Wembley. At the training ground beforehand, Graham Taylor had gathered the players together and slowly read out the team he wanted to play. '. . . number 9, Ian Wright . . .' must have been the sweetest words Ian had ever heard. He clenched his fist and internally screamed 'I've got it!'

The selection put him on a par with the likes of Gascoigne and Lineker, players who'd travelled the orthodox route to this peak: junior, reserves, first team, internationals.

Publicly, Ian proclaimed how flattered he was to share the lime-light with such vaunted sportsmen, having missed out five years on the professional ladder. He has often heaped adoration on Lineker's professionalism; his unruffled dedication and incredible scoring record, and claims to have learned a lot about positional awareness, how and when to make runs at international level, from the man many saw him replacing.

Privately, though, Ian saw international selection as his birth-right, and considered himself the best man for the job anyway – if he didn't think that, he reasoned, he had no business putting on the famous white shirt.

Such breakthroughs brought renewed attention from the bigger English clubs. By the season's close, it was almost a certainty that Ian was going to leave the club that had made him.

Steve Coppell looks back on that time as a watershed both for his side and for his tenure at Selhurst. The much-heralded approach from George Graham came in pre-season but Steve wanted some time to convince his prime asset to stay. It was clear from the outset that Ian wanted to stay in London, he describes himself, after all, as a 'London Londoner'. He didn't want to move from the south London he's known all his life. Ask Steve if there were any other big clubs who were in for Ian and he absolutely rules that out.

'I think he was set for Arsenal, and Arsenal were set for him,' says the manager, still with a tinge of weariness in his voice. 'Those were difficult weeks while he was publicly transferred before he was gone. I think that was the only time when we had a more difficult relationship, because obviously I wanted him to stay. I think his going was a signal to everyone that we weren't ambitious. But I fully understood.'

Steve also squashes another idea that has emerged from the Selhurst terraces, that had the Liverpool ban still applied, Ian would have stayed in SE25.

'I think it would have delayed the inevitable,' he suggests, and then offers an explanation as to why: 'I have played at United and played in front of big crowds week after week. Even when we (Palace) were third in the table our average was 15–16,000 or so. The stage to play on is the big stage, not on the supporting stage; you've got to be there at the centre.

'If I was him I would have wanted to have gone. He wanted to play to 40,000 crowds. He's an exciting player, scores exceptional goals. We didn't teach him anything. He got his experience at Palace but everything else is his own doing.

'But I was looking at my situation and the hard work I'd put in at the club and I thought, "Well, I don't want him to go", simple as that. It sent a message to everyone, and I didn't like the message it sent.'

The uncertainty affected Ian's game. During that period, Palace actually played Arsenal – and lost 4-1 (with fellow Black-Packer Kevin Campbell, whom Ian would ostensibly unseat, notching two).

The question arose, though, had Ian fallen out of love with the Palace? There were reasons. Ron Noades is a personal friend of Ian Wright, but that's not what he is best known for. Ron, thorn in the side of the FA hierarchy, second-hand car dealer and property developer, left Wimbledon and bought a controlling interest in the Selhurst club in early 1981. Well-meaning but likely to use a sledgehammer to crack a nut, he was renowned as a direct talker, a no-nonsense chairman and had thus become a figurehead of sorts in the wider game.

Shortly after the tenth anniversary of his accession, Channel 4 broadcast an investigation into race discrimination in British football, and Ron was quoted extensively. The film documented the stereotypes and prejudices which riddled the modern game and which militated against the progress of black and Asian players.

Apparently most incriminating of all, the Palace chairman was heard nonchalantly to claim that 'When you get into deep midwinter in England, you need a few of the hard white men to carry the artistic black men'. On the face of it, this was an extraordinary betrayal of those 'artistic' black players who had battled for Palace over the previous decade – in all kinds of weather – from Vince Hilaire through Tony Finnigan to the pre-eminent members of the present side: Ian Wright, Mark Bright, Andy Gray, Eric Young and John Salako.

Ron Noades was indignant at Channel 4 and claimed he was misquoted: 'Channel 4 cut it in such a way as to twist my words consciously,' he complained. He pointed to the fact that when he was chair at Southall FC he'd insisted on recruiting black players – Cyrille Regis amongst them. But the main point of contention can never be justified in any context.

When questioned by writer and Palace fan, Tor Øystein Vaaland, as to whether there was an innate distinction between black and white players, as before, Ron was still inclined towards the old school of opinion: 'Well there was, but the difference is now less. The blacks are technical, we saw that when we were in South Africa during the summer of 1992. But on the other hand they are not as well organised or technically skilled. The difference is less so in England than Europe or elsewhere.' So now our blacks are better than their blacks?

After the documentary's screening, the press was full of news of the tremors from the chairman's bombshell and how they were reverberating round the Palace dressing room. Ron himself claims that his comments caused no friction either at the time or afterwards, and had no effect on any transfers.

Whether the furore actually hastened Ian Wright's departure from Selhurst is hard to say; he'd already made up his mind that if someone came in for him, the time was right. He spoke with Ron Noades personally concerning the matter and was said to be reassured by what he heard. But loyalty is paramount in Ian's mind, and he may have felt disillusioned by the public airing of Ron's views, ostensibly concerning himself and the brothers at Palace.

Steve Coppell doubts even that. 'I don't think it had any part in his decision,' he reckons. 'I think his only motivation was football. You know, Ron and Ian have a good relationship even to this day. I genuinely don't think that affected Ian. Ian's motivation was to play in front of big crowds and to win trophies. And although we had finished third the season before, it was a fair bet that we weren't going to be contenders for the championship every season.'

In mid-September of the 1991/92 term, Ian signed for Arsenal for £2.3 million. Mark Bright stayed put and, so often regarded as a Robin to Ian's Batman, proved everyone wrong by claiming the club scoring record with nine goals in eight games banged in after the departure of his partner.

When he left, Mark wrote a touching note to his friend reminding him of 'the part he had played in putting Palace on the map'.

At Palace, a panicking Steve Coppell bought the hapless Marco Gabbiadini from Sunderland as a replacement. Mark Bright quickly noted the difference. 'No disrespect to Marco Gabbiadini,' he told the *Independent*, 'but all the players said, "it's only now we realise just how good Ian was". It's like marriage; sometimes you don't realise how good it was till you separate.'

Ron Noades was unrepentant: 'I treat my players like stocks. Ian Wright was 28 years old when we sold him. How much longer could we have expected him to play at the same level? Not long. Well, yes, it is possible that we sold him a year too early.'

George Graham was out playing golf at a Football Writers' Association day when the news came through that Ian had signed. But it wasn't fairways and greens that Ian was fixing his attention on but the cool classicism of Highbury's marble halls. It was the fairytale palace of his dreams. He had really arrived among football's aristocracy.

At the press conference to parade his priciest acquisition, George declared to journalists that he wouldn't guarantee Ian pole position: 'Wright will not necessarily go straight into the first team,' he claimed. 'I have six forwards challenging for places and in Smith, Merson and Wright I have arguably got three of the top men in England.' Alan Smith had notched 27 goals and donned the Golden Boot the previous season, Limpar and Merson were both capable finishers, and the bustling Kevin Campbell was emerging to fulfil the promise he had shown in the reserves. After a shaky start to their defence of the First Division championship,

Arsenal had shoved fifteen goals in three games past Palace, FK Austria Memphis in the European Cup and Sheffield United.

Highbury terrace regulars might have been forgiven for querying whether Ian was actually surplus to requirements – another enigmatic signing by inscrutable George, who had a legendary dislike of 'stars' and their wage demands. Arsenal had been linked with more prime hunks than Elizabeth Taylor during George's tenure, and the reports had never come to fruition. Why suddenly pay £2.5m for a man pushing 28 when Campbell was on song, and in the Gunners' kindergarten Paul Dickov and Andy Cole were graduating with honours?

Ian knew he needed a great start after such a dramatic and highly-publicised move. He even felt compelled to query the transaction himself: 'No-one's worth that amount of money,' he suggested, in mitigation for himself.

Ian hit the ground running, and had a formidable start to his career in the famous red-and-white Arsenal strip, scoring once in the debut against Leicester in the League Cup and three times at Southampton – not for the last time – three days later in the most stunning League debut Arsenal's faithful had seen. Delighted travelling fans, surprised at the initial outlay, warmed to their most expensive signing, mockingly chanting 'What a waste of money!' to the heavens. Ian followed up with strikes against Chelsea (his first home goal) and Leicester again in the return and was well on his way to stealing his strike partner's Golden Boot.

People had been expecting a lot, but not that much. The old Ian may have tried too hard and flunked his chance. This was a new model, though, a made man, a 'don'. He'd already achieved enough in the League and Cup at this level with Palace to master his nerves. Now it was time to accept his due from his fellow players.

Ian had changed; increasingly so after the split with Sharon the year before. With his new-found wealth had come more refined aspirations.

Ian was as working class as they come. Throughout the pre-football years of employment strife, he and his family had sometimes gone without the things he'd have liked for them. His family background in Brockley had been comfortable and unextravagent;

he and Sharon had lived in a modest home on the same Honor Oak estate for years before the split.

But even at Palace, with more cash than most of his old friends could ever dream about, he was free to indulge the passions he'd suppressed – this he did with the alacrity of a Lottery winner.

Some time before Ian had bought himself the stylish rag-top Mercedes he'd always coveted, but in 1990 he had a prang in it and was banned from driving for speeding – 'driving like Ayrton Senna', as Ian himself put it.

The ban brought about a special chance meeting. Ian had to travel around by bus and taxi, or get one of his friends to ferry him. For a man of the street, it was little hardship. One day Ian happened to bump into an old friend at a bus stop in Croydon. Her name was Deborah Martin; he recognised her from when she was a kid on the Honor Oak estate, the same age as 'Rocky' Rocastle and four or five years younger than Ian. She'd grown up now.

They got talking. She knew something about Ian's success and fame but she wasn't fawning because of what the older boy she'd known years before had become. In fact, she was so down-to-earth, it was refreshing for Ian to talk to a woman who was so genuine. Most of the women he met in night-clubs these days seemed drawn to his persona rather than the bloke behind it.

Deborah was motivated too, vibrant, self-contained; confident in herself. She had carved out a decent career for herself in banking, working at Barclays Bank in Croydon. Ian joked that he could do with some help in the financial arena, and she laughed.

Deborah left an immediate impression on Ian. She wasn't impressed with his status, she was interested in him as a person. There was no 'side' to her. She was funny, warm, attractive, and there was a spark about her that Ian found irresistible. He was overwhelmed. There had been a few women since he split with Sharon, but Deborah was so genuine that he fell for her immediately.

Within six months, Debs had moved in with Ian to his luxurious new four-bedroom home – the archetypal footballer's house with a 'trophy room' – just south of Croydon, and they were engaged to be married.

Deborah was the perfect foil for Ian: steady where he was moody; mature where he could be infantile; practical when he was splashy; unassuming while he was surrounded by hangers-on; normal when his profession could be so fake. She was also the reliable type. Family meant a lot to her too. He could build a proper life away from football, a sanctuary, with Debs.

The couple share many of the same interests too: going to the movies, clothes, Italian and Chinese food. Deborah even dutifully tapes football matches or basketball for Ian if he wants. Debs is the backbone of the home. She's the one who's there when Ian's away, and he's out a lot. She's also assumed the leading role in the feel and decor of the house.

Debs is very homely and assertive, which is what Ian needs. There's a furious debate within the black community at present concerning successful black men who date white women. Some radical commentators have pointed to that as proof that the slave mentality is alive and well: a backlash to the depiction of black women as 'superwomen'. In an ideal world, colour would be irrelevant, but the discourse and division between black men and women, especially in the States, has meant that the issue is a very piquant one. In some quarters, two black people together is still seen as a threat. A white partner makes you more like 'one of them'. Both Ian's long-term relationships have been with black women. He's a roots man.

He and Debbie enjoy quiet nights in when Ian's not playing or at some promotional function; they get some Chinese food in (Ian is never seen in the kitchen), hire a video and put their feet up. She also handles another important function: as someone who rose to become a Personal Financial Advisor at Barclays, she looks after her husband's burgeoning capital too.

'It wasn't a problem to Debs that I had three kids [Brett was born after his split with Sharon to another mother] because she knows what I'm like,' Ian once asserted. 'I've never been the type of guy to have girlfriends everywhere. I reckon I've only had five girlfriends my entire life. I'm not the type to mess around with girls, and Debbie could see that.'

Others might not have been able to handle the children, or the fame. Ian claims Deborah's coolness about him being well-known was a major factor in their relationship blooming. He wants respect from people for who he is inside, not what the public thinks of him.

Debs and Ian were married in June 1993 on Necker Island, the Caribbean hideaway owned by Richard Branson, boss of Crystal Palace's sponsor, Virgin. Just under a year later, on the 22 May 1994, Ian had finished playing against Norway, a drab 0-0 draw, when word reached him that Deborah had delivered their first son – and Ian's fourth boy – Stacey: the 'Staceman' to some of Ian's friends, who say Ian never stops talking about him. He never forgot his other boys, but now he had a new family and different life to lead.

One pal of several years' standing, Winston Husbands, carries out all the electrical requirements of the Wright household through his small company, Herwin Services. Winston also serves 'Rocky' Rocastle, who recommended him to Ian, David Seaman and Paul Merson. He's glad to call the couple his friends and is struck by how happy and close they are. Deborah is 'a very warm, very genuine person who is always encouraging towards me as a small businessman'.

He can see that Ian only has eyes for Debs too. 'There's a lot of women who like the guy off bad,' Winston attests. 'But he's a family man. He's married his own kind, an ordinary woman, and respect to him for that: Deborah is a lovely woman.'

By the time he met Debs, Ian had also grown as a person and changed his take on life in a variety of ways. His responsibilities as a successful Afro-Caribbean man underpin his approach. He has a lot of black friends whom he will help out in simple ways.

If a friend is negotiating a contract on a building site somewhere, and it might swing it if Ian Wright the footballer goes along, he will make sure he accompanies the guy, puts in a good word and shows an interest. He won't make a big deal of it, or seek personal kudos out of it.

Why? For the same reasons Ian will never turn down the request for a signature, no matter how badly he's played or pissed off he feels, he'll do it because it will always remind him of how he was or might have been, of how he always wanted to be a footballer, and that he grew to learn there are duties intrinsic to that privileged role. His status has to have some use apart from making it impossible for him to lead the life he used to. If he can use it to make someone's life a little better, that's enough.

More than most people – and certainly more than most footballers, who are generally a nonchalant, spoilt bunch – Ian recognises that sometimes people need a little luck or help to achieve their dream. His life hasn't been easy but he's got more than he ever dreamed of now, so why not pay some of it back?

Ian hasn't changed except in the comfort of his lifestyle. He's still cool, not at all stuck-up and very straightforward. 'He's a calm and collected person. He knows who he is and has a surety of confidence about himself. He is a roots man in the sense that we get on very well – there's a mutual respect,' says Winston Husbands. 'He's a trusting person when he knows and respects you.

'There are so many people that admire him, but if it's gone to his head I haven't seen it. He knows his own potential but it hasn't gone to his head.'

Ian has never cut anyone out of his life without good reason. But his public profile had grown with the Highbury move, and he'd begun to suspect the intentions of the tabloid press towards him. He had to take steps to protect aspects of his life that could be misconstrued if reporters wanted to do so. Like most working class lads in London, Ian knows and likes people whom such luminaries as Gary Lineker wouldn't touch with a barge pole. But if you grew up in south London, you couldn't avoid knowing the odd rogue. And maybe even liking some of them.

On one occasion some years ago, Ian wanted to visit his old teacher Eric Summers. The only trouble was that Eric had to take a job – short-lived, as it turns out – in a club that, unbeknown to him, had a dodgy reputation. Eric hadn't seen Ian since he'd left school, and always told people he'd love to see his old pupil.

Out of the blue, one night Ian pulled up in his Shogun Jeep outside the venue with his old mate Andy Gray. He knew the place was full of villains – the press would have had a field day if they'd got hold of the story. Andy Gray came in and told Eric, 'Ian's out there.' But Eric didn't realise what he was saying. A little while later, Andy reiterated, 'Did you hear what I said? Ian's out there in the Jeep.' He didn't want to get dragged into the club. Eric found out later to his cost that it was a dodgy place, with lots of drugs and stuff. Eric rang Ian and apologised, saying, "I'm sorry, I didn't realise you were out there." '

With celebrity comes responsibility. As a black man, Ian is aware that, unfair as it is, he represents more than just himself as an individual in the public eye: he is a symbol for the Afro-Caribbean population of Britain.

The popular tabloid newspapers, so often filled with negative images and stereotypes of black people, see a story in his rise 'from the ghetto' to megastar status. But any weakness is regarded as a kind of inevitable reversion to type: that dreadful old fiction that 'you can take the boy out of the ghetto, but you can't take the ghetto out of the boy'. As one of the few Afro-Caribbean men in such a vaunted position, Ian recognises that he has to be extra vigilant: 'whiter than white'. Look at how they crucified Michael Jackson and James Brown and see how seriously they take Linford Christie, John Barnes and Chris Eubank. All superstars draw flak in this country, but black luminaries make the best target practice.

The way to avoid the fall from grace is to run a tight ship and avoid fools. Ian has kept in touch with the people whom he knew he could rely on to be staunch and discreet. It meant he had to withdraw from the sort of behaviour he got away with in the old days. 'When he was at Palace he was still one of the boys,' says one old spar. 'It's only since he went to Arsenal, bought a new house down at Croydon, that things have changed. The man's looking after his career.'

In fact, he was surrounding himself in a protective swathe of those who loved and respected him. Ian is a man who inspires and expects loyalty. He takes people at face value. He's reliable and supportive to the many people who mean anything to him, and he doesn't see why anyone should act any differently towards him.

He responds strongly if that code is broken. A few years ago, he summarily sacked a cleaner who had told the papers something she shouldn't. Ian hates some writers and has a lot of enemies in the press. He feels he's misrepresented again and again by people who don't know him. Like all footballers, he reads the *Sun*, the *Mirror* and the *News of the World*, and he's been stitched up a few times, misquoted and given an unjust reputation. The exceptions to Ian's aversion to journalists are Lee Clayton on the *Star*, who actually began work around the same time as Ian started at Palace and was one of his first interviews; Paul McCarthy from the *News of the World* and Richard 'Dickie' Pelham, the *Sun* snapper who stages all those crass photos of Ian dressed as a gangster, wearing a wig or blowing a saxophone.

More often than not, those are the people who splash the headlines for Ian when he wants a story placed in the papers, because he trusts them not to distort things. Again, this is Ian's way of repaying respect and loyalty.

That's the thing with Ian. When you're in, you're in. When you're out of favour, there's no way back.

7 'You'll Never Score for England'

'People say that Ian wouldn't be the same player if you took the fire out of his game. It could be that his prime motivation is to prove critics wrong. Forwards, especially, are criticised if they are not scoring and they love nothing more than proving the knockers wrong.'

Don Howe, England assistant coach

THE FA CUP FINAL at Wembley in May 1990 had established Ian Wright at the forefront of most commentators' thoughts on the best successor to Gary Lineker for England. Even the most Quixotic, the most myopic, recognised that the Palace striker deserved a run.

'Ian does have weaknesses,' the saintly Gary himself was later quoted as saying. 'He's not particularly strong on the ball. But he has that priceless ability to help himself to goals. I'm as convinced as anyone can be that he's my successor.' It might have been equivocal praise, but as far as passing the baton went, it was fair enough.

Even though the following season (1990/91) provided fitfully good hunting for Ian (he only managed 19 all told, a disappointment in his terms), his potency in a campaign that saw Palace permanently encamped near the First Division's lofty peak could not be denied. It was rarefied air for the club and the Wright-Bright duo was primarily responsible for taking them to it.

In December 1990, Steve Coppell picked up the Barclays 'Manager of the Month' award. By the middle of that month Palace were in third place, a position they would maintain for the rest of the season – the best top-flight finish in their 90-year history.

Around this time, England manager Graham Taylor was looking forward to the European Championships in Sweden in 1992, a tournament his team had high hopes of qualifying for.

'It was only my fourth game in charge,' says the manager, who has now returned to club football with Wolves. 'I had taken over the side that had finished runners-up in Italia '90. And I was looking, originally, for a sort of an evolution, not a so-called revolution. But as players' injuries crop up, as Terry Venables is finding himself, you get opportunities.

'Obviously Ian Wright was being pushed. He was scoring goals like nobody's business and the Cameroon was an ideal game. The first game I took over was a friendly, but the next two games were qualifying games in the European Championships. So, for me, the first real opportunity of a friendly game I got, I brought Ian in. He was in fact my first new player.'

And so the call went out for Wright, who had occupied Graham Taylor's thoughts before. Their paths had crossed three seasons earlier when manager Graham and his Aston Villa grandees were slumming it in the old Second Division along with Palace.

Ian wasn't surprised at being called up; it was what he'd deserved all along, even though the barren spell he was stuck in – one goal in twelve League starts – was hardly ideal preparation for his international debut.

When the national boss watched his debutant at the initial England training session, he was taken aback by Ian's enthusiasm, which made even Paul Gascoigne seem like a shrinking violet. In fact, Graham was a little concerned; he thought Ian was 'hyperactive'. The unabashed exuberance, the mimicry, the play-acting, the liveliness; he was later to say to Ian that he was glad he only had him every six weeks and not every day.

It was the sort of behaviour that had tested his teachers' patience at Samuel Pepys, but Ian had never been as excited at school as he was about being part of the England set-up. He'd only been a pro for five years: he reasoned that the equivalent in the average footballer's career would be a call-up at twenty. Brilliant!

The Palace hitman was largely included to see how he shaped up at international level. Graham Taylor always maintained that if there was a massive gap between standards at the top of the old First Division and the Second, there was another major step up to be made into the international game.

'It's a different type of step,' he confirms. 'Not necessarily how you play, but you have to have a temperament, you have to have a personality, you have to be able to cope with it all the time. All those things have to be taken into consideration.'

Thus were sown the seeds of doubt which lingered in the England manager's mind, throughout his tenure, over Ian Wright's psychological competence at world level.

There were no doubts, however, in Graham's mind what Ian's assets in the domestic game were:

'His first strength is his goalscoring, there's no doubt about that. The ability of this man to score goals from all positions is very, very important. It's his game . . . and the fact that he wants to score goals.

'I felt this boy – late starter to the game, desperately wants it – has the ability to turn on half a sixpence and (with) fierce, fierce shooting, pace, spins off people – once he learned the international game and could settle a bit of maturity about himself, all he needed was goals early on. And the longer he went without them, the more I began to get that feeling.'

On 6 February 1991, a dreadful evening's football against Cameroon, was memorable solely as the coldest English international night on record. Lineker's two goals put the lacklustre Africans out of their misery, tights and all, and reaffirmed the Spurs striker's sovereignty over his position. Ian was unexceptional, running hard but missing what decent opportunities he was presented with. 'In that first team,' points out Graham, 'you've got to remember he was new to it all. And it was just a question of him going out there and seeing what happened. It was a freezing night and the Cameroon players weren't interested in playing. I can't say I particularly blame them, but there had been a terrible problem with them, because they'd stayed in the hotel till five o'clock until they'd got certain money in cash and all that kind of thing. It was a difficult introduction for Ian.'

A first cap was his, but for Ian, it was like going back to the early days at Selhurst Park: he had everything to prove and no time to do it in. Graham Taylor's sense of his striker's desperation to score was spot on. It's a rare chink in Ian's armour, an inferiority complex: if he isn't scoring what is he doing?

'It's a mystery to me, as well as other people,' he told writer James Lawton in December 1994, 'why I haven't scored more goals for England. I suppose there is a bit of insecurity. When I play for England I look at some of my team-mates who are rock solid in the England set-up – David Platt, Paul Ince, Alan Shearer

– and I think they can afford to make a mistake, miss a goal, and I can't. So often when I get a chance I want to do it so badly.'

Ian was determined to get a few notches next to his name as soon as possible to justify himself. Missing chances, any chance, mattered. And hadn't he always scored on his debuts?: for Greenwich Borough, Palace (and later Arsenal). There was a nagging doubt in his mind that he would be found out at the top level, and he didn't like it.

The problem was, whereas as a club player he was able to turn it round and reap revenge a week later, for England it was a long wait before the next game, and you never knew if you would be selected.

The next opportunity Ian had was a month later against the Republic of Ireland, when again his early Selhurst days came to mind. Graham Taylor employed Ian, as he was to do for many matches to come, as a super-sub, replacing Gary Lineker in an attempt to break the stalemate and shake up the Irish defence with a bit of raw and unpredictable aggression: 'What d'you reckon, Lawrie? – Wrighty comes on and scores a blinder!' But Ian got little change out of Arsenal's David O'Leary and Paul McGrath of Villa (in fact he'd played against both twice already that season, without scoring). At least Graham Taylor had him in his thoughts.

Three months later in another friendly, against a USSR side riven by the recent end-of-empire events back home, Ian was paired up front with Alan Smith, a future Arsenal team-mate. Again, Ian failed to find enough openings or capitalise on what few chances he had. Smith grabbed one, Platt, surging from the back, nabbed two.

The biggest thing for Ian was when he was selected, at the end of Graham Taylor's first year in charge, in June 1991, for the England tour of Australia, New Zealand and Malaysia. But Ian didn't respond in the way the manager wanted, either on or off the pitch. He was selected for just one of the four matches. His Palace team-mate John Salako played in every one.

Graham Taylor won't be drawn on the reasons for Ian's omission, but on a tour abroad Ian's playful tendencies were to the fore, and reporters with the party in the South Pacific related that he didn't respond well when left out of the side.

He still displayed an impatient naiveté at international level that concerned his manager. 'When we went to New Zealand and Australia I think that Ian – even though he's a mature man in many respects – I think there was still possibly . . . some sort of growing up at international level that he still had to do.

'And on that tour, because we didn't go ahead with him the following year [in the European Championships] and he missed out, I think Ian probably thought he'd not exactly blown his chances, but hadn't done himself justice.'

The New Zealand game, in which David Hirst came on as sub and scored five minutes later, was Ian's last England match as a Palace player. It was also his last game for his country for nearly a year. Ian had played four games without scoring – an unsettling record, even if he'd been sub in two.

After his disappointing attitude on the South Pacific tour, Graham Taylor may have been of the opinion that he would wash that man right outta his hair. As it turned out, the national boss kept Ian in the frame, especially once he'd signed for Arsenal, an essential move in the England manager's view, but one which would 'make or break him'. To Ian, though, it simply appeared that, with one of the great stages of international football beckoning in Sweden, he was barely even close to a walk-on part in the mind of the man who mattered.

'I always thought my goals would be enough to get me through in the end,' he admitted afterwards, 'even though people had been saying for ages I'd be the striker who would be left out.'

To say he was extremely disappointed is not to know Ian when he's down: his face was as long as a baker's round. Apart from his scoring record for Arsenal, 26 goals in his first season with the club, he was playing the best football of his career, and his profile was higher than ever. It was just a shame that Benfica had booted the Highbury club out of the European Cup before he had a chance to prove himself against continental defenders.

Ian's last, cursory chance of a role in Sweden disappeared after the European Championships warm-up game in Budapest against Hungary in May 1992.

When the squad was announced, the only Wright on the list had an 'M' for Mark next to it. (In the event, the Liverpool defender withdrew from the squad.) Ian was crestfallen, and felt robbed. What did he have to do?

'I find this hard to forgive,' he told James Lawton of the *Independent*, two years later. 'That was my time. If he had given me my head then, trusted me a little bit, I think my career for England would have gone differently. I was scoring so many goals for Arsenal, and I won the Golden Boot.

'I don't feel bitter, just that somebody has deprived me of something that was mine.'

Understandably, given England's ignominious slump in the Swedish tournament after injuries to John Barnes, Paul Gascoigne, Paul Parker, Lee Dixon, Rob Jones and others, Graham Taylor is defensive about his omission of the country's leading scorer. 'I'd left Wright out because with Lineker there I couldn't see Wright getting in at all,' he says. 'And although people say, "Oh, you could have taken him for the experience", with only twenty people going you don't think about taking someone just for the experience, particularly when you bear in mind I decided to take Shearer for the experience and for a specific role, as opposed to Wright.

'People could say to me, "Yes, but if you knew Gary Lineker was going to go, and you were looking to Wright, you probably should have taken them both", and in a party of 22 I could have done, but not in a party of twenty and eventually, with the Mark Wright situation, a party of nineteen, it wasn't on.'

It has been said that what Graham Taylor and his second-in-command Lawrie McMenemy rejected in Ian Wright was his lack of flexibility, and McMenemy was quoted as saying they preferred players who could play in more than one position 'because you've got to play so many games in such a short space of time. If Gary Lineker hadn't been there, Ian Wright would have been a certainty, but we certainly didn't ever expect we would play the two of them together in a team.'

Gary Lineker always liked the ball played to feet but, deprived of Barnes and Gascoigne, the supply of accurate passes was always going to be limited with a midfield mastered by the likes of the bellicose David Batty.

Ian Wright, by contrast, favours the ball to run on to and is more likely to create something out of nothing. But the England management team had concluded he would provide no new channels to goal that Gary didn't already. As it was, under trying circumstances, Gary underperformed by his own lofty standards.

'You might say Lineker didn't perform. I have to be careful what I say. A lot of people just won't accept that performance,' remarks Graham guardedly.

It may simply be that after Ian's occasionally negative attitude in the South Pacific, Graham felt he couldn't risk a repeat if Wrighty was shuffling around in the stiffs. 'To be fair to Graham Taylor,' Steve Coppell told the *Independent*, 'Ian is not a very good substitute. He's got enough confidence in his own ability that he wants to play; and if he's not playing then he's not good to have around as part of a squad.'

Whatever the reason, while England ran aground in Sweden, their natural 'Lineker-in-waiting' was kicking cans back home in Croydon.

Or, to be precise, Ian Wright was trying hard to enjoy himself in Miami with his old mate and former Arsenal colleague, David Rocastle and their respective wives. Ian intended overlooking all the games but caught one or two. Part of the reason they chose America was because televised European soccer is a rarity (though Ian loves to shop in the malls there).

It was hard for Ian not to feel wronged: 'I had this buzz, which wouldn't go away: "I should be there", I kept saying'. And so said all of us.

So was Ian Wright always intended as a new Lineker in the boss's eyes? 'That was very much a media thing,' stonewalls Graham, 'because if you remember when Alan Shearer came and made his debut against France in '92, he scored and he was called the "new Lineker".

'There isn't a "new Lineker". It's "Ian Wright". Ian Wright and Gary Lineker are different types of people, and they're different types of players. They both can score goals. Then Lineker has this tremendous goalscoring record at international level which, for whatever reason, Ian, it has to be said, wasn't able to achieve.'

Graham wanted a different type of team, one which didn't channel everything to one goal machine.

'If anything was going to replace Lineker, it was going to be

Shearer and Wright. That's as I saw it. There's a line of thought where you don't actually need partnerships. Lineker's partnership eventually came with Beardsley, if it was a "partnership" – in many respects Gary Lineker played on his own.'

But with the World Cup qualifiers looming, Graham was aware that he needed the two strikers, and their contrasting styles, to work quickly together, and that despite the hollering for Deane, Ferdinand, Hateley, Hirst, Quinn, Bull and, suggested *The Times*, 'even Collymore'.

'I felt the one-off approach of Wright would be compensated a little bit perhaps by Shearer's more team ethic,' reveals Graham Taylor. 'That's not to say Ian is anti-team – he's not – but Ian's a goalscorer. Shearer would contribute that little bit more in other things, and he had had the experience as a 20-year-old of the European Championships.

'I felt if we were going to have a partnership, at that time, in late 1992, it was going to be between those two. In fact, if you look at my team selection for the first game against Norway, you'll find we were looking for that to be our new partnership upfront.'

Initially, and in general, the England manager was impressed with the way Ian reapplied himself to the national team against Norway and Turkey that autumn after the mortal disappointment of missing out on Sweden. Ian was dynamic in the Turkish game, and broadened his game to a more team-oriented approach.

'Turkey was definitely my best game for England,' he said, shortly before the San Marino game the following February. 'I'd got it into my mind that if I didn't do it in that one I could say good-bye to international football. Graham Taylor stuck by me after I missed a few good chances against Norway and it came right.'

There was no managerial genius behind Graham Taylor's approach, no sorcery or manipulation. He just told Ian to go out and play like he did for Arsenal.

'The manager knows what I can do. It's just a matter of time. I'll score a goal and everything will be perfect. No problem. You have to be confident at this level, but you have to be capable of doing the business as well.'

Always sensitive to such things, Graham Taylor detected the fragility of Ian Wright's ego behind the shield of his larger-than-life personality. But he also saw a huge difference between the Ian Wright that first joined the England set-up as a Crystal Palace player, and the Ian Wright that had matured and developed under George Graham as an Arsenal player.

There were still areas that needed to be ironed out, not least, as the England boss saw it, his holding play and distribution.

'His weaknesses were that there are occasions when, if you're talking from a team point of view, the ball doesn't always stick with him,' asserts Graham. 'He's quick at times and sees things, and you can't always rely on the ball staying there on occasion. He wouldn't always be at his best.'

Ian was nowhere near his best in the Norway game. The manager subbed him after 25 minutes of the second half. The loose Shearer–Wright relationship hadn't solidified, and the 'less flexible' Wright was sacrificed.

It was a complete relapse for a striker who by now seemed impermeably confident at League level. Steve Coppell could see his former star going through the same motions he had in his early professional career. Clearly, Ian was simply too anxious to impress again, just like his Palace salad days.

But the ex-manager still stood by the man he'd groomed from non-League to international level: 'I might be simplifying things,' he remarked, as Ian struggled to make the England starting line-up, 'but I just look at his goals and say, "Who's scored the most?" From that point of view, you've got to look at Hirst and Wright. If you start getting involved in blends, I think sometimes you're overlooking the obvious. If you have two strikers who score goals, presumably you've got a better chance than if you have one striker who scores and another who makes.' – e.g. Barnes, Sharpe.

In Ian's opinion – a view shared by critics of his direct style – he hadn't proved himself for England unless he had scored, and that he patently had failed to do. Ian felt he still had much to achieve at this level. He knew he was capable of doing the business, but time as ever was working against him.

In truth, Ian had already begun to think that the European Championships had been 'his' time. Perhaps he was also thinking he was past his international sell-by date. It didn't stop him banging away of course.

Although Ian's performance against the Turks a month later at Wembley had been one of his best from a team point of view, again he failed to break his duck. Moreover, the press had cranked up the disagreement over his exclusion from the European Championships squad, commenting on his lack of goals and his lack of guile against grade A defenders.

They also began to lap up subtle hints dropped by Graham Taylor calling into question Ian Wright's quality at the top level as well as his disciplinary record for Arsenal. No-one could destroy Ian's self-belief, but the fitfulness of his England career from now on would puncture his ego again and again over the next year.

Once he was in the Highbury goldfish bowl, trouble stalked Ian and there were knock-on effects for his national reputation. In late 1992, after he had 'slapped' Spurs defender David Howells during a typically tense north London derby and was subsequently punished, Graham Taylor felt moved to direct a thinly veiled warning towards his aspiring striker, innocuously couched in the phrase 'the behaviour of international players at their clubs is important'.

The response of Stuart White, writing in *The Times*, was understandable: 'With one rash and ill-advised blow, Wright may have punched a hole in his international career and might even have terminated it.'

Ian's good behaviour after the Howells incident probably spared him a heavier FA ban and the termination of his international career; Graham Taylor felt he had been punished enough and had responded properly.

In fact, time has not healed the wounds inflicted on Graham Taylor by the bloodthirsty press and there are hints that he has come to sympathise with Ian's treatment by the media. 'There was so much highlighting,' he remembers, 'so much pressure and Ian would get upset if he thought there were unfair things. And he did feel that at times he was treated unfairly.'

But Graham's honesty sometimes undermined his players and caused resentment. In Ian Wright's case, his candour fed a perceived clash between the two. When quizzed about how the lengthy 'Howells' suspension would effect Ian's preparation for the San Marino game, Graham replied, 'That's his problem.'

Graham denies a personal rift, though. 'He never said anything to me. But you could see that sometimes when he was involved in talking to the press. He was never nasty. But you just felt that he was resentful. Ian tries to be honest and answers openly, and when that gets misused or abused, I think he probably felt people were getting at him. Of course, that only comes with maturity. Later on, you just have to say that's how it is.

'There are occasions when you've got to take a step back and just think about it,' muses the ex-England manager. 'You need that at international level in your playing too. You need to learn now you're being marked a little bit closer and firmer, you're having your shirt tugged, don't react to that. All of that you can only do by playing. And I think that he played enough games under myself to have learned that.'

Ian has claimed that he immediately 'feared the worst' about Graham when, after a brilliant World Cup, Gascoigne was dropped for the new manager's first match against the Republic. 'I was stunned,' he said. 'And then I thought, "If he can do that to Gazza, what can he do to me?" He did it to me in a big way, but that's history.'

It was thought that it was the inconsistency that disturbed Ian and other players, but much of it, the manager maintains, was forced on him by circumstances.

'Nobody would have liked it better than me,' he insists, 'that in the Norway game, when we had Ian and Shearer as our forwards, if they'd both stayed fit and both scored goals. I would have picked them both for ten games. As it happened Shearer was only fit for three of them.

'We had drawn with Norway 1-1 and been very unfortunate not to beat them – that was in the October – and our next game was at home to Turkey and we won 4-0. Gascoigne came on and got two goals, we pretty well played the same team. I know it was only two games, but everything to me was looking okay. By the time February came it had gone.'

Before that Norway game, there had been an ominous moment at a press conference. Graham Taylor was indicating that there was 'light at the end of the tunnel' for John Salako, Paul Gascoigne (whom he wasn't expecting 90 minutes from in the match) and Paul Parker. 'I'm determined to see us through to the USA in '94,' he declared. 'To do that I'll continue to pick the best squad, to lobby for a better deal for the national team and to motivate players.' As he finished speaking, the lights in the room suddenly went out.

After Turkey, what England and their manager desperately needed was to play another game a month later to keep up the momentum. Instead there was a three-month gap after the 4-0 win before the San Marino ritual slaughter. By that time, Ian was injured again.

As far as Graham Taylor is concerned, San Marino was Ian's Waterloo. Unlike Napoleon, however, Ian's downfall was his absence from the battlefield.

He had pulled a groin muscle in scoring both the Arsenal goals that demolished Nottingham Forest in the FA Cup fifth round. 'I'm hoping it's just a little muscle twinge and not half as bad as everyone thinks,' he said afterwards, forlornly. Ian had been on fire in the domestic game, with sixteen goals under his belt.

The England medical team gave Ian intensive treatment at the squad's Buckinghamshire HQ, but to no avail. Ian had to miss out on the feeding frenzy against the Group 2 small fry. (Norway had gone into double figures against them.) Team-mate Paul Merson knew what it meant to his Arsenal pal. 'I just feel sorry for Ian,' he sympathises. 'I dread to think what he would have done to San Marino.'

'To me, the San Marino game at home was the one Ian didn't need to miss,' believes Graham Taylor. 'He needed to be there. We'd lost Shearer, we'd lost Pearce, in that three-month gap. We'd started to lose Gascoigne because by that time he'd stopped working on his fitness.

'We had to push Platty forward alongside Ferdinand, and I remember David Platt being ever so pleased he was playing up front against them: he could get some goals. And he scored four.

'If you think back, Ian then got four goals in the return game away. Now what it would have been like . . . On little things like that, careers depend.'

Ian's goal famine at international level – now seven games without troubling the statisticians – was in complete contrast to his League and cup form, where he was on the way to adding 30 strikes to his name for Arsenal that season.

This discrepancy became a source of national amusement. A *Times* sports writer suggested that all his England caps should be embossed with small ducks. Others pointed out the irony of the advertising campaign, 'Behind every great goalkeeper is a ball from Ian Wright'. Not at international level there isn't, they smirked.

Billboards for Nike featuring Ian had appeared at the start of his international career that alluded to the 'next Lineker' tag: 'Gary who?', they cheekily and indiscreetly proclaimed. What a hostage to fortune that line proved. As Ian's inability to assume the Lineker mantle became more obvious, the former Tottenham striker's publicity machine produced the trenchant response: 'Lineker 48; Wright 0'.

Not for the first time, Ian was aware that along with the light of publicity came the heat. Opposition fans were quick to latch on to any opportunity to turn that up.

Always a focal point for their animosity, Ian now endured chants of 'You'll never score for England!' wherever he went. When Arsenal met Yeovil in the 4th round of the Cup, he gestured the 'flying V's' back to them when the nagging refrain rang out – even though he had scored a hat-trick. The message had hit home, and it hurt.

Graham Taylor could understand Ian's problem. 'If he'd scored early on in his England career, if he'd played in the first San Marino game and scored the goals that Platty did, I think we'd have been talking about a different Ian Wright,' he maintains. 'I don't blame Ian for that. He knows, as well as I do, that anytime it could go in.'

The problem is that no-one has actually pinpointed Ian's international deficiencies – clearly even the manager himself. The idea that he was just trying too hard has gained popularity as a result, especially amongst his England colleagues. Les Ferdinand was quoted as saying as much.

'I think the point about Ian "chasing time" is a good one,' contends Graham, 'because I felt he always felt he had to score to justify his place, because the reputation would be, "Well, what else has he done?"'

'I very strongly made a point to him, when we beat Turkey 4-0 and he had gone down the left side, driven in a great cross and Shearer came across the defender, which he's good at, and headed it in. After the game I said, "If you're not scoring, don't you worry about it: that'll do me!"'

'It works both ways, because even though he's now scored all these goals, and recently at European level too, you have to learn about man-marking of the highest level against you. And the defenders are usually hard people: they're as quick as you and they're skilful. So you have to learn all about that.'

The fact is that one of Ian's strong points is his ability to twist and turn round the Premiership's defensive leviathans. At international level, however, smart sweepers are capable of mopping up most of the balls that are Ian's bread and butter.

There's more to it than the learning curve Graham Taylor refers to, though. It might be simplistic, but Ian's game wasn't necessarily suited to the way Taylor's England team played.

Arsenal play a deep, half-field pressing game, working to achieve things on the break, which provides plenty of space for forwards when they surge towards goal. It suits Ian's pace and opportunism perfectly.

The national side, as befits the elevated standard of opposition they face, tend to move forward more patiently, allowing defences to cover and crowd the area. This is not where Ian is at his best and, after the Lineker experience in Sweden, Graham Taylor was never going to build his side around one player. Furthermore, Ian has always enjoyed playing alongside a big target man, someone to take the heat off him. At Palace, it was Mark Bright; at Arsenal, it was often Alan Smith. And for England . . .?

Interestingly, Ian is probably better suited to the direct approach advocated by FA Director of Coaching and Education Charles Hughes, with whom Graham Taylor was frequently said to be at odds. As Nils Middleboe, the Scandinavian who made his name with Chelsea, once wrote, 'To systemise is to sterilise'. He may have been writing before they changed the offside law, but he had a point.

In May 1993, Ian again found himself sitting in the wings as others acted out the unfolding drama of England's failure to reach America '94. On a bitterly cold night in Chorzow, Poland, Ian watched as England's middle was overrun and outmanoeuvred. Graham Taylor was famously dismayed by the first half performance, describing the men who should have been his midfield generals – Barnes, Gascoigne and Palmer – as 'headless chickens'.

The mood on the England bench has been captured for posterity (if that's the right word) on the video *Do I Not Like That*, originally titled for television – more prosaically and fairly perhaps – *The Impossible Job*.

Viewers were alarmed at the seeming shallowness of thinking among the England hierarchy that night. Perhaps they were tongue-tied by the incompetence of the performance, but when Graham Taylor turned to his assistants and mused aloud that Wrighty was made for a game like this, he sounded like nothing more than one of the fans that had travelled over from London N5.

'I actually turned round to Lawrie McMenemy and Phil Neal and said, "This is made for Ian Wright, this game, this is made for him to go on and score." And that was it. I told Ian, "Go and score". It was one of those things that just happened ... I'd thought it before and it hadn't.'

Ian had seventeen minutes to prove himself, which in international terms is roughly equivalent to the moments between the traffic lights turning green and the driver behind you hooting. As it was, with six minutes to go Ian cruised on to a typical Arsenal ball from deep-lying Tony Dorigo to beat goalkeeper Bako with a first-time shot. Ah joy. His first goal for his country. Oh, and a point saved.

'Somehow,' attests Graham, 'when you look at that – and I'm not trying to defend myself – I could have given up on Ian, and some people would have. You're talking about how many times has he played before he's scored?

'By the time the Poland game came, he'd had seven appearances and not scored. So that's the thing that's not quite read properly, because if I hadn't still had that faith in him, he wouldn't have been there.'

Faith is a powerful motive for Ian. When he invests it in someone, he expects it to be returned. Retrospectively, he didn't always feel this was the case with Graham Taylor.

'I wouldn't blame Graham Taylor,' he confessed to football glossy *Four-Four-Two*, 'but people say I've got sixteen caps and five goals. They don't say I've only played seven games and come on for nine as a substitute. I've never played two games on the spin. I've never had a decent run in the side. I've always had to come in and work hard to get chances.

'Maybe I've missed a few chances but I still think I deserved a chance to get a run in there to get my confidence going. But Taylor never really allowed me to get that. But he never ever made me feel I wasn't good enough to play for England – I always knew that I was.'

Perhaps frustration and disappointment have clouded Ian's memory, but there were several contentious issues there. Firstly, and perhaps tellingly, he complained about having to work hard for his chances. Well, welcome to the international scene, mate. Nothing is handed on a plate at world level. That other Premiership strikers admire the fact that he can create 30 goals a season in such an unadventurous team as George Graham's Arsenal seems lost on him.

Furthermore, and most contentiously, Ian complains that he was never given a proper run in the side. Yet even though he dropped Ian after the Antipodean trip, and overlooked him for the Swedish jaunt, the England manager continued to buy into Ian Wright's stock long after many in and out of the game had disinvested.

For the second year running, Ian found himself in America because of Graham Taylor's team selections. This time, however, the rest of the team was with him. The 1993 American tournament – another tiring and distressing summer tour for the England team – nevertheless provided Ian with great opportunities to capitalise on his initial investment against the Poles.

It had been a good build-up for him. Paul Ince and he had become firm friends. Superficially they had the same outlook. Similar backgrounds. Same ebullient, playful manner. David Platt took to calling them the 'twins' because when they went shopping they always ended up liking and buying the same things. It was the sort of bonding Graham Taylor was looking for with 'Club England', his attempt to recreate a clubby camaraderie at international level.

The approach was vintage Taylor. The first media-friendly England manager was also, while at Watford, the first manager to introduce a clause in players' contracts that tied them to 'community' duties in their spare time. The international squad – albeit a more extended one than Graham wanted – was beginning to gel. But on the pitch, everything was coming unstuck.

During the game in Foxboro against the USA, Ian had plenty of excellent chances to score. But they were the sort he would treat as mere *hors d'oeuvres* were they to present themselves at Highbury.

Here, in the white national jersey he seemed to want to make too sure he hit the target and Tony Meola produced a brace of brilliant saves to deprive him. Even though he was sub in that game, Ian's misses were all the worse for the final scoreline: 2-0 to the Americans.

Ian Wright's sense of his own mortality in the international arena was never greater than after that woeful tour. Shortly before the second Polish game, in September the same year, he revealed, 'I play every game as though it might be my last. You have to because there are so many quality strikers around.'

It was an ominous sign for someone of his habitual confidence; as if he was saying to the England boss that he would understand if he was overlooked. But scoring Premiership goals like the sensational juggling act against Everton, as Graham Taylor himself admitted at the time, rendered him 'very very difficult to be ignored at international level if you haven't got other forwards who are putting the ball in as well.

'This boy does things you don't coach, and as long as you've got it within the framework of your team, off you go. There is that unpredictability about him, but it has to be translated into goals.'

If Alan Shearer had recovered from his long-term injury, Graham Taylor might not have felt inclined to pursue things with Ian. But he liked him and he admired his League performances. And Les Ferdinand, who had come into the picture too, hadn't exactly lit up the scene.

Ian was still a fully paid up member of the national coach's attempt to build a cosy team atmosphere around a consistent core of players, an atmosphere akin to that of a First Division squad.

'He very much contributed to "Club England",' says Graham. 'People may look at my reign and say it was a mistake to try to get that. I think you can [achieve that] with a group of people, and I tried to introduce that at international level off the pitch.'

There was no problem between Ian and Graham, though there were mutterings, amplified by the national newspapers, from both about each other. It wasn't personal: it was business.

'I've always got on very well with Ian,' smiles Graham. 'He will have his own opinions, but I always found him, generally speaking, good to work with. I liked him and still do; his enthusiasm and humour were infectious. I always remember his big smile.'

The England manager believes an anxious moment actually occurred off the pitch for Ian at the very start of his England career. In October 1990, England were scheduled to play a friendly match against Poland and the team gathered for a social evening beforehand.

This was really the inaugural meeting of 'Club England'. And it was Ian's first involvement with the international set-up. He was to be a non-participating sub. But he performed impressively when called upon a few days before the match.

That night, the squad had a meal, went to the theatre and returned for a karaoke evening at the Royal Garden Hotel in London. According to tradition, the new boys were called upon to show their singing capabilities. As Graham Taylor's first freshman, Ian was called upon to sing. He chose a classic soul number.

'He sang very well, he was very good,' recalls Graham. 'And Steve Coppell said to me, "Have you seen him dance?" But he says it was the most nervous thing he did.'

Of course, it wasn't always like that. The surly side of Ian, the childish mucking about with Gazza or, latterly, his great friend Paul Ince, inevitably reared its head on occasion.

'I think sometimes there's a front with him,' says Graham. 'I found on a couple of occasions when I spoke to him on my own he could be a serious young man. And sometimes it was his honesty that got him into trouble. 'I like that kind of person. But he could be up and down, couldn't he. I would rather say that and be honest about him.

'But I'll be honest. I had no problems with him. I never felt I had any personal problems with him. He was up and down, can't be still, always on the move. There's times when you need a rest from that, and as an international manager I could [get it].'

But if Ian mostly impressed Graham as a man once he'd matured, as a player he was still sub or subbed more times than he cared to remember.

Obviously being sub is better than not being named at all, but everybody wants to play. You're there; you want to be one of the eleven. A policy Graham Taylor introduced as international manager was naming the team the weekend before.

He would leave the subs usually until the Wednesday, the day of the game. But anybody who wasn't on the bench was allowed to go home because the disappointment was so intense.

Even at Palace Ian was never the best person to have around if he knew he wasn't going to be involved in a game; no player likes being sub, but Ian could be downright sulky. Just as his infectious enthusiasm lit up the most laborious training session, so his sourness could contaminate the mood of others. It didn't mean he resented the manager's decision – he would be the same if injury ruled him out. It just meant he was desperately disappointed.

Ian never responded in an adverse manner to his England boss's decisions to select him as sub. But after a while, the super-sub apprenticeship he'd already been through at Selhurst Park began to grate again – especially as, unlike when he first turned pro, he wasn't producing the goods. But he never gave Graham Taylor the impression that if called upon he wouldn't go on and do it.

Graham Taylor stands by his selection decisions principally for one very simple reason: Ian's fitness to play. He believes it was injury that curtailed Ian's international career, tying the manager's hands.

If Ian wasn't up to speed, he would be loathe to capitulate to the problem. Even going back to the days of school Ian was always desperate to play. No way would he allow anything as incidental as injury to stop him. Would the same apply with England? You might risk a half-fit kid in the Invicta Cup; but in the World Cup?

'Ian had some injuries during that time,' reveals Graham Taylor. 'He must have got over a dozen or so with me – the greater part of his international caps. What I found is that when I selected the side against Norway for our World Cup qualifier, by the time we'd played our tenth qualifying game, Ian had played in five of them, he'd been substitute in three and he'd missed two through injury. Now the three that he was substitute, if you look, he was having knee injury problems.

'When we went out to Poland and Norway Ian, in fact, was complaining about knee problems. In fact, he hadn't played for Arsenal. And he hadn't reached a stage at his international career where you could say, "Well, I know he's not really quite fit, but I'm going to play him." A club manager can do that. How could you say that at international level? You can't.

'So if you're asking was he a success or a disappointment, I'm saying that to a degree he was a success, but he wasn't a total success. There were so many occasions when I had him and he was either carrying an injury or, let's say, I had discussions with his club who said, "Look, we're going to let him come, but he's not really fit." 'Now as an international manager, whatever people may say, you sometimes find yourself in a position where you can't actually say, "Well, he's come but his club manager says he's not really fit and I'm going to play him." It was very very difficult.'

Graham Taylor claims to have records covering all the times Ian was supposedly less than 100% fit.

'If you remember,' he argues, 'there was that period of time where George [Graham] just played him for certain games and then just left him out. And he was always left out around international games. It was not an easy thing to control and do.'

One particular occasion stands out: the fatal defeat in Norway, when the English bulldogs rolled on their backs and waved their paws feebly in the air.

'I'd made this tactical decision,' says Graham, 'and I was criticised because we lost. If we'd won, I'd be the greatest thing that ever lived. But I was very much of the firm opinion that Norway were wary about playing us. And I wanted Ferdinand to play very similar to the way he had against Holland in the 2-2 draw, and I thought Sheringham's touch and height would disturb Norway. And it just didn't work out.

'Everyone talked about Pallister at the back and the changes, but the two disappointments for me in the Norway game were the strikers. I tried and hoped that we could push on to Norway and get at them, particularly with Ferdinand and Sheringham. But it didn't work. So we brought Ian Wright on, and obviously we were hoping he would come up with a goal.'

But Wrighty came on and failed to make the hoped for impact. England lost.

'I remember after I'd had him as substitute against Norway. And coming back on the aeroplane Ian went to the doctor and asked for something for his knee. I remember thinking, "I was right not to go in with him from the word go." Now those kind of things I can talk about.'

More to Ian's detriment, at the end of the 1992/93 season when he was having trouble with his knees, the renascent Les Ferdinand was on form. Ferdinand – almost alone – had played very well when England drew at home in the capitulation against Holland, 2-2 – the infamous 'Do I not like orange' match.

But Les had still only scored three goals for his country. There still seemed no consistent strike force that Graham Taylor could settle on. Before the San Marino game, Graham Taylor had tried eleven strikers in his 27 games in charge. Disturbingly, only the Alans – Smith and Shearer – had been given successive games during that time. Ian wasn't the only casualty – physically or professionally – during the period.

'I don't look upon Ian either as a major success or a major disappointment,' explains Graham. 'It would have been far better for me if he'd been fit for all of the ten games. And he wasn't. He was picked for 50%, he played eight out of the ten. And it's very difficult as an international manager, because people often say they have to have a run. But that's tricky, particularly when you're trying to qualify for competitions, and you only have twelve games in a season.'

Graham Taylor has support for his view that Ian is wrong to feel he wasn't given a fair chance under his regime. Amongst those who agree is Steve Coppell.

'I don't know whether you should expect to have a fair crack of the whip,' contends Ian's old boss. 'You just get an opportunity and if things fall nicely, then the opportunity goes well and you establish yourself; if you struggle, then the opportunities become rarer. Ian had the chance. The fact that he didn't establish himself I'm sure is a major disappointment to him personally, but he's still done all right for himself.'

Ian needed to score, wanted to score. It's a perennial problem with strikers at international level. They sometimes feel it's their only chance to retain their place. Everyone wants a 'good run'.

Kevin Keegan said that until he had twelve England games under his belt he didn't feel like an international player. Keegan was good enough to be able to earn those dozen games, or the circumstances were right for him at that time. Football isn't always like that.

It's ridiculous to allow that latitude for any number of players; you just can't do it. The reality of life is that at international level you have to deliver, and decisions are made quicker and earlier; it is too much of a luxury to allow people eighteen months to find their feet as an international player.

Graham Taylor cites Luther Blisset, whom he managed at Watford, as another example. 'He only played fourteen games for England. Prolific goalscorer, scored three against Luxembourg, but couldn't find the goals at international level. And he was a very similar type of player to Ian. But I always remember saying to him, "Look, you've got those fourteen caps son; there's many people don't get those."

'It isn't a question of not having faith in them, or anything like that, because once you've given somebody twelve or more opportunities, be it as substitute or whatever, you've done as much as you can as an international manager.

'I never saw Ian as a successful goalscorer at international level. His game is based on goals, and one has to say that Poland and San Marino were the only two occasions he scored.'

Ian himself appeared to acknowledge his failure at the highest level. Incredibly, before the San Marino game, when it was virtually done and dusted that England had failed to qualify for America, Ian began to step back, to withdraw from the reckoning. He talked favourably about other strikers, to the England manager's astonishment.

He would say things on behalf of his friends, particularly his close black friends: 'What about Andy Cole?' or, 'Well my time's up, it's obviously not going to come for me again. Andy Cole, he's the next one ...' Graham Taylor used to try to encourage him, 'You've got no need to say that son, you can play till you're 35, why shouldn't you be in the England squad?

'Ian came into the game late, and there is this desire in him. You look at him now – 31 – and there's no reason he can't play for another four or five years,' says Graham. 'He should know what the international scene is now. He's scoring goals. In my opinion it's really up to him now. People like Fowler and people like Cole shouldn't really be seeing the England scene if Ian's doing the job. He's got that experience behind him. There's no need for him to turn round and say, "What about the young ones?" '

For the San Marino game, however, Andy Cole lined up on the bench.

When the now departing manager addressed his disheartened team after the match, it was without rancour. 'Look, we've all got our careers to look after, and nothing will please me more if the majority, if not all of you continued to be selected by the next manager,' he told them.

And indeed, Ian was selected by incoming boss Terry Venables, even if, under the former Tottenham manager's regime, he was required to adopt alien roles. At least, he was 'still around' as he describes it. Terry gave Ian his first run of consecutive games against Greece and Norway in May 1994 – as sub. After USA '94, England played the hosts at Wembley. Ian came on for nine minutes at the end. Ho-hum.

'I would think Ian would be disappointed now,' says Alan Smith, Ian's Arsenal team-mate, 'because he didn't get in that squad at the end of the season [the 1995 Umbro Tournament]. Only Terry Venables knows really what he thinks. But you only have to look at the squad, don't you. For some reason he's not in it, so draw your own conclusions.'

Nevertheless, Don Howe, Terry's coach for England, has been impressed by Ian's flexibility where Graham Taylor saw little. 'I've found him very disciplined in his game,' claims Don. 'If Terry Venables has asked him to adjust his game he has done it – no problem. When we tried the Christmas Tree formation he did well for the team in an unselfish role, even though he considers himself an out-and-out goalscorer.'

Still the goals fail to come – not one in the vengeful 5-0 demolition of World Cup qualifiers Greece. Ian has still only scored five times in twenty appearances.

'Perhaps he just needs to break the ice before he gets the goals flowing,' says Don Howe, comfortingly. 'Perhaps it is just bad luck – it's not as if he has been missing chances he would normally put away. He has not seemed to get those same chances. Perhaps it is because he is more unselfish and conscious of his responsibilities to the team.

'But I wouldn't agree with those who say his style of play isn't suited to international football. He has shown throughout his career that he is capable of finishing in a wide range of ways. He can shoot with either foot, score with his head, he gets on the end of crosses, turns inside the box or runs in on goal. He has just not shown his club scoring form for England.'

His boss Mr Venables might not agree. If the second Polish game was Ian and England's 'High Noon' under Graham Taylor, the clash with Romania, one of the revelations of America '94 a few months earlier, was more like black comedy. England were like dwarves: outpassed, out-thought and out of touch. Tight-lipped and ashen-faced, the England manager appeared to consign certain players to history. He'd already warned that 'Caps must be earned, not tossed around like confetti'. Now it seemed time for some divorce writs to be handed out

One of them appeared to be aimed at Ian Wright, who played perhaps his least competent match at international level in his first start under the Venables reign. Required to cover deeper, to allow Le Tissier and Lee room on the flanks, to burst forward whenever possible, and to break down Romania's passing game from the back, Ian appeared positionally naive and his first touch and distribution were found wanting. The England coach singled out people's champion Matthew Le Tissier and Ian for criticism. 'Tried and found wanting' was journalist Joe Lovejoy's observation.

'I asked both of them to play the same way that they do for their clubs,' Venables claimed, 'but it wasn't as simple as that. The Romanians were sending them backwards and giving them decisions to make: "Am I going to follow you, or are you going to follow me?"When they were in doubt, they opted to do the defensive job.

'Romania dictated to us, and we followed them, which took us away from the forward areas. We've got to improve our team play so that when the ball goes forward we've got three men up there, not one.'

Increasingly, Ian's inability to replicate his domestic strike ratio and the subsequent failure to reproduce his normal team contribution seem to have put paid to his chances of figuring in England's starting line-up for the 1996 European Championships, when 'Football comes home'.

When Terry Venables spoke of having a 'fairly settled side' by the time of the 'dry run' Umbro tournament in June 1995, he was clearly thinking that Anderton, Wise and other auxiliary strikers would perform the Wright role better. Despite a dismal showing against Brazil, Japan and Sweden from teams compromised by injury and (in some cases) threats of incarceration, the Arsenal striker is unlikely to fulfil one of his remaining dreams: to play for England in a major tournament.

Perhaps that's why his omission from the European Championships in Sweden still rankles. In that sense, his criticisms of Graham Taylor carry a bitterness that is understandable but unfair.

There's a mood to reappraise the Taylor Era: the record of his first ten games in charge – seven wins, three draws – is actually better than Terry Venables', whose team had won five, drawn four and lost one over the same span.

Whatever, there's no bitterness between the ex-England manager and his first new recruit, just history.

'I liked Ian Wright, I liked him as a lad, and I know if we met now there would be no problem,' says Graham Taylor now. 'I saw all those quotes afterwards, where he probably felt that I was never sure about him. Let me tell you this: if I hadn't been sure about him, he wouldn't have been in the squad.

'That's what gets me when people say, "He's not too sure . . . Well he hasn't played me". But for god's sake you're named in the national squad, the manager's got to be sure about you.

'And that's the kind of comment that sometimes Ian makes. He sometimes speaks as he feels at that time, and he plays like that too. My only regrets are that he didn't score earlier and that he missed the San Marino game at home.'

For Steve Coppell, the manager who perhaps knows Ian best of all, it's quite simple. 'I just hark back to the day when he walked into our office,' he says, 'and he was wide-eyed and determined to do well.

'I think if you'd said to him at that stage, "Listen, you're going to get promotion, you're going to be transferred for a lot of money, you're going to be a big hero in London, have your name on billboards right across the country and you're going to play for England": I think he'd have been quite happy with that.'

8 'Ian Wright Wright Wright!'

'He's almost uncoachable, so I can't claim any credit.'
George Graham, ex-Arsenal manager

'Some people claim he has changed his style at Arsenal, but Ian has played with fire in his belly throughout his career. He would not be the same without the aggressive streak.'
Mark Bright, ex-Crystal Palace striker

ALTHOUGH IAN ACCEPTED each new shift in his life, each breakthrough, with the same mixture of alacrity and indebtedness, he was surprised at how familiar each environment was to him once he got there. Although there were fresh challenges, there wasn't anything he couldn't cope with. Everything was just as he'd always pictured it. And although he wouldn't say as much, it was actually easier than he thought; perhaps because he wanted success so much, he'd thought it all properly through and worked hard for everything that came his way.

On arrival at Highbury, he announced it was 'my place, my fairytale place'; and it did turn out to be his field of dreams. Ian's hat-trick League debut is one of Arsenal's all-time great overtures. He followed it up with a phenomenal strike rate: 26 in his first season to nick the Golden Boot off Gary Lineker's toe (combined with those he'd already notched at Palace); by the end of 1992/93 campaign he'd claimed 56 goals in 79 appearances. There was something charmed about Ian from then on; he became their milestone man. Another 35 goals came in 1993/94, followed by 30 in 1994/95.

Ian reached 100 goals for Arsenal in 143 games and less than four seasons – more quickly than any other Highbury finisher. He is only the 14th player to reach a ton of goals at a single club (and he did it at Palace too, scoring 118 for them).

Sod's Law of Old Boys operated as usual: with the delightful contempt football has for the sensibilities of the dejected, Ian became a centurion on 1 October 1994 – against Crystal Palace. Supporters of other clubs can take comfort from the fact that Ian scored nearly 25% of them against just four teams: Southampton, Sheffield Wednesday, Nottingham Forest and, of course, Crystal Palace. Saints fans will appreciate that he scored nearly one in ten of his goals against them.

It doesn't end there. In registering his first goal in Europe against Odense in 1993, Ian also scored Arsenal's 100th against continental opposition. Then there's the record of scoring in every match of the European Cup-Winners' Cup in the 1994/95 campaign, until the Paris final, during which Esnaider snatched immortality from Ian by hitting the target and going one better. Still, undeniably, the Arsenal hitman has the Midas touch.

Ian was made by the move to Highbury's marble halls, professionally and fiscally. He was welcomed with a wage that put four figures in his account every week, even before he thought about income from endorsements and public appearances. Ian's name was added to every PR company's list of invited guests.

The revision of his contract in July 1995 stretched the figure to a reputed weekly haul of £10,000, since he and Tony Adams had clauses allowing them to renegotiate their terms if an incoming player earned more than they did. Not bad for a player who originally claimed he'd cost too much. And another good reason to welcome Glenn Helder, David Platt and Dennis Bergkamp!

A 'name' as soon as he hit Highbury, Ian was inundated with offers of freebies, TV chat show invitations and media events. But he was mature enough to keep his head by then.

Ian remained loyal to Nike at a time when others might have chosen to cash in on their new found currency and crank up the wedge. In return, Nike upped his remuneration along with his involvement. He is now required to make TV ads, star in billboard campaigns, appear at various stores around the country and turn up at soccer camps – wearing his Nike gear, of course. Nike request eight or so appearances a year, many of them abroad.

There are other lucrative deals too. But Ian has been able to exploit his new prominence in more altruistic ways for the benefit of his community and others. Ian works a lot for various voluntary organisations, especially those involving children. He never forgets his own underprivileged upbringing and, as one of the relatively few footballers who saw something of the outside world before entering the game, he has a more compassionate take on the circumstances of those whose lives aren't as blessed. In the words of Smashie and Nicey, Ian does a lot of 'charidy' work, but doesn't like to talk about it.

For Graham Taylor, Ian Wright's late start and background have had a big impact on the player. 'Lads who have come into the game from a professional background, they know they can get a job if it goes wrong. But if you get other lads who'll come into the game from what they consider next to nothing, they don't want to go back there.

'And I think that late start definitely produces a different mentality; they're more rounded, they know there's other things going on in life. Football can be a very closed world. A lot of professional footballers are a bit like teachers, with all due respect – and I've got a daughter who's a teacher. You go to school, you go to college, you go back to school. And what's going on in the rest of the world?'

If you want to be a made man, you have to act like one. At Palace, Ian would always return after senior training to work with and encourage Alan Smith's youth team. He would attend the school matches of his sons Shaun and Bradley and inspire the other kids. Now he started doing the same for the Arsenal youth team. Over the years, his presence has had a talismanic effect on the kids. In his mind, it's a way of amending the touchline support he never had as a child. Ian likes to settle scores like that: quietly without fuss. Last season, he followed the Arsenal juniors' progress in the Youth Cup, which included a clash with Millwall, the club that rejected him at fourteen. Ian recognised one of the men in charge at the match and made a point of going over and speaking to him. It's not just that Ian wanted to see him squirm (though that's always a possibility), but that in football you meet the same people over and again, and Ian's not the sort who will blank you over something that wasn't your fault.

Ian's commitment to Arsenal is total. To get to their training ground, it's a three-hour round trip in half-decent traffic conditions from Ian's home just south-east of Croydon cruising through the heart of London or steaming all the way round the M25.

Part of the package at Arsenal was a sponsored car from the

range at Highbury Ford (replaced each year) which Ian drives to Highbury on match days. His other cars already included a white convertible Mercedes (a cool £68,000 worth of Hollywood horsepower) and a Shogun Jeep. The beloved but accident-prone German sportster was pranged again in a smash with a neighbour in 1993, since which time Ian has enjoyed the even more luxurious flair of a soft top Jaguar XJS.

But the luxury Ian has always craved is a Harley Davidson. George Graham, like all good fathers, sensibly forbade him to buy one. Sneakily, Ian had one tattooed on his thigh instead. And a Harley seems to have become inextricably linked with Ian's eventual departure from Arsenal in two or three years time. 'I'm not going to walk away from this place when it is over for me. I'm going to ride away on a Harley Davidson to tour Europe, in leathers, in style,' he has said, time and again. Even in rebellion, Ian does the right thing, goes by the book. But where does that leave Debs and Stacey?

For the first four years of their relationship, Debs progressed through the ranks at Barclays and by 1993 she was a Personal Financial Adviser. She was earning a good wage. One of the perks of working in banking is the favourable rates of interest on mortgages. Debbie could probably pay off the monthly house payments herself. That sort of self-reliance is as important to Ian as it is to her.

The Brockley days of strife had been consigned to the past though not forgotten. Ian and Debs had begun to lead a comfortable life but, with the recent changes, new commitments meant that Deborah would see Ian even less.

'The ultimate goal is to take the family with us wherever we go,' Ian declared. 'It's hard on Debbie. She's had to take a sideseat to my career, sacrificing her job to look after the home and family while I'm away. But she knows it's not for ever and when it's over, I'll have a lot of time to spend with her.'

One consolation is that Ian is a more rounded and self-assured man than before, and he is devoted to their son, Stacey. When they can get someone to look after their young son, the couple frequent a tried and trusted roster of local restaurants, especially Italian, for the modern footballers' fodder: pasta. Ian will have a Fusilli Napoli, washed down with a few Peronis. If Ian's out on his own, he'll pop into one of the fast-food stops in the T.G.I. Friday chain for his regular scoff: Cajun chicken sandwich.

Ian's a beer man, too. Drinks Bud, but not to excess: you won't see him drunk and skint and running to the press like some broken down footballers; as his old teacher Peter McCarthy once predicted, Ian was never going to go the wrong way. He still haunts the night-clubs of London with old friends: Emporium, Gas Club, whatever's in vogue. Towards the end of the 1994/95 season at Arsenal, Ian bumped into seventies maverick Frank Worthington, who had, as revealed in his memoirs, been regarded as a booze'n'fags merchant. Ian was made up though; kept eulogising about the long-haired Leicester lothario saying, 'He's a legend, man.'

Off the field, Ian is a footballer's footballer if only others knew it. He has respect for plenty of today's stars, especially the entertainers like Matt Le Tissier, Peter Beardsley and Ryan Giggs. Giggs, of course, plays for the same side Ian's best friend Paul Ince used to.

Ian was immediately drawn towards Paul Ince when the two met in the England set-up. They are kindred spirits in many ways: both are black Londoners; both enjoy a popularity with crowds rivalling that of a burger van at a Buddhist convention; both are incorrigible kids, prone to antics like cutting down their England training joggers in hot weather or indulging in mud fights; and both, Ian was interested to discover, shared the same 'fire in the belly', the hunger that makes a winner.

Ian and Paul talk every week on the phone and see a lot of each other when they can. When Paul signed for Internazionale of Milan – rivals to the team Ian adores – it was Ian, Debs and Stacey who flew out to share the Ince family's last holiday before joining the Italian elite.

Home and family are very important to Ian. He and Debs adore movies. They are a great escape from pressure. Ian loses himself in them. His taste is wide and illuminating, taking in the comedies of Woody Allen and cerebrally violent films such as *Taxi Driver* or *Pulp Fiction*.

His great passion – bordering on obsession – is the discerning end of the Mafia genre. Francis Ford Coppola and Martin Scorsese are his favourite directors; De Niro and Al Pacino the actors he most admires and emulates. But then, like Jimmy from *Goodfellas*, Ian's the type who roots for the bad guy in the movies.

He's seen *The Godfather* trilogy, *Scarface* and *Goodfellas* so many times he's devoured them line by line, and can spout each nugget of smart, malevolent wisdom before the actor delivers it.

When one of those movies is on TV, he'll get on the phone to his friends to run through the screenplay euphorically as it happens: the delivery of a fish to Don Corleone's *capo*, for example, 'That's a Sicilian message. It means "Luca Brasi sleeps with the fishes" ', or Al Pacino's warning, 'Fredo, you're my only brother and I love you. But don't ever take sides with anyone against the family again. Ever.'

You want to crack Ian's face into a smile? Quote from *Goodfellas*: 'Two things: never rat on your friends; always keep your mouth shut'; or 'Whadya mean I'm funny? Funny how? Like a clown? I'm here to amuse you?' Ian loves the Joe Pesci character. But when someone says of him, 'He's got too much to prove – that's dangerous', he might feel it's a little close to home.

Those films are universally admired, but there's a resonance in the wise guys' cool ruthlessness, their warped but vehement sense of honour and strict family values, that Ian finds intoxicating. His life has been mundane in comparison, but there must be times during the cut and thrust of 90 minutes' battle when he wishes a centre half would sleep with the fishes.

By the time he got to Highbury, Ian's other tastes were changing too. The street gear was still his favoured garb for an informal evening out or for training: R.A.P. or whatever was the latest hip label and style. It's a cultured ragamuffin look, and says to the world that Ian is still in touch with his roots.

Increasingly in recent years Ian has expressed a bizarre respect for aristocratic 'Englishness': the tradition, the impeccable deportment, the look. He has gone on record as respecting Prince Charles for the way he handled the apparent attack by a gunman down under (in Australia) in the middle of a speech: 'He is an upper-crust Englishman at his best,' says Ian. 'For me he is the ultimate, a hero even, and I don't care who knows it.'

That's ironic when you consider the English ruling class's attitude towards the likes of Ian, calling into question black players' loyalty and commitment when representing their country (as relayed through the *Daily Telegraph* letters pages).

Ian's wry sense of humour on the subject was evident as far back as September 1993, when England faced a crunch qualifier against Poland. The team had been pilloried for its lack of application in recent matches – in particular John Barnes became scapegoat. Ian was asked by journalists if the team felt confident. 'If we felt any other way we wouldn't deserve to be in the squad,' he blustered, adding with a twinkle: 'It's the bulldog spirit man.'

Ian's English gent image might well be a calculated affront to the racists on Ian's part; an impertinent way of expressing his own British identity and wrongfooting the bigots who would deny him that. (He actually looks most comfortable in casual designer wear.) The other point is that such icons as the Royal Family still present a mythical image of British 'fair play' that wasn't much in evidence when Ian's parents arrived in the UK, or when Ian was growing up in south London in the seventies.

There's a class angle to it too. Quality is the obsession of the 'made-it' working class. Ian's background is humble, though in the demographic jargon of the adman he is aspirational middle these days. In reciting his respect for the 'upper-crust Englishman', he lurches towards the inverse snobbery of the working class social climber.

Ian has also said that he subscribes to the old Arab adage that you can know a man by looking at his shoes. At Cup Finals, for example, he studies the Duke of Kent's shoes, so shiny you can see yourself in them – and maybe that's the point. But it's a condescending and irrelevant concept. At eighteen, what would Ian's shoes have looked like?

It would be sad to think that the humble footballer who once thought his transfer fee was a joke had turned into one of those people who know the price of everything but the value of nothing. And, thankfully, it is still far from the case. It's more likely such 'personality-forming' information comes from the miscalculated suggestion of one of his management handlers.

Ian does admire quality, though, and can afford to invest in it. For the last few years his shoes have been bought from Church's in Kensington, hard-wearing loafers made to his personal specification. His enthusiasm for a quality chukka knows no bounds: Ian makes Imelda Marcos seem as shoe-shy as Sandie Shaw, and his suits are made by Sousters of Luton. He chooses classic, conservative cuts, but with a personal twist.

Ian has broadened his reading matter in recent years too. Between Croydon and London Colney, he spends a lot of time in the driver's seat and passes the time engrossed in 'talking books', audio versions of best sellers. His favourites include all-time classics or the pot-boiling legal dramas of John Grisham such as *The Firm*, and he has a penchant for fast-moving, accessible spy thrillers.

Pride of place, though, is given to the tape of Arsenal fan Nick Hornby's brilliant evocation of the obscure life of the football supporter, *Fever Pitch*. When Ian met Hornby at a function, he was in awe, and proclaimed the embarrassed writer was 'a genius'. *Fever Pitch* is the cherished read of most thinking footballers.

But Ian's no stranger to Shakespeare's works: his cousin, soap star Patrick Robinson, was the first black actor to play Romeo at the Royal Shakespeare Company. 'I never miss him in *Casualty*,' Ian has said, adding in that disarming way, 'but I'd rather see him in Shakespeare. He plays a blinder.' Ian himself has tentatively confessed an interest in playing 'a bit of comedy'. Don't hold your breath.

Ian is actually a more cultured man than people give him credit for. After seeing *Four Weddings and a Funeral*, he developed a taste for the poetry of W. H. Auden. His music taste now ranges from the soul and reggae of his youth through to world dance music, jazz, techno and quite a bit of rock. Ian has long been fascinated by the music world, ever since he used to see the sound systems 'stringing up' in the halls and houses of Brockley as a kid.

Good fortune has allowed him to indulge his passion further than most with the funky street beat single 'Do The Right Thing' which did quite well in clubs (especially around N5). The motivator behind the recordings has been Pet Shop Boy Chris Lowe, a fanatical Gooner (one of the duo's big hits was called 'Being Boring'). He has encouraged Ian to express himself and there is another backing track waiting for Ian's impressive vocals to be overlaid. Ian is unusually reticent on the matter. 'I enjoyed it so much,' he said. 'But we'll have to see if I have any real talent.'

He stays hip to the tip, though, through his contacts with younger DJs on sound systems and friends and recording artists in the music industry. Cheating time still, he currently dresses like an adolescent 'junglist' with the bandanna and pirate's earring.

Another of Ian's overriding passions is computer games. *NBA Jam* is in keeping with Ian's lifelong penchant for basketball; PGA Golf is another. A 'Gameboy' is never far from his grasp on the team bus, or even the pitch inspection at a European final if there's a new skill to master, a personal best time to reduce or someone else's bench mark to obliterate – usually the incentive which fires him up the most.

But then that's Ian's most overriding quality: his competitiveness. 'He's insatiable to win at anything,' suggests one friend. 'Nothing is done by him without the intent of winning. You could be walking down a street and he'll say "Race you to that tree".'

In basketball, it's still Ian's big dream to be able to slam dunk (though friends claim he was able to as a youth), because it's an emphatic act of conquest and that's what winners do. He enjoys tennis, too: when he's with the England party, he plays a lot against Paul Ince, Paul Merson and Gazza, if they're there. He wants to beat them hollow every time. Wouldn't play otherwise.

And that's the quality he brings to the football pitch. Ian is so confident it's almost corrosive. 'Ian is calm and collected even before a big game,' says a close friend. 'He doesn't feel any pressure, no matter what the game is. He knows every time he steps on the pitch he's going to score. He can't go out on the pitch without thinking, knowing he's going to score.

'It's the other players who feel the pressure, like Kevin Campbell. Ian's too good to worry about criticism of his game. Criticism of his temperament and his reaction upsets him – because it's unfair.'

In the dressing room Ian is unreal. 'He's potty,' said Paul Merson. 'Shouting, dancing, on fire.'

'He gets very hyped up before a game,' smiles Alan Smith; 'very up, very loud and demonstrative. I think he does that more than anything to get himself going. It's just something that he does:

warming up, kicking balls about and having a laugh and a joke with everybody else.'

There isn't a sound system in the changing area though, unlike the old days of 10-Em, Greenwich Borough and most celebratedly at Selhurst Park. 'Well, George Graham didn't allow it,' says Alan. 'I've heard Bruce Rioch might allow that if the players want it. I'll have to get my Perry Como tapes together.' Sadly, of course, Alan's 'magic moments' will never grace Highbury again after his retirement.

Perhaps George reasoned that his star striker was entertainment enough with his impersonations, singing and general hyperactivity – he certainly didn't need any more stimulation. 'Ian is one of the game's great enthusiasts,' said the former Arsenal gaffer. 'With most players, it's a case of winding them up before a match. With Ian the opposite applies. He's so determined, you need to relax him before the kick-off.'

Ian will inform his team-mates with the assurance of the hitman that he knows he's going to score. On odd occasions he's even more certain: 'I'm going to get two today,' he predicts, ''cause I missed a couple of chances in training.'

Tony Adams, a huge influence on Ian during his Arsenal career, has adopted that credo. He'll watch Ian scud a half-chance into the hoarding, then clench his fists and mutter, 'You're all right, Wrighty, you're all right', knowing that in Ian's mind that will mean the next one will stick.

Ian Wright's elevation to the big league was made comfortable for him by previous associations. He already knew David Rocastle since the scuffed knees of his Honor Oak days; Michael Thomas and Paul Davis were fully paid up members of night-club goons the 'Black Pack'; Lee Dixon, David Seaman, Tony Adams and Alan Smith were in the same England set-up.

Even George Graham was familiar to him in a way. He was reminiscent of the type who had been amongst the most significant figures in Ian's professional life: those strict figures who demanded and returned respect. There was a direct line of ascent from Syd Pigden, through Eric Summers and Steve Coppell to George, the Caledonian iceman.

George admired Ian's hunger for the game, his aggression, pace and skill: qualities he himself was known for. The fact that Ian got off to such a flying start at the club surprised no one who had trained with him, including George.

But Arsenal was a step up to a more technical level of football. At Highbury it's not good enough to get your sums right; you have to show good methodology too. Every player has to justify his actions within the context of the team's performance. It's a sound philosophy if consistency and Championship challenges are customary obligations, rather than blessings as at some other clubs.

George wanted to work on aspects of Ian's game that were still too raw. 'When he first came to the club he'd go where the ball was and just try and get involved all the time,' recalls Alan Smith. 'But George Graham was very much one for team play and everyone doing their part. I think he had to let Ian get on with it slightly, because if you try and curb him you'd probably take away something from him.

'I don't think he'll ever be a natural passer of the ball. He does like to make those 40-yard passes at times, when he miskicks and they go straight to one of their players, but the gaffer always used to scream at him not to give the ball away. And after a few years of having that bawled at him, he's probably a bit more careful he doesn't give the ball away now.'

George also hammered away at Ian about his positional sense – a weakness since school days – while encouraging him to keep unleashing the renegade in him. And there is no doubt that Ian has a special gift for finishing and for consistently scoring distinctive goals that few can match. By allowing Ian latitude, George, the great disciplinarian, also unleashed the devil in his striker.

One man who has followed Ian's career with interest is his childhood hero Stan Bowles. He didn't know of Ian's worship of him, but there was an empathy nevertheless. 'I think Ian Wright would have been a star in my day too,' says Stan, in a rare tribute to a modern player. 'His character, he's a great goalscorer. I've seen most of his goals and I'd put him up there with the all-time greats. It's especially hard in a team like Arsenal. I was lucky, he has to make his own chances.'

Both players are respected for their off-the-cuff brilliance. 'If you don't plan anything,' postulates Stan, 'you can do whatever you like with it. I think Ian's the same as me in that respect. Of course he keeps scoring these fantastic goals and they can't all be flukes.'

And then there's that extra dimension: temperament. 'People used to say "Just calm down". Then something would happen and you'd lose your temper next game. You just can't legislate for it. Without that part of my game I don't think I would have been anywhere near as good as I was.'

At Arsenal, Alan Smith was immediately taken with Ian's swashbuckling style. 'I remember the last game of his first season at Arsenal against Southampton,' he recalls. 'Ian was going for the Golden Boot, and he was determined to get it. He scored one and missed a chance, but then with a few seconds to go he took it from David Seaman and ran nearly the length of the pitch and scored. He was so determined he was going to get that Golden Boot.'

There have been so many classic strikes with either foot. Characteristic is the direct, wrong-footing run at a defender on the edge of the box: first this way, then that, through, and *bang!* Or the simple move he's been executing all his life: beating the offside trap, skipping on, getting the ball under control, dancing up to the 'keeper like a matador, waiting for him to twitch before delivering the *coup de grace*, sending the ball the opposite way.

But the one that displayed everything good about Ian Wright was the mouth-watering strike against Everton at the beginning of September 1993, when Seaman's long dead-ball clearance was deftly killed and controlled by Ian, who then sent Matthew Jackson the wrong way, looping the ball over the Everton man's despairing head with the other foot, gathering it again and instantly lobbing it with an instinctive subtlety over Neville Southall to universal astonishment. Classic Wright.

But classic Arsenal?

The Highbury club, perennial kings of proficient monotony according to detractors, had at least shaken off the old 'Lucky Arsenal' cat-call during George Graham's reign. Extraordinarily strong-willed teamwork was the hallmark of the side that won the Championship in 1988/89 and 1990/91, the incredible domestic double in 1993, and the European Cup-Winners' Cup in 1994.

But as Lee Dixon noted, 'Individually we're not the most gifted players in the world but as a team we'd give anybody a go.'

With Tony Adams and Steve Bould formidable at the back, Lee Dixon and Nigel Winterburn the surging wing-backs, a midfield – surely one of the best England has produced – based on David Rocastle, David Hillier, Paul Davis and Mickey Thomas, the wingers Brian Marwood and Anders Limpar and Paul Merson linking up with a strike force of Kevin Campbell and Alan Smith, Arsenal had been able to produce goals from everywhere.

In the second Championship under George, the Arsenal top scorers notched 27, 16, 13 and 10 respectively, a pretty even spread of goals. The following season, Ian's first, it was an even healthier 26, 17, 14 and 13, with the new boy supplanting Alan Smith. But by the next, 1992–93, the top four tally ran 30, 9,8 and 6; recovering to 34, 19, 12, 7 the one after. More tellingly, since Ian's second season, the main men in the Gunners' midfield managed just five goals in 216 games before the '94/'95 campaign.

Ian was performing better than George Graham could have hoped for, but the balance of the team was changing. It's not Ian's fault that he was too efficient a goalscorer, but Arsenal are a Championship side, and they haven't seriously challenged since George constructed the side as a supply line for his voracious goal machine, Ian Wright.

Another corollary of Ian's advent has longer-term repercussions: his arrival in the Highbury nest forced other fledglings out. Ian's presence effectively capped any ambitions Andy Cole had of making it in north London. Given the briefest glimpse of light during the pre-season Makita tournament, for Cole the Goal the line of accession was now cut off.

In a straight adjudication between Cole and Campbell for a second string prospect, George settled for the steadier of the two. (The Arsenal hierarchy were concerned that Andy was always nightclubbing; in fact, Andy was most often simply staying over with his sister in nearby Enfield, where he retains a flat.)

Andy moved on to Bristol City amid rumours of alleged misdemeanours. Cole's eventual fulfilment at Newcastle, coupled with Campbell's withering on the vine, threw George's decision into sharp relief.

'That was a terrible shame for Andy,' said Ian. 'But, in another way, it was the making of him. He knows that every time he scores it is just a little more embarrassing that we had him once and let him go.'

But it was Ian Wright's arrival and dominance that forced George's hand, and perhaps prematurely.

Ian wasn't one to freeze out other strikers himself – even if he always considered himself the best at his job: 'No one can test!' In his England career, Graham Taylor had queried why Ian would put a word in for his perceived rivals including Les Ferdinand and, latterly, Andy Cole, when he was still in the international frame.

Ian and Andy were friends at Highbury, often staying behind after training at Arsenal's London Colney training ground for extra shooting practice. Wrighty it was who dubbed his junior spar Andy Van Cole after the mighty Van Basten.

Kevin Campbell's situation was different. He'd already forced his way into the team and proved himself. On Ian's arrival, he was the one to step down in the early days. He was still in for European Cup matches in 1991, but only because Ian's registration with UEFA wouldn't clear until the third round (by which time Arsenal were already out).

Kevin could justifiably lay prior claim to Ian's role, and George was mindful of that in the way he would 'big-up' the young Lambeth boy (as well as the restive Anders Limpar) in the press.

It sounds odd, but from a team perspective Ian unwittingly ushered in an uneasy period upfront for the Gunners. Although goals would come, no single partnership gelled for any length of time. The only consistency was Ian Wright's appetite for goals. Arsenal fans would learn to sing, with a due sense of irony, '. . . and it's I-an Wri-ight, Ian Wright FC!' There was increasing danger in an orchestra that only performed when its lead violinist carried the tune.

Alan Smith was the senior incumbent at that time, Golden Boot winner and classic Graham man: one-for-all, diligent and extremely effective. Physically comparable to Mark Bright, with whom Ian had struck gold at Palace, Alan's character couldn't be more different from that of the rumbustuous Eagles pair.

They were all about robust verbals and frenetic energy. Alan is more a pipe-and-slippers man and his calm potency is ridiculously underrated. But the symbiosis George hoped for between his two senior finishers never materialised.

Alan only knew of Ian through what he'd seen of Ian at Palace, though they had played together for England against Russia at Wembley. 'It worked out quite well for me,' he recalls. 'I scored and we won 3-1. I don't think Ian had one of his better games for England; he was brought off in the second half. I just remember it from my point of view that I'd scored at Wembley.'

Perhaps it was that inauspicious international start that should have alerted George: Ian was replaced by Peter Beardsley after 70 minutes. Whatever the truth of the matter, there were immediate problems with the Wright-Smith axis.

'Well I'll be honest," says Alan. "I don't really think we clicked as a partnership, Ian and myself. I don't think myself and Ian have really been on the same wavelength; which is strange really, because a tall target man like myself and someone like Ian normally go together well. And Mark Bright and Ian went together well.

'But for some reason my goals dried up when Ian came – I didn't score half as many.'

Where Wright'n'Bright was like fire and ice, too often Wright'n'Smith was simply tepid.

'When I say the chemistry wasn't right,' offers Alan, 'I mean we're two totally different types of people, but that shouldn't really make a difference. Ian is very much an individual type of player.

'He plays off-the-cuff and I don't think really anybody knows what he's going to do next. Which makes him difficult for defenders to play against, but not always easy for me to play with because, you know, I don't know what he's going to do. Sometimes it's just difficult to get an understanding.'

With Mark and Ian at Palace there was a sense of telepathy between the two. Steve Coppell organised the team to provide the long ball to them and their individual enterprise would do the rest. Mark Bright's goal tally had benefited from Ian's direct assistance, even if it was often in the same way as the dog capitalises on the scraps from the master butcher's table. But they'd regularly score in the same match.

Lee Dixon explained the team's predicament with candour to Tony Willis of the fanzine *One-Nil Down, Two-One Up*: 'Wrighty is a phenomenon you can't really explain. He's a goal-machine. But he's different to Alan Smith. Alan will never go over the top and chase balls and score from the edge of the box. Wrighty, on the other hand, will never hold the ball up for ten minutes when you need a breather at the back.

'We play two different games when Alan and Wrighty play together. If I get the ball when Wrighty's playing I look up, see him making a run and knock it over the top. With Alan, I look up and play it to feet.

'When they play together the players tend to hit Alan and then Wrighty gets frustrated because he's not getting the ball. I enjoy playing with both of them but I don't know if they can play in the same team.'

'It was a case,' admits Alan Smith, 'a lot of the time, of the manager changing the partnership: played me for long periods, and then he played Kevin Campbell. He tried to work it out like that.'

This was the other option at the gaffer's disposal: to team up Ian and Kevin Campbell. They were similar types of player. Ian was the senior partner though, and often gave the impression that he wanted Kevin to do the hod-carrying job for him, badgering him to load his barrels like John Salako and Eddie McGoldrick used to.

That's not Kevin's game. He's a bustler, a runner, a mixer, a finisher, not a target man and provider, as he'll no doubt prove at Nottingham Forest. He and Ian could be effective together, but Kevin seemed unwilling or unable to step out of the senior striker's shadow, which was not in his favour: the body language between the two – Ian haranguing him for daring to try a shot himself! – said it all.

Steve Coppell's words spring to mind: how Ian's assurance, his can-do philosophy can make him so demanding of other players: 'He can verbally be a big problem . . . if someone's weak enough to be affected by it, then Ian can affect them.'

Ian had moved one step further since leaving behind his Palace days. As a 'made' man, a gifted, golden-booted, gold-toothed articled Don, Ian was now held in awe by many younger professionals. To watch Ian post-match is to witness a stream of his peers press flesh and pay homage to him, especially the black players. And Ian accepts their observances with a mixture of gratitude, jocularity and something of the air of a benign African king:

the man has presence and charm. Ian's a big personality and, if people can't live with it, that's their problem.

But it was also George Graham's problem. In that first season together, Alan and Ian only appeared three times on the same score sheet: against Notts County (2-0), and in the rabbit shoots at Sheffield Wednesday (7-1) and Southampton (5-1). It wasn't the dynamic duo the manager had hoped for. At that time, Ian and Kevin Campbell proved a more fruitful combination, sharing the honours six times.

Kevin and Ian knew each other a little before Ian came to Arsenal, but they hit it off and became big mates once he was there. Ian was like an older brother to Kevin and his character on and off the pitch dominated the younger player. Kevin was one of the few players who used the nickname Ian acquired at Palace and uses when referring to himself: 'Satchmo', after Louis Armstrong.

And it was said at the time that Ian would push the case for Campbell being his partner at Arsenal instead of Alan Smith, who wasn't affected by any stick of the type Ian still liked to dish out to his fellow players.

Lee Dixon wasn't alone, however, in suggesting that Ian's braggadocio style had obviated the need for a big target man, and that he didn't see how George could play Alan and Wrighty together without compromising both.

Alan Smith doesn't feel that Ian's canvassing on Kevin's behalf influenced how the gaffer voted. 'Well maybe he thought if they're good friends off the pitch it'll work on the pitch,' reckons Alan. 'and it did at times. But the manager, George Graham, would have looked at how it happened on the pitch; if it worked, it worked and he wouldn't care if they were friends or not.'

George himself showed no signs of preference for a particular pairing – as long as it included Ian. 'If a partnership was going well he'd want to stick with that, keep it together,' maintains Alan. 'But if things weren't happening he'd want to chop and change, sort something out that did work.'

It wasn't enough that Ian was on fire if the rest of the team was simply smouldering.

Moreover, Ian's solo performances allowed George to live a lie: by 1993, his was an ageing team that was to become a one-man band incapable of challenging for the Premiership, which was considered Arsenal's birthright. Former Arsenal winger, Brian Marwood felt compelled to comment, 'I look at Kevin Campbell and players like that, very much living in Wright's shadow. I think the whole scene at Arsenal has been geared towards what Ian Wright's doing and not on what the rest of the team has been up to.'

When Ian is missing, Arsenal are a different side, and not necessarily less effective – even if they lack flair – a fact noted by the big screen operators at Highbury. When Arsenal beat Blackburn 1-0 a few years ago in Wrighty's absence, a message was flashed up from someone in 'Boringdon'. Ian was sanguine about the reputation. 'Opposing fans even sing "boring, boring Arsenal" when we go out for our pre-match kickaround. It's part of our history.'

The problem with relying on a single player is the same as that of the one-club golfer. Teams learned that if you stopped Ian Wright playing, you mostly stopped Arsenal.

Of course, that was easier said than done when Ian was flying. And he was nearly always flying. Ian scored a dozen vital goals and almost single-handedly propelled Arsenal to their amazing feat of winning both the FA and League cups in 1992/93. But George Graham's team had changed from one of flying wingers to a team playing the 'channels'. It's worth noting that teams with effective wingers have won the Championship five times out of the last seven seasons –including Arsenal, twice, with Marwood and the Limpar down the flanks.

It wasn't as if Ian demanded the switch: his game had to change too. 'When we played together at Palace,' recalls winger Eddie McGoldrick, who followed Ian to Highbury a year later, 'Ian was very demanding of the sort of cross he wanted. There were balls coming into the boy all the time.

'At Arsenal, Ian has had to be less reliant on wingers. He scores more individualistic goals. The service at Palace was centred on Ian. At the Gunners, he's looking all over the pitch for the service. He has become a much better player.'

The Arsenal staff worked hard to hone their rough diamond. 'The training at Arsenal is very different from Palace,' reveals Eddie. 'Steve Coppell concentrated on recreating the matchday style of play: lots of crossing and finishing and concluding the session with an eight-a-side game.

'George Graham and Stewart Houston emphasised a more technical style; lots more ball work, grids, three-on-three. You had to retain the ball, pass and move.'

Fellow striker Alan Smith has noticed an immense improvement in Ian's overall play since he joined, especially as regards his running off the ball.

'When he first came to the club,' says Alan, 'he'd go where the ball was and just try and get involved all the time. But George Graham was very much one for team play and everyone doing their part – I think he had to let Ian get on with it slightly, because if you try and curb him you'd probably take away something from him. He's just progressed as a player, his technique.'

In Eddie McGoldrick's eyes, the Arsenal touch has produced a far better all-round player. 'Ian is very adaptable,' says Eddie. 'The influence of George Graham and Stewart Houston shouldn't be underestimated.

'Ian's learned to be unselfish. He knows that he has to bring other players into the game. And he gains as much satisfaction now from taking a defender out of position to create space.'

It's often been said that Ian didn't respond well to close attention, that his touch wasn't up to it. Graham Taylor certainly felt that Ian's holding play was inadequate, and Ian's inability to reproduce his League form in an England shirt led to dark murmurings about his quality against the continental defensive style: one, ironically, that he'd come to admire in his favourite foreign side, AC Milan.

Ian never saw the shadowing of English centre backs as a problem. The 1994/95 season provided another perfect example against Wimbledon, when Ian appeared to have been shepherded out of danger to the touchline wide of the goal by Reeves' attentions. Then with a shimmy and lightning turn, Ian left the player for dead and clattered the ball against a post. Alan Smith picked up the empty.

Ian's hunger for goals remains insatiable, but he has learned patience at Arsenal. 'It doesn't matter who the defenders are,' he points out. 'No-one can shut me out for a whole game. If they stop me for 89 minutes, I'll score in the 90th.'

Nevertheless, Ian's frustrations have led him either to go roaming out of position – George has deputed him to the wing (his old school position) at times – or to come into conflict with his marker.

One current Premiership centre back describes what it is like to mark Ian Wright: 'His strengths are his pace and that he's a great goalscorer. And he always works hard; he's always a handful.

'He's not physical, but he does a lot of talking on the pitch, trying to aggravate and irritate the opposition. So you always have to keep a cool head when you play against him. He talks a lot of . . . how can I put it politely: crap. He's always been after me for a certain reason, but I don't care.

'He says personal things, not that bad, but things to upset you, unsettle you. He's quite unusual in that. You've got a couple in the Premiership, but he's probably the worst. His mate Mark Bright is quite bad as well.

'I don't usually say much back to him, but he's a player, you can talk some sense to him as well, so that's the good thing. I'd never say "unlucky" to him though!

'I don't mind marking him, it's just he gets so hyped up when he's playing. He's not a very friendly player to play against. It's part of his game, and probably why he's done so well. He has to be in a certain frame of mind to produce good games, Wrighty, and I think that's why he plays like that: He's a real handful on the pitch: you never know what he's going to do.

'The first 30 minutes, if he's doing well, he'll always keep going, but if you give him a few whacks, like any other striker, he goes a bit quiet. Even then, he's always a handful for 90 minutes; he doesn't go really quiet like some strikers do. He just starts moaning even more if he's having a bad time.

'Wrighty dishes it out to his other players too: it's part of his game. He's a very nice guy off the pitch.'

Over the years, Ian has had run-ins with many centre halves on the pitch: Alan McDonald, Kenny Monkou, Steve Bruce, Steven Pressley, even Gary Mabbutt . . .

The incident with QPR veteran McDonald occurred in January 1992, in the middle of Champions Arsenal's worst run for four years: it was their sixth game without a victory, and they'd only scored one goal in five games.

Ian received his seventh caution of the season after a challenge which left the centre half on the floor with a chest injury. McDonald was benevolent to Ian afterwards: 'It wasn't the challenge that injured my ribs,' he conceded. 'I did it when I fell to the ground.'

Ian was already wondering if referees had marked his card: 'Look at me,' he requested. 'I have to challenge big blokes, blokes who are over 6ft. I didn't do that sort of damage. I'm not malicious; I'm not dirty. This is getting out of control.

'I don't expect experienced players saying these things about me and getting me the wrong publicity. I just want to score goals. I don't think I deserved to get booked.' Ian's anxiety was heightened by the effect his reputation might have on Graham Taylor's selections for that summer's European Championships in Sweden.

In March 1995, the Bruce episode came during a similarly barren spell. Manchester United won 3-0 in a bad-tempered affair which left Arsenal perilously placed in the table. Ian was cautioned for a tackle on 'Dolly' (or is it Daisy?) in the 43rd minute. He was visibly furious at the booking, and gestured at Bruce as Keith Cooper brandished the yellow card.

Ian was still fuming as the teams walked off and there was a flare-up in the tunnel during which Ian was alleged to have struck his opponent in the face – presumably to reset Bruce's pugilist's proboscis. Most interestingly, United are a side with whom Ian is very friendly – Paul Ince was still playing for them of course.

Southampton's Monkou is the frequent object of Ian's retribution, in terms of verbals and goals. Ian takes particular delight in scoring past the Saints, but he reserves his most acerbic comments for the lanky Dutch central defender and his apparent intimidation tactics.

'He gets away with murder,' Ian has alleged. 'The fans don't see or hear the things he does. He always tries to turn the fans against opposing attackers.'

As a species, Ian would like to see centre backs on the endangered list. He has a policy to shut the bad ones out of his life. 'If they can gain any advantage by stopping me from concentrating on my game, they'll try it,' he said. "Now, if a player tries to wind me up, I just won't speak to him. If you have a shot and a defender says "Unlucky", or if he tackles you and when you pick yourself up he asks if you're all right, then you'll talk to him, because you know he is going to be hard but fair.

'The ones who are nasty don't like it when you don't respond. They try even harder to stop you, and then every time you get the better of them it's like a notch for you. Your confidence grows, theirs drops, and you find they've got less to say for themselves the longer it goes on.

'But you also get defenders who want to kick you all over the place and have a go verbally too. I've learned. I won't talk to them. I'll give them my answer when I beat them with the ball, or score a goal.' But what if the answer won't come: something's got to give.

Ian's reputation within the game is mixed. There are some who approach him with reverence, others who respect his record and put the disciplinary side down to the same enthusiasm that brings the goals, and those who simply dislike him for being 'mouthy'.

Henry Laville demurs, recognising his old school mate still. 'You can see it, he's got what every good player has. His attitude is, "Hey, this is me you know". And he's got that little bit of nastiness still, and you just think, "Yeah, that's Ian, man. Go ahead. Go ahead, bro".'

Ian is an entirely different person off the pitch: warm, relaxed, funny. Not everyone has seen him like that though. Knowledge that Ian is not like his public image has encouraged the formation of a protective coterie of friendly black footballers, a sort of Praetorian guard, who'll loyally support and shield their friend.

Ian needs good publicity, but even with his friends at the *Sun* and *News of the World* doesn't seem able to garner it. His 'agents' also appear reluctant to scotch the popular view of the man as a ragamuffin brute.

Discipline is the main barrier: the 'bad temper' as Stan Bowles euphemistically puts it. It was George Graham who suggested 'You have to accept Ian, warts and all'. But since the hitman's move to Highbury, and his questionable disciplinary record, more and more people have questioned George's imperative.

Ian's lack of self-control revealed itself early in his career at Arsenal. At Boundary Park in November 1991, allegedly spitting at Oldham fans and using an 'improper gesture' cost him a £1,500 from the FA. Ian had been booed and spat at by some home fans for fouling Earl Barrett. The fact that Ian scored a typical eleventh hour equaliser didn't endear him to the Lancashire crowd.

Eyewitnesses claimed Ian spat back after the final whistle and the evidence was captured on Granada TV cameras. He and Paul Merson were also seen to make provocative gestures to the crowd. Again, Arsenal's bad form may have been a contributing factor: the defending Champions had won only one of their last seven games, and had been knocked out of the League and European cups.

George Graham was annoyed with his striker. 'The crowd were spitting at Ian, but you are not allowed to spit back. He should have accepted it and done nothing.'

But he recognised the wider issue of crowd intimidation. 'It's happening regularly now,' he said. 'Players must ask the PFA what is their line on players being spat at.'

The Professional Footballers' Association's line turned out to be equivocal on the subject of Ian's reaction: 'You can't condone it, no matter what,' said secretary Gordon Taylor. 'But there is increasing evidence of physical and verbal abuse of players.'

The following spring the FA investigated Ian's behaviour during a game at West Ham amid allegations of abusive language. Ian collected five bookings that season, most of which were avoidable.

The 1992/93 season began in now characteristic style. At the end of August, Ian was reprimanded for an unprovoked attack on Oldham's Neil Pointon. Weeks later at Wimbledon (where former fellow Honor Oak inhabitant Steve Anthrobus came on as sub), Ian emerged from a scrap – which George Graham was later to downplay, in the way managers do, as 'handbag stuff' – with a damaged finger and an arm in a sling.

It was classic Wrighty: scored twice; elbowed defender; got injured. (Ian seemed to be on the treatment table more than in training that season.) He was the 13th player to be booked in Arsenal's first seven games.

David O'Leary, who pulled Ian away, said the hothead 'just needed calming down'. Ian himself admitted 'there was a bit of a skirmish. Suddenly I turned round and there were three of them all ready to eat me.'

At the end of an incredible season for Ian, during which he powered Arsenal to the unique distinction of winning both domestic cups, there was more trouble for the eye-catching finisher. After the FA Cup final replay in May 1993, he faced a 'disrepute charge' for making a gesture at a linesman. It was missed by the referee, but the FA responded to complaints from members of the public and a 'member of the association' who had witnessed the moment on TV. Ian was fined £5,500 the following pre-season for debasing the climactic occasion of the football season. But you have to wonder, would the FA have responded as strongly – indeed would the members of the public been so keen to report him – if the transgressor had been Mark Hughes or Dean Saunders?

It was the second time Ian had been judged in a 'trial by television'. But the previous occasion was the nadir for Ian's reputation both inside and outside the game.

At Highbury, towards the end of November 1992, almost exactly a year to the day when Ian had been hauled over the coals for the Oldham spitting incident, Ian was seen to respond to a foul by Tottenham midfielder David Howells by turning and delivering a swift right-hander to his opponent. The incident was captured by cameras and replayed on television. Initially Ian protested that he 'didn't punch him, I am only guilty of raising my hand.'

As had become his habit, George Graham at first turned a Nelson eye to the incident, complaining about the overall performance of referee Alf Buksh and demanding that the London referee be banned from officiating at a Gunners match ever again. (The outburst earned him a £500 fine.) 'Ian's temperament is something he's been working hard on, but it's difficult because he gets maximum publicity whatever he does,' he commented. You felt that George's support was partly because he encouraged aggression in his players, particularly when results weren't going their way.

On *Match of the Day*, Alan Hansen and Ray Wilkins were unusually animated. 'There is no place in sport for what he did,' quoth 'Captain Scarlet', forgetting that boxing is a sport. 'He's got to sort himself out,' suggested the vigorous Mr Wilkins.

In the face of video evidence, Ian admitted acting instinctively and hoped any FA action would not jeopardise his career. He was banned for three matches and warned obliquely by England boss Graham Taylor about the importance of discipline at the top level.

Ian was deeply depressed by the 'Howells incident' and the impression it gave of him. After that, photographers followed him everywhere, and match reports concentrated on his 'flaws' rather than how he was playing. For a time, he considered jacking it in or going abroad to escape the pressure.

During his suspension, Ian had time to think things over and resolved never to get suspended again unless it was for accruing too many bookings in the general cut and thrust of his game.

George Graham let the FA handle the matter, though he had private words with Ian. George used to bring players in like that, talk to them before training in his office at London Colney and then send them out to do the normal training. That's how he liked to handle it.

'George Graham has been brilliant about it all,' said Ian. 'Arsenal are a club steeped in tradition and have a reputation to uphold; and he could have taken a very different attitude, but he's stuck by me all the way and I'm very grateful for that.

'I was embarrassed by the Howells thing, and I suppose Arsenal must have been too, but it was just an instinctive reaction. I feel I got taken to the cleaners for it. I'm not saying what I did was right. I know I shouldn't have raised my hand. But I feel they went the whole hog on it.

'There have been four or five incidents since which were much worse – real fighting on the pitch – and no one was made an example of like I was. I have learned from that. People will see that.'

Just weeks earlier, George had commented, 'We may have one or two problems at the moment but discipline isn't one of them. And as long as I'm here it won't be.' But the evidence flies in the face of that promise. And it could be that George's indulgence of Ian's ref-baiting has ill-served his star striker.

Ian's sponsors, Nike, might have been quietly rubbing their hands together over all this. This was surely the stuff of McEnroe, Botham and Cantona? They'd already run antagonistic billboard campaigns playing on Ian's anti-hero image.

'All those blokes are the best at what they do, but they are also always in the news – for one reason or another,' offers Nike's Jim Pearson. 'Wrighty – like a lot of top players – will occasionally get into trouble on the pitch. But that's just part and parcel of being a star. It might be what sets him apart.

'Just about everyone is going to have a bit of bother every now and then. But that doesn't automatically make them a problem player.'

What's good for company profits doesn't necessarily bring peace to the player and Ian isn't happy with the nasty reputation he has earned in recent years: it diverts attention away from his positive achievements. For a player who so craves respect, it's a PR disaster. But Ian's advisers haven't seemed keen to respond with a public charm offensive and as a result the player has reaped the whirlwind.

Nike's contentious 'Gary Who?' promotion, targeting the boy Lineker, one of football's few universal charmers, was miscalculated and badly timed. It was humiliating for Ian, but more publicity, by reference, for Nike.

Other campaigns have locked onto Ian's cool, killer image: 'Behind every great keeper is a ball from Ian Wright' and the TV ad 'Can I kick it?', which portrays Ian as a sullen, shady, dangerous man do little to dismiss the widespread view of Ian as a nasty bit of work.

Supporters and journalists were also quick to latch on to Ian's volatility. We all know the press like to pump things up, but Ian's disciplinary record is a condom inflated to the size of the Graf Zeppelin. And once the tabloids say it, we all go along with their thinking. The more publicity Ian got – either for goalscoring or indiscipline – the more opposing fans were incited to dislike him.

There are plenty of players with snidy reputations who haven't suffered the same treatment as Ian Wright. The fans' vituperation is given extra impetus by the fact that he is the man most likely to puncture the dreams of your team. His protests are dismissed as spoilt brat whinges; his tears in the Paris St Germain game didn't unleash the same wave of sympathy that Gazza's did in Italy. Ian has failed to project his warm, vulnerable character and his attitude doesn't look likely to soften with age: he's too proud to appear contrite.

'My reputation goes before me,' Ian has complained, innocent-ly. 'I get booked for things other players get away with.' With a touch of the John McEnroes, he speaks of his 'enemies', as if there is some arcane group of conspirators out to do him down.

'People believe I'm a villain,' he once complained. 'I can feel them turning against me. It's horrible and it's making me very angry. When I play games away from home, there can be so much hatred coming from the terraces every time I get the ball, I believe if those fans got hold of me they'd kill me.

'And I don't know why it happens.' Perhaps he should ask his agent.

Part of the reason also lies in the 'them and us' siege mentality George Graham brought about at Highbury. Even before Ian arrived, George's teams had received fines totalling £70,000. In fact, there seems to have been a kind of 'autumn dementia' throughout his tenure at the club: in October 1988, Paul Davis was fined £3,000 and banned for nine matches after breaking Southampton player Glenn Cockeril's jaw; in November 1989, Arsenal were fined £20,000 after a fracas at Highbury with Norwich; in October 1990, they were fined £50,000 and docked two points following a brawl at Old Trafford. It makes a mockery of the FA 'bung' inquiry, which claimed to have been lenient towards the disgraced manager in view of his 'exemplary' disciplinary record.

Ian's own controversies complete the sequence of early season madness: at Oldham (October 1991); against Howells of Tottenham (November 1992); and at Wimbledon (September 1993). In September 1994, there was the clash with referee Robbie Hart over Ian's 'muppet' jibe and, soon afterwards, George Graham's humiliating 'bung' scandal originally broke cover.

'This is not something I am proud of,' George confessed after the United debacle. 'And I must make sure it does not happen at Arsenal again. If I am in charge of discipline of the players, then I have to take responsibility.'

'Before the punishment was handed out,' says Alan Smith, 'I don't think anyone thought it was that serious an incident, the Man United thing.

'When the punishment was handed out and the manager got fined and the players got fined, I think then we realised it was a very serious offence and the board took a very dim view of it because it wasn't good publicity for Arsenal. After that he wanted everybody to just tighten up a bit, make sure nothing like that happened again.'

But George was a shrewd operator and would use the idea that the world was against Arsenal to create a siege mentality, as a spur to urge on his players. 'He's always been one ... he likes his players to talk to the ref,' says Alan Smith, 'or sometimes have a moan to the ref: keep chipping away at the ref enough and he'll give some decisions your way – I think that was the philosophy. A lot of times, you know, the players would disagree with him on that.'

Without doubt, Ian was strongly influenced by the domineering George Graham, who had been so good for his overall game, and took his ideas to heart. 'This discipline thing has given some people a chance to have a go at us,' he commented. 'And it makes me all the more determined to do well.'

So Ian continues to hassle the referee, give players stick and wind up crowds. He was banned three times during the 1994/95 season and amassed over 41 penalty points. Yet it is not fair to suggest, as some Palace adherents with foggy memories are wont to, that Ian has had 'all this stuff pumped into him at Arsenal'. To be fair, Ian has always been the same player – he has only been sent off once, and that was against Bournemouth for two over-zealous tackles back in 1988 wearing Palace colours.

What has affected his game more than most people realise is the referees' interpretation of FIFA's clampdown on loose tackling and dissent. There's little doubt that any team would have been penalised as much with Ian in their side as Arsenal were in 1994, when the new rules made the previously cavalier Bould and Adams regard strikers' ankles as if they were booby-trapped. Ian has always been inclined to lose his rag. That's why he needs someone there to help him find it again, to stay cool and keep his powder dry.

Take the 'muppet' incident, for example. Robbie Hart booked Ian for an overzealous lunge at Norwich's John Polston and brought Arsenal's haul to four bookings in the first five games (it contributed to Ian's three-match suspension in November). The FA looked witheringly at Ian's description of a top referee – 'muppet' is one of those words for idiot that does the footballers' rounds.

But a matter of days later, Ian had constructed a passable re-definition of the term. 'A muppet is a thing that can't think for itself,' he reasoned. 'This was not meant as an insult, it was meant to indicate how these new rules have changed referees.

'I thought the most important skill a referee could have was old-fashioned common sense, the ability to judge between a nasty tackle and an accidental or clumsy one.

'These days they have a yellow card in a special pocket so they can get it out quick. You get booked for anything at all now. They're just not using their common sense ... a robot could do what they're doing.

'I have been booked too many times this season and I am the first to admit it, but I don't look upon myself as a nasty player.

'If there was a way I could stop these bookings happening, I would do it straight away. But I can't see that I'm doing anything differently now. I will try and explain this to the FA. The point I have tried to make is a serious one.' His criticism of the new emphasis in FIFA rules was taken up by many others, including the saintly Glenn Hoddle, a man Ian has rarely been in the same camp with.

Ian is taken seriously by few of the very breed he is so often penalised by that it is refreshing to talk to Alan Gunn, now an FA observer, who was a referee for eighteen years and who officiated at the 1990 FA Cup Final in which Ian starred.

'I always had a very good relationship with Ian Wright,' he asserts. 'Wrighty off the pitch is a fabulous bloke. Yes, he gets wound up in games, but so do lots of players.

'I've probably cautioned him, but the important thing to re-member about Ian is that you have to have a sense of humour. He responds to that. I also made sure that I kept talking to him.

'What I like about Ian is that he makes a point of saying hello to me when we bump into one another when I'm acting as an FA observer. Some players just ignore you.'

It works both ways. Alan's remarks about keeping the channels of communication open with Ian are well-founded. After a game against Leicester last season, Ian complained bitterly about the ref sending him to Coventry. 'The referee didn't want me to speak to him at half-time and he booked me on the way off. It's so stupid because I'm trying to get rapport with refs. Sometimes I think I just can't win in this area. So what I do is play my game, score my goals and say to fans, "This is me, judge me on what you see, what I do, what I am." '

It's fair to say that referees read the pen-pics in the programme before the game and are often influenced by reputations: ask Vinnie Jones, Dennis Wise . . .

The fans' view of Ian is audible as soon as his name is read out before kick-off. In most cases it's based on a healthy regard for his finishing skills. But in the case of one club it runs much deeper.

Crystal Palace fans have a love-hate relationship with Ian Wright: they used to love him, now they hate him. Well, that's not strictly true: some still recall what he did for the south London club between 1985 and 1991 with pride, and accept that footballers aren't married eternally to a club for better or for worse.

In fact, Mark Bright was one of the few ex-Eagles who returned to the nest in alien colours to a decent reception, and Ian, initially, was treated pretty much the same way; certainly at Highbury in 1992 that was the case. But already Ian was determined to sink the dreams of the fans who once worshipped him. Footballers often feel inclined to exaggerate their loyalty to a new club's supporters, but George Graham was shocked at how keyed-up Ian was in the dressing room before that first game against his former team-mates. He had to calm Ian down before he imploded.

But the killer blow in Palace fans' eyes came in the Coca-Cola Cup semi-final in 1993 at Highbury, when, to cap the imminent expulsion of the Eagles from the competition, Ian ran to the coterie of Palace fans and kissed his Arsenal shirt. It didn't help that Ian had scored in both ties. And it didn't help either that the former Selhurst hero had been subjected to vitriol rarely dished out by Palace fans.

The old anthem where his name was chanted to the chorus from Arrow's soca classic 'Hot Hot Hot', was amended, swapping Ian's surname for a slang term for masturbation, complete with appropriate hand gestures. Far more malicious was the acrid little ditty to 'Michael Finnigan': 'Ian Wright is illegitimate/He's got Aids and can't get rid of it . . .'

Little wonder that Ian is contemptuous of the terrace regulars of Selhurst Park. It puts into even sharper focus Ian's dedication of his goal in the FA Cup Final to Steve Coppell, whose side had just been relegated.

The interesting dilemma here is that of Nesta Wright, Ian's mother. She went to see Ian at Palace several times: they are her team. But she doesn't like to watch him at Arsenal, and has only been there once or twice. It could just be the Thames barrier – Highbury is north of the river. Or it could be that, like a lot of Ian's friends, she felt Ian didn't need her physical support anymore. After all, like family, you can't change your football team. Ian's affection for the club, as distinct from the fans, remains undiminished, though. He is still friendly with chairman Ron Noades and many of the players, and has been know to catch the Eagles playing if he's injured (or suspended).

'I had a good relationship with Ian, which continues,' says Steve Coppell. 'I haven't seen him for a long time but whenever we see each other, we get along well together. Even now I get great satisfaction from seeing him play and seeing the great goals he scores.

'I was proud as punch that the day he got married, he phoned me up from Mauritius [sic]. I was delighted about that.'

'I love Palace and I love Steve Coppell,' Ian vowed, the day before that first Coca-Cola match. 'There are players there I've got a lot of time for because we enjoyed some good times together. If we do stop them, I'll be quite sad.' But not quite sad enough, perhaps.

Still, Ian's respect for his former manager is undiminished; he still calls him 'The Boss'. 'George Graham has been excellent in improving my technique and so on, but the transition from non-League to international football is down to Steve. He's done everything for me. I can't praise him enough for the time he took with me and what he's given me.'

Ian's attitude to fans is ambivalent. He often appears not to care how much people dislike him as long as his Highbury worshippers wear 'God' and the number eight on their replica shirts. But unlike Gazza and other controversialists, opposition fans complain that you can't 'have a laugh' with Ian; he's too keyed-up. It seems a shame that someone with such a joyous side to his personality can't transmit that to people for 90 minutes on a Saturday. Mind you, joking with the fans wasn't going to get Ian in the gaffer's good books.

Like many in the game, Ian feels that fans aren't held accountable enough for their actions. Name players like him walk off the pitch at the end soaked in spit, ears ringing with bileful insults. One thing that is certain though is that a spitting, menacing horde isn't enough to silence a man of Ian's upbringing and pride.

In 1994 at Highbury, a fan threw an empty miniature whisky bottle at Ian minutes after he had celebrated a goal. It might have been different if the opposition hadn't been Tottenham. Ian loves to beat Tottenham, if only because he knows how much it means to Gooners. To Spurs adherents, Ian should be treated as Satan's very spawn.

In return, he's a wind-up merchant, wrapping his finger round a post when there's a corner at their end, idly giving the 'spin-on-it' finger to them. One Tottenham fan even reported him for celebrating the goal in that 1-1 game – admittedly for looking at the Spurs supporters as he went crazy. Martin Samuels in the *Sun* pondered what things had come to when a player couldn't even celebrate a goal without complaint. The mood was moving in Ian's favour.

What may have turned things for him was an incident at Millwall in the FA Cup in 1995. As a Palace player, Ian had enjoyed deriding the supporters of the club that rejected him as a youngster – and there could have been some residual vindictiveness in him after doing so. But as a black man, Ian was all too aware of the racist reputation of some of the habitus of the Den.

A few years ago, Ian claimed to have been hit by a coin thrown by a Millwall fan. Despite the great strides made by the regime at the New Den to eradicate the bigots, there is too much history and bad blood between Ian and Millwall for him to remain silent. Before the Cup clash in 1995, Ian decided to crank up the volume of the dispute by announcing over Arsenal's 'Club Call' line that he was expecting a bad reception at the club and that the source was racism.

In some ways, he was simply stating the facts as a black man who had grown up in the locality and knew his neighbours' form.

Ian's visit to the New Den was predictably vociferous and clamorous. Ian was spat at and abused throughout. His words had brought out the worst in the crowd. Ian had done no-one any favours – not himself, not the anti-racist cause, not Millwall FC. He had broken the unspoken rule of current players not to incite racist abuse by directly acknowledging it.

Among those disappointed by the episode was former Millwall player Andy Massey, the junior pro who used to look after Ian during his fleeting time at the club. 'The crowd go mental don't they,' Andy groaned. 'Ian used to support Millwall; he's even said that himself. I put it down to the papers – they try and cause so much fucking trouble over this. They try to blow it out of proportion. Where we used to live we all supported Millwall – he wouldn't have been able to support any other team anyway.'

Team allegiance is nothing where race is concerned.

The ultimate goal would be to achieve so much in the game that you transcend issues of race, that you belong to the pantheon of English football stars neither because of nor despite the colour of your skin. You are there because you are a brilliant footballer.

Yet in the mid-1990s, sixteen years after Viv Anderson and Laurie Cunningham became the first black players to represent their country, players like Ian Wright, Paul Ince and John Barnes have to contend with attitudes, in administrators as well as audiences, that question their resilience and their commitment.

The 'cricket test', that measure of loyalty to the national side snarlingly devised by former Conservative Party chairman Norman Tebbit and picked up on by right-wingers such as cricket fan and extremist correspondent to *Wisden*, Robert Henderson in 1995, applies to football too. It is the bastard son of 'Noades' Law'.

John Barnes, one of the greatest footballers to emerge from the English system, discovered that when he joined Liverpool in the summer of 1987. Barnes is an intelligent, sensitive man, who happens to be a skilled footballer and who also happens to be black.

The Merseyside city, legendary hub of the triangular slave trade, was renowned for the bigotry of its footballing adherents: Liverpool fans were fond of reminding anyone who would listen, 'There is no black in the Union Jack, so all the niggers fuck off back!'; Everton would rally with 'Everton are white!'.

Kenny Dalglish once made a joke of having little figures on a board to explain tactics. All were red except one which was, Dalglish explained, for 'Barnesie'. The figure was, needless to say, black. Dalglish at least recognised the fact that before he is a Liverpool player, Barnes is a black man.

The Jamaican-born player's standing at the club, and in the city, depended on him not appearing 'to have a chip'. John Barnes quickly decided retreat was the better part of valour. It didn't stop the players giving him a derogatory nickname rhyming with Molby's 'Rambo'. 'He calls us honkies and we all take the rise out him,' revealed John Aldridge's book at the time.

Dave Hill's portrait of Barnes, *Out Of His Skin*, also provides an insight into the man's disarming self-deprecation. On his first day at the training ground, John Barnes and two other players were served tea – well, the other two were. 'What am I, black or something?' joked Barnes to universal laughter. Then there was that infamous line in the 'Anfield Rap': 'when I score the crowd go bananas'.

For some Afro-Caribbean people, Barnes was a sell-out. From a middle class military background (his father, Colonel Barnes, organised the Jamaican arm of the invasion of Grenada in 1985), he appeared alongside a West Indian cricket legend on the campaign platform in 1987 to show his support for Margaret Thatcher's Conservative Party.

This was the same Margaret Thatcher who had declared that immigrants were 'swamping our culture' in 1979. It was the same Tory Party that had brought in the 1981 British Nationality Act, which compelled some British people of Caribbean background to pay for their citizenship.

There is a logic to Barnes' position regarding racism in football and many others have subscribed to it. If you acknowledge the bigots in the crowds or on the pitch, you validate it in the eyes of the perpetrators. It means they have 'got to you' and the chances are it will put you off your game.

Ignoring the presence of racist abuse is not to pretend it is irrelevant but to defuse it. Those who see that hooting or jeering has no effect on a performance are unlikely to persist for long unless they are that even sadder breed motivated for political reasons.

The more self-confident amongst those still turning out every Saturday tend to codify complaints in generalities about the scourge of the game rather than their own specific experiences.

A player such as Ian Wright loudhailing in the press the fact that racist abuse is ruining football for them is likely to prompt an immediate redoubling of the boo-boys' efforts. There's also the matter of trust: few black players would allow the white tabloid media to speak for them.

Once a footballer has quit the playing side, it is only rational that he should speak out. Brendan Batson, now Deputy Chief Executive of the Professional Footballers' Association (the players' trade union), and ex-Chelsea defender Paul Elliott have been un-shackled by retirement from active duty and are outspoken in their views on bigotry in our national game.

During his time playing abroad, Paul Elliott had terrible trouble in Italy from racists, especially in the south. 'At Bari and Napoli,' he complained, 'the crowd were so vehement – animals – that I had to be escorted off the pitch by police.' Over there, the clubs didn't give a damn, the football authorities didn't give a damn and his fellow professionals didn't give a damn either.

But there are some still playing who have dared to go further and Ian Wright is one of them. In an era when Arsenal put up a mural in place of their North Bank that featured not even one black face (an oversight apparently pointed out by Kevin Campbell), and when Subbuteo have only just bowed to pressure and included a couple of 'brothers' in their England team, the game needs some people to speak out – when will a white player feel so inclined?

Ian Wright is routinely called a 'black bastard'. Players try to wind him up, and the basest way is through his colour. To confirm that it upsets him is to invite more of the same and do all black footballers a disservice. Barnes himself believes Ian is singled out for more abuse because of his transparently volatile nature.

There are those who believe that the Campaign for Racial Equality's laudable 'Let's Kick Racism Out Of Football' campaign has eradicated the scourge from the terraces. But as John Barnes pointed out in a television interview, 'You haven't got rid of it, you've just suppressed it. To get rid of racism in football you have to get rid of racism in society.' Just because they keep quiet, doesn't mean they've seen the light. But it's a damn good start.

The great farce of the 1994/95 season was the way Eric Cantona's response to the goading of Crystal Palace bigot Matthew Simmonds was portrayed as inevitable, that Cantona was somehow justified by the nature of the abuse.

That is an insult to every black player who has suffered the torrents of abuse, week-in, week-out about the colour of their skin. No black player has ever reacted like that, and it's doubtful whether he would be treated as indulgently as the Frenchman if he did.

That is not to say that the situation hasn't nearly arisen. During the Tottenham derby, the same day that the whisky bottle was thrown at Ian Wright, it was also said that a fan tried to run on and attack the striker. A close friend reveals that it really fired Ian up: 'He didn't sympathise with Cantona's actions, but he understands his frustrations. He thinks fans get away with murder. Ian has been spat at too.

'He'd have no qualms about beating up on a fan who came on the pitch to challenge him. That Spurs fan running on to the pitch – Ian said, "It doesn't matter how big he was, I'd do him. He might knock me down, but I'd get in some good punches".'

Debs recorded the now notorious Palace-United match for Ian. When he saw it, he couldn't believe his eyes. In the light of his own track record, it's interesting that he sees no future for the Frenchman in this country. 'How would Eric have handled what I had to go through at Millwall the other week when 90 per cent of fans were screaming and swearing at me from the first minute to the last?' he queried of his friend Paul McCarthy in the *News of the World*. 'That's what it will be like for Cantona whenever he goes out on to the pitch again.'

Meanwhile during the 1994/95 season there were rumblings on the Highbury terraces about Ian's worth for the first time. He only scored eighteen goals in a League season riven with suspensions. One fan wrote to the *News of the World*: 'Ian Wright has a lot to thank George Graham for. The Arsenal boss brought him from Palace and put him on the big stage. And how does Wrighty thank him in time of trouble? Instead of scoring the goals he's capable of, he acts like a spoiled brat.'

Ian needed to work on his PR, and at last there are signs of a new maturity in Ian's approach. Against Auxerre during the Gunners' defence of their Cup Winners' Cup title in 1995, Ian claimed he was 'punched, spat at, kicked on both ankles, abused and trodden on. I refused to be intimidated. They tried to get me, but I wouldn't retaliate.

'They failed because I kept my cool. I did it for the team because I knew how important it was.

'That was my stage, my type of game.' Ian also had something to prove after being dropped by caretaker manager Stewart Houston. 'This was my answer,' he stressed.

The real crunch for Ian, though, had already passed. In 1993/94, Ian ventured into Europe for the first time. Arsenal had won both home knockout tournaments the previous term, but their current league form was poor. Few gave them much hope of progressing against sophisticated opposition that included two Italian teams: Torino and incumbents Parma. And after his mixed showings in the white of England, fewer still imagined Ian Wright could handle continental defenders, feeling that he would be too vulnerable to their gamesmanship.

However, George Graham had learnt from his European Cup defeat by Benfica, when Arsenal had thrown everything at the Portuguese, had enough chances to win (three knocks on wood, an uncharacteristic point-blank scuff from Tony Adams), and been outrun in extra time. This time, Arsenal would be tight, combative and play to the strengths of the English game. 'Keep the opposing supporters quiet,' said Gunner Graham. 'Then you know that you are doing well.'

With David Seaman's 'emergency knees' on permanent standby and Tony Adams the rock of the defence, goals were coming where necessary in tight encounters. Arsenal progressed smoothly to the semis to face Paris Saint-Germain. Ian seemed to have proved the critics wrong in one respect: he had scored three crucial winning goals along the way. But he had been booked, and in the Cup Winners', a second caution meant immediate suspension.

George had decided to drop Ian for the away leg of the previous round against Torino. There were two reasons for this. Firstly, George was not interested so much in getting a result in Turin as in not conceding anything. If relief was needed from the pressure

Arsenal would naturally be under from the Italians, Alan Smith was the sponge, the man who would gather the ball and hold it up until support was forthcoming. That ability is not Ian's strongpoint.

The second reason was forced on George. 'The Torino game away was one where if Ian had got booked he would have missed the final,' says Alan Smith. 'It didn't really matter in the end anyway, but no-one was to know that at the time.'

Ian was disappointed at his omission. 'I remember the team meeting and Ian was obviously quite surprised to be left out,' recalls Alan. 'I don't know if George had told him beforehand. Maybe he had, but I just remember Ian's face and he was very upset about it because it's a nice stadium there in Turin and I think he just wanted to play there.

'But that was the manager. He was always quite brave like that: doing what he thought was best. In the end we got the draw and everything was fine.'

Alan sticks by Ian with regard to his coping with the close attentions of foreign defenders. 'I think if he'd played more games he'd have got better at it. Maybe in the early stages he wasn't so good with a close marker, but you could say that about anybody really. The more touches you get the quicker you get used to it. And as we went through the campaign I think he showed that he could handle that.

'You're not really used to it in the English game. I don't know whether that affected George Graham's thinking. I think he just didn't want Ian to get booked, and he thought we could do the job without Ian.' It didn't stop Ian commenting to the press about George's decision. So the threat was still hanging over Ian when Arsenal faced PSG in the Parc des Princes, where Ian's goal won a magnificent draw, and two weeks later at home: one match away from the final. In some ways it didn't matter that Arsenal had won; or that they won with a formidable and daring 4-3-3 formation that threw the opposition's marking by putting Ian on the wing – once again showing their manager's tactical brilliance; it didn't matter that Ian Wright had headed them to a draw in the first leg, or that this was one of the all-time great English performances in Europe: one of measured endeavour and resolve, epitomising the 'mental strength' of George Graham's team.

All that mattered was what happened in the 43rd minute. It was a physical encounter. What the French sports paper *L'Equipe* called 'une affaire des hommes' – men's business. Danish referee Mikkelsen had already cautioned two players and was struggling to control the mood. Arsenal were protecting a precious lead supplied by Kevin Campbell. It wasn't going to be easy.

Then, in a position of no evident danger, Ian tracked back the Paris defender Roche, who was in his own half near the touchline. Ian forgot himself, slid in, missed the ball and caught the player fractionally late. French players hounded the referee – in a way that must have been familiar to Highbury regulars since George Graham's arrival.

What happened next might have propelled Ian instantly into the hearts of the British public, almost as quickly as Gazza's tears in Italia '90. The yellow card was shown to Ian, and he suddenly looked like the child you might have seen on the Honor Oak estate: vulnerable, hurt, desolate and lonely. He was going to miss the final he'd always dreamed of. The TV cameras followed him cruelly. 'I went down on my knees, covered my face and prayed it wasn't true. But deep in my heart I knew. It just hit me and I felt the tears welling up. I said to myself, "No, don't break down, take it." That just made it worse. My stomach knotted up, my throat got a lump in it, and I just let the tears come.' The Highbury faithful sang Ian's name; it was one of those rare, genuinely moving moments in football.

Could you blame the French for intimidation? Alan Smith thinks not. 'The actual booking, Ian was the first to admit, it was really silly. Ian was chasing the fella, it wasn't as if he was being fouled or anything. And it was pure enthusiasm really that made him dive in from behind and catch the lad.

'Half-time he was beside himself with grief really. Everyone was trying to get him to calm down because we still had a half to go and try and get into the final.'

Ian walked straight into a nuclear blast from George Graham. The gaffer told him to go into the bathroom for his own good to calm down while he continued his team talk. George didn't speak to Ian until a few seconds before he went out again.

'I think it's fair to say he was inconsolable,' says Eddie McGoldrick.

Players drifted in to try and bring Ian round: Kevin Campbell, Alan Smith, Tony Adams and Paul Merson. The best way to get to him was to appeal to his sense of responsibility, his loyalty to his mates, to the club. 'We said he had to do it for the team,' recalls Alan Smith. 'He'd not want to let the team down, and we still weren't in the final at that stage, even though we were 1-0 up. So there was 45 minutes of a lot of hard work to be got through. Ian was as important as anyone else.

'And eventually he did calm down and went out and did his job. It must have been very difficult.'

Before he went out, George Graham stopped Ian and put an avuncular arm round him. 'You have to show real strength of character out there,' he said. 'You mustn't let this get to you or you're letting the whole team down – and that would be totally unacceptable and unprofessional.'

That shook Ian. He left the tunnel not feeling sorry for himself, but determined to help the lads into the final.

Arsenal won through, with Ian showing enormous fortitude, contributing as much as anyone to the victory. But knowing he was going to miss the biggest occasion of his life, Ian's mood cast a shadow over the celebrations.

Not for long, though. Supporters recall seeing Wrighty leaning out of the dressing room window minutes after the final whistle, spraying champagne along with Paul Merson and laughing and joking with ecstatic supporters, singing 'One-nil to the Arsenal!'. Inside, he felt hollow. But there was no way he was going to sit in the corner of the dressing room creating doom and gloom at a time of exhilaration.

Later Tony Adams and his wife Jane put their arms around Ian and they all cried together. Everyone knew what it meant to the Brockley boy.

In retrospect, Ian would come round to the view that it was better he was sacrificed than inspirational skipper Tony Adams. 'If anybody had to be sacrificed, it's better it was me and not Tony,' he told Paul McCarthy at the *News of the World*. 'Without me, the lads can win the cup; without Tony it would be a lot more difficult. I just thank God it wasn't Tony. That would have been disastrous.

'But I tell you, it's hard to take when it hits you as hard as this.

I've had some bad times in football as well as good. But this is just about as low as I've felt. It's worse than missing out on the World Cup finals.'

Before the final against Parma in Copenhagen, Ian was bubbling as usual. 'He made sure he was really involved,' remembers Eddie McGoldrick. 'On the bus to the stadium he was winding up the lads, encouraging the team, saying "We can do it." '

Alan Smith, the man who scored the winner with a classic volley, concurs. 'He always seemed to be his same self. But probably underneath he was covering it up. I know I've heard him say it really cut him up the way things happened.

'But I can imagine it: first European final and you're missing it, and you just don't know if you're going to get the chance for another one. Anyone would be really upset.'

After the game Ian was as involved in the celebrations as anyone else. There was a sense that they had won it in part for him. Young midfielder Ian Selley even offered his medal to Ian. It was a tremendous triumph, but Ian somehow felt cheated. The big stage had eluded him for the first time. His transition from ageing non-Leaguer to European champion was not complete. His England career was in doubt, and he might never reach another final.

'We have laid a foundation of hope at Highbury,' trumpeted George Graham. 'If you lose hope, or lose belief, you may as well get out of football.'

Ian Wright's greatest hope was that this wasn't his last chance.

9 Shooting in the Twilight

'All my life I had been looking for something, and everywhere I turned someone tried to tell me what it was. It took me time . . . to achieve a realisation everyone else appears to have been born with: that I am nobody but myself.'

Ralph Ellison, *Invincible Man*

'The Arsenal move is the best thing that has happened to me, other than Steve Coppell taking me on. Everyone has been marvellous to me, and if it's goals they want as gratitude, then I won't rest until I've scored all I can.'

Ian Wright

THE 1994/95 SEASON was the most sensational in Arsenal's history since the day modern founding father Henry Norris was kicked out of football in 1925 over financial irregularities – including the 'unauthorised use of a chauffeur' (for what purposes it is not made clear).

In the worst example of that annual 'autumn madness' under George 'Napoleon' Graham, 'The Merse' was on the rocks over cocaine 'addiction'; Ian Wright was on his way to amassing over 41 penalty disciplinary points; the team looked perilously close to plopping through the relegation trap-door for the first time in 76 years; and the manager himself was soon to be sacked by the Highbury board for being discovered doing what plenty of others have done before him – accepting a huge ex-gratia wedge for being so nice as to buy Pal Lydersen and John Jensen via the mediation of Scandinavian soccer agent Rüne Hauge.

Ironically, it was Ian Wright's former boss, Steve Coppell, as chair of the FA's 'bungbusters' inquiry, who pointed the finger at the Highbury gaffer, indicating that, having seen the evidence, he did not see how George could escape charges. Ian made no public comment on the Merson and Graham strife, but in keeping with his principle of not wishing to drop someone who's done nothing wrong to him, Ian backed the two of them all the way. Ian doesn't condone the use of drugs – of course. But he is compassionate enough to realise that Paul's was a personal problem that demanded sympathy not chastisement. Ian's criticism of Paul was purely professional: more and more he complained about the service Merse was supplying him with.

The George Graham episode was more hurtful to Ian. He owed a lot to the gaffer. George had brought out his all-round game, allowed it to blossom. And he'd also stuck by Ian when other managers might have turned their back on a controversial player. Charlie Nicholas, Paul Davis, Michael Thomas and David Rocastle had all fallen foul of the manager. But George never ranted on about Ian. Ian repaid respect and loyalty in kind.

In all the breathless excitement, the only cheer for the Gunners on the eve of a new year appeared to be that John Jensen had scored his first – and possibly last – goal for the club.

All of this uproar gave the lie to George's sometime assessment of the club he loved. 'We were boring when I played, we were boring in the thirties and no doubt we'll be boring in the next decade. I don't mind as long as the trophies keep coming.'

In fact, Arsenal entertained everyone except themselves and their fans in 1994/95. An 'end of empire' atmosphere haunted the majestic trophy room. This was a stately home in crisis and the team's form suffered accordingly: they were out of both domestic cups by mid-January (the Third Round FA Cup clash with Millwall marred by crowd trouble) and never in the hunt for the Championship. A final position of 12th was the worst in George Graham's reign.

Just as the Conservative Party is a structure for maintaining power rather than changing society for the better, so Arsenal is a club formulated to acquire silverware rather than decorate the playing fields of the Premiership. They were doing neither. From the bowels of the marble halls came the lament: 'something must be done!'

Stewart Houston, George's right-hand man since 1990, was handed the reins in a steady-as-she-goes move in February after the dismissal of George Graham. He assumed control of a side in the middle of a League slump during which they scored more than once in only two outings out of nineteen. The mighty man between the sticks, David Seaman, was troubled for weeks by a tender fractured rib.

All of which diverted attention away from a fantastic achievement by Highbury's top Gunner. Ian Wright reached his century of goals for the Reds on 1 October against his old pals, Palace. Andy Cole stole the Golden Boot from Ian in 1993/94, and there was never any likelihood that he would win it back this term: by October, he'd only notched four League goals. Still, Ian was charitable enough towards his former training ground spar, even if, as is so often the case, the advice Ian imparted seemed often to be aimed at himself: 'The one thing I say to Andy is never get bored of scoring goals. Never get relaxed about it, never take those goals for granted.'

Ian's goals were pretty much all that was keeping Arsenal in Europe. With all the other distractions, Arsenal's success in the defence of their Cup Winners' Cup trophy sneaked up on everybody, including some at the club. Not Ian, though. He had directed much of his energy into Arsenal's raids on the continent. He was determined to lay to rest the haunting memory of missing last year's glorious occasion. Goals against Omonia Nicosia at home and away (on a pitch so bad Lee Dixon suggested the groundsman should be drug-tested) and in both clashes with Brondby had brought a surge in confidence and the Gunners faced a tricky meeting with French stylists Auxerre in the quarter final.

Once the FA and Coca-Cola were out of the way, Ian focused everything on spurring the Gunners to a second successive Cup Winners' final. 'We always knew this was our best chance of a trophy,' he said. In the Premiership, Ian often appeared less enthusiastic and seemed less hungry. The arrival of young forward John Hartson from Luton for £2.5m might have been expected to quicken his step, but it was the Welshman who impressed alongside the established Highbury star.

Ian was given to complaining to his team-mates more than ever if they failed to supply the ball to him whenever possible – not always with justification: his finishing instinct was fitful and his first touch and team contribution, especially after the introduction of £2m Dutch international winger Glenn Helder, were inconsistent.

In the light of all this, Ian was devastated by George's dismissal not just for the manager himself. As the player most photographed at the troubled manager's side, and the main beneficiary of the gaffer's reorganisation of the side, he was identified as George's boy. A different manager, a new broom and fresh tactical approach could signal his subordination in the pecking order at Highbury. To many people, he *was* the Arsenal team.

Ian's fears appeared justified when Stewart Houston dropped him for the clash with high-flying Blackburn. The striker was in the middle of the worst goal drought of his free-scoring career: he troubled the stats people just three times in 26 League games. It was the first time he had been dropped since he arrived, though George had left him out of one or two European games before for tactical or practical reasons.

With the Auxerre return game just days away and the tie poised at 1-1, this was the last thing Ian wanted, and he made sure he worked on the new manager in the build-up, comparing his approach to George Graham's. 'It hurts,' he said. George used to 'give me a kick up the arse every now and then', whereas Stewart was more taciturn. It was clear Ian still felt he responded to the stick more than the stonewall.

It was difficult for Stewart, who as coach was closer to the players than the aloof George, but he guessed Ian would give his answer in the all-important Auxerre match. Of course, the striker responded in typically instinctive fashion, capitalising on the only moment of defensive confusion in the French defence to throw his whole body into an early, superbly flighted side-foot, more like a cross-field ball, into the net from 25 yards. The assassin had seized his one opportunity and struck. Game over.

The milestone man had equalled another scoring record: that of John Radford's goals in Europe. The caretaker manager was visibly relieved. 'Ian Wright is the man!' he beamed. 'I sensed before the game that he was up for it. It was an absolutely fantastic goal, the sort of exceptional thing that he does so well.' You sensed somehow in those words that Ian had the upper hand.

Ian scotched rumours of a rift. 'Stewart was right to drop me at Blackburn,' he conceded with largesse. 'We are all professionals and I accept that. We have taken a lot of crap this season and the only way to put that right is by going out and doing it on the pitch.'

Sampdoria in the semi-final were another proposition. The Genoa club were riding high on the reputation of Italian football: Serie A clubs looked even money to win all three European trophies at one point. And they had little regard for English football or Ian Wright.

Sampdoria's coach Sven Eriksson had done his Premiership homework and was cagey: 'He is quick, sly and troublesome. Our defenders will have to be on their guard.'

But his sweeper Ricardo Ferri was less respectful: 'Everyone talks about Ian Wright, but he is no phenomenon. He's nothing special. Wright has got a lot of goals in the English league. So what? You can easily do that by just using a bit of pace.

'Ian Wright would not score as many goals if he was playing football in Italy. He may be good for the English game, but he does not strike me as a player who can make the difference in a match.'

It was the wrong thing to say, and definitely the wrong man to say it about, as the Palace boo-boys had learned. There's nothing that inflames Ian's hunger more than disrespectful slanging like that.

As usual, Ian made his mark with a goal to slip past John Radford's European record, but Steve Bould made the difference, coming from the back twice to give the Gunners a tenuous 3-2 lead to take to Italy. 'One chance, just one chance' was Ian's mantra in Genoa as he inspected the pitch nonchalantly, clutching his 'Gameboy'.

Against the odds, and against a parsimonious defence, Arsenal pulled off an amazing result, scoring twice to level the scores at 5-5.

Ian showed his best predatory and vengeful instincts to loose himself from Ferri, the man who had written him off, to steer home from six yards on the hour – Ricardo Ferri sleeps with the fishes . . .

Stephan Schwarz – scoring his most important goal in a too short stay at Highbury – added the second with three minutes to go. Ian could hardly watch the drama unfold after extra time. Arsenal's cool penalty shoot-out win was well-earned – with the injured Seaman saving three times. Ian instantly dropped to his knees and gazed heavenward.

This born-again mood was reinforced afterwards. 'I could not even begin to tell you what I went through,' he told reporters. 'I just want to thank God. It is a blessing.'

All the players were ecstatic, but Ian especially so. He had set out to avoid disciplinary problems in the campaign and had done so; he had also been sharper at scoring than he had been in the League, where his temperament was still a major problem. He'd reined himself back and got what he wanted. There was a lesson in there somewhere, if only he'd learn it.

And so to the final; very nearly an all-London affair with Chelsea, who lost out to ambitious Spanish club Zaragoza. Arsenal were only the sixth club to return to the Cup Winners' Cup final – Parma were the last – and no team had ever won the prize twice in succession.

Before the game an erstwhile Tottenham rival, the midfielder Mohamed Ali Amar, a.k.a. Nayim, honoured Arsenal's strong team mentality and three individuals worthy of his team-mates' attention: Adams, Merson and, of course, Ian Wright. 'Like our striker Juan Esnaider, he has to be angry to get the best out of himself. Wright can turn a game upside down.' How modest, in retrospect, the Moroccan was being.

Zaragoza had a reputation for travel sickness – their record away in the tournament wasn't impressive. It was something special for Ian to walk out on to the pitch at the Parc des Princes in Paris and savour the atmosphere of a final that he would actually play in. The landmark specialist was hopeful of completing a remarkable sequence in the final – uniquely, he'd scored in every game of the campaign so far. 'It would be terrific to be remembered for that but I'll be happy to set up a chance for somebody else to score the winner,' he remarked.

The final was a dour, bad-tempered affair. Lee Dixon and Paul Merson had shaved their heads for charity; it seemed to affect their performances. Ian, his collar tucked in as is his habit, was shepherded by the sharp, smart Caceres and played just behind John Hartson who, it was hoped, would take some of the heat off Ian and allow him an opening.

Early on, Hartson tackled Nayim from behind awkwardly. 'I'm going to kill that fucking wanker,' pointed the Moroccan, who clearly hadn't forgotten any of the English he picked up in his five years at White Hart Lane. Ian sidled up to him and suggested in no uncertain terms that he should get up and be a little more reserved in future. Arsenal fans resurrected the Tottenham connection and abused him from start to finish.

Merson was hacked. Barbeza was felled. Winterburn looked off the pace after a similar challenge and was stretchered off – bad back. Aguado pushed Ian Wright over in the box but wasn't penalised. Keown's nose exploded in a head-to-head with his own man, Adams. Back home, not even the surging engine of Brian Moore's TV commentary could rev up a dull game.

At half-time, ITV ran the Nike ad depicting Ian as some sort of Yardie shootist: 'Can I kick it?'. 'Yes, you can'. 'Can I kick it?' It ends with Ian's maniacal scream *'KICK IT!!'* You could sympathise with his frustrations.

In the second half, Arsenal fans were subdued until the Merse had a floating header cleared off the line. The Aragón fans' drums beat an ominous rhythm. It was touch-and-go – the perfect opportunity for Arsenal to cause an upset.

Ian was confounded by the attention of Zaragoza's tight markers and was becoming irritable – might this provide the spark?

But it was that Esnaider fellow, the one Nayim had likened to Ian, who exploded, picking up the ball outside the 18-yard area and firing it past a static David Seaman. It was a brilliant execution, worthy of Ian himself – and it was the Argentinian who claimed the record of scoring in every round.

It looked all over, but you never get to ten on the count with a floored Arsenal, no matter how hard the punch. Minutes later, someone latched on to a Ray Parlour through ball to stab home in the box. Ian Wright punched the air and ran left, taking three or four triumphant team-mates with him to celebrate his goal. But it was John Hartson, wheeling right as the net billowed, who had scored. Bizarre.

On 86 minutes, Arsenal had perhaps their best opportunity to clinch victory when given a free kick 30 or so yards out. Stephan Schwarz and Paul Merson stood over the ball. The Swede lunged forward and delivered an innocuous shot. Ian Wright was livid. 'I know,' complained Merse, 'I told him to just stick it in there!'

Ian was more animated now, but unable to shake off his marker. The sweeper ruled out his usual runs behind. 'Just give it me here,' he wailed, slamming his chest. Ray Parlour was running hard but producing little; Paul Merson kept conceding possession.

Esnaider was having more luck. He was called offside in a close decision, and pointed to the linesman. 'Death,' he mouthed. Later Steve Morrow cleared off the line – with an arm.

As extra time dribbled away, commentator Brian Moore began to build up for another heart-stopping dead-ball shoot-out. 'Who's going to be the hero . . .' he began, as Nayim picked up the ball just inside his own half and saw it bounce invitingly. He looked up and . . .

Well, the rest is history – or aerodynamics: Nayim's extraordinary bombshell was the last kick of the game. The Spanish fans sang their anthem – one of those soppy waltzes favoured by continental teams – then 'Y Viva España', and Arsenal fans drifted away crestfallen, their dream shattered.

And so Ian looked to the future again. A new season and a new manager. The appointment of Bruce Rioch could have been the best thing to happen for Ian. Quintessentially an Arsenal man: stiff-backed, clean cut, likes discipline. Ian might wonder about the trouble in his new boss's past – the scraps with his players for example – but there seemed little doubt that Bruce Rioch placed his faith in Ian. Ian himself showed uncommon enthusiasm for the new season.

When Dennis Bergkamp signed, Ian immediately drove up to Highbury to meet and welcome him. As a student of the European game, Ian knew all about the Dutchman's electrifying skills. Similarly, when it was announced that David Platt was Arsenal-bound, an excited Wrighty rang up to check the news. Shortly afterwards, Ian renegotiated his own contract, pledging to see out his days at the marble halls on ten grand a week.

A few days after Dennis's signing, Ian found himself queuing in a petrol station, frustrated by a badly parked car. He was about to berate the driver, when he recognised the rangy build and spiky blond hair – it was the Iceberg himself.

Already the two have struck up a personal understanding. Likening his new partner to Stefan Petterson from his Ajax days, Dennis told the *Mirror*, 'He has the ability of all great strikers – he only needs one touch to get it right.'

Off the pitch, Dennis was surprised by Ian's ebullience. 'I've never come across anyone like him before,' he said. 'He can make a joke out of anything. He dances around, he gives us all advice and he cheers whenever we score. He never keeps still. Even though he's 31, he behaves like he is only 21.' Others have found that can be a little wearing; would mild-mannered Dennis feel different in six months' time?

In Italy, Dennis was known as 'Beavis' for his resemblance to one half of MTV's gormless cult cartoon characters. Ian acted decisively to show his displeasure when a few daring souls decided to call him 'Butthead'.

Whatever, the arrivees re-animated Ian Wright. He wanted to be better than all of them again.

How will Ian develop in the twilight of an amazing career? There's no chance of him playing out his days by dropping down the divisions like a punch-drunk duellist, as some forwards do. But what about dropping back in the team? England coach Don Howe: 'The question now is whether he starts to drop deeper towards midfield as many great goalscorers have done as they've got older. But If I was his manager I'd tell him to go out and keep doing what he does best – score goals.'

In truth, Ian's distribution is not really strong enough for that forward-supporting role, but his other assets remain unharmed by the passing of years: he was 32 in November 1995, yet still among the paciest in his squad.

'He has this huge hunger for the game,' says Eddie McGoldrick. 'He's got that willingness to keep on learning and he looks after himself. From what I can see he's just as quick today as he was when I met him back in '89.

'You never stop learning in football, right up until you've finished, and Ian is so keen to keep on improving and keep on scoring goals.'

Few doubt that Ian will make hay however he plays. 'I don't see any reason why he can't carry on for another three or four years at the very top,' says Alan Smith.

Before the season began it appeared he would play upfront alongside John Hartson, with Dennis Bergkamp and David Platt at the front and back of a diamond midfield formation. Out of the open-heart surgery of an uncharacteristic season has come an un-clogging of the arteries at Highbury. The stars would never come before; now they flock. Entertainment was once subordinated to the process of winning trophies; now Arsenal have acquired some of the modern game's great crowd-pleasers.

The football flowed fitfully at Highbury.

'Ian's not been happy with the amount of goals he has scored this season,' says Eddie McGoldrick. 'His goals have been in the cups; he wants to be on the League charts.

'A lot depends on steering clear of injuries, especially now he's getting older, but he's been fortunate since that 1990 leg break and I can't see any reason why he can't carry on. I'm sure Arsenal fans and everyone at the club will be keeping their fingers crossed that he can.

'There are not many Ian Wrights about.'

Football is all about dreams, the possible and the improbable, those who realise them and those who sink in them. In an odd way, Ian Wright's reputation does put him on a pedestal, and comes close to earning him what he's wanted since he played at being Gerd Müller, Pelé or Stanley Bowles as a kid. That he is one of the most disliked players in the Premiership is in itself the most sincere kind of respect: we hate those players who are most likely to do our team damage and sink our dreams

Peter Prentice, the Palace chief scout who 'discovered' Ian has a term for Ian Wright's success. 'It was a fairy story really. You might see 200 or so players come along under similar circumstances but no one else has done anything like Ian.'

But no fairy godmother ever waved a wand and magicked a Brockley kid into the England squad or to winners medals or Golden Boots. You have to do that all by yourself. It takes endeavour and dedication of singular measure. Ian's got just that.

'Don't get me wrong,' Ian once said. 'Everything I've got, I worked hard for. I knew I was good enough to make it, but Steve Coppell was the only one prepared to give me the chance to prove it.' It was precisely that balance of respect and self-motivation that Nesta Wright had inculcated in Ian from youth.

Jazzie B, the Funki Dred entrepreneur who created the Soul II

Soul empire, was driven by a similar hunger. He articulated the ambition of many sons and daughters of Caribbean migrants in *Touch* magazine. 'When I was in school, it wasn't just like me and the guys playing football, it was like *I wanted to be a footballer man* ... And how bad I wanted to be a footballer. And my coach would say, "work hard, work hard". And you know true, I life is that still. It does get a bit hectic where man want you to do this and man want you to do that, where the decision lies right there in front of you. And again, you might complicate things. Listen. Man fe believe in themself. I believe in myself and what I am able to do. And knowing that the cap fits and I wear it.'

Ian doesn't subscribe to the 'what goes around comes around' theory. He knew the cap he wanted to fit him. He has always acted on the agencies in his life to achieve his ends rather than rely on the providence of others.

If it hadn't been football that he succeeded in, it would have been something else, not some submission to the inevitable tribulation of 'the ghetto' as is often erroneously trotted out in profiles of the man. If Ian chose to be an actor, one side of him would always hold that he was better than De Niro; the other would worry he'd make it past non-verbal vignettes on *Castles*.

But there's more to Ian than that, if only people were allowed to see it. He retains the sort of Biblical conservatism that his mother imparted: a passion for tradition and distaste for political correctness married to a sense of injustice for the poor, the underprivileged and the oppressed. In recent years he's become more comfortable with himself, but he still presents a difficult image to the outside world. Even his later willingness to cite religion as an influence by thanking God for the bounty he has provided Ian and his family with is tinged with scepticism.

So what is the real Ian Wright like? Perhaps two exist: one loudly obscuring the other in the public gaze. There's Wrighty, 'Satch', the brash, happy-go-lucky, hedonistic, spiteful man who holds court over his peers – the spitting footballer – kissing his teeth and loudly proclaiming his Jamaican background: 'Eh, man wh'appen? Ta raas! Me get vex out there y'kno.' Then there's Ian: quiet, stable, cultured, homely, socially responsible – the sensitive family man – the man who's interested in his friends and how they're getting on.

The two even dress differently. There's the young footballer who popped back to Samuel Pepys School with his trademark New York cap at a jaunty angle, spending a fortune on the latest cool US sports gear, keeping up with the music-led fashion trends; the ragamuffin hip to the street vibe in his Shogun Jeep, defying the promptings of Old Father Time and spending his holidays in Miami. He has played himself into the upper middle class echelons, and aspires to an increasingly cosmopolitan range of interests but Ian still largely draws on the black working class culture which moulded him.

And then there's the lover of elegant Italian couture: the man who buys his classic footwear from the classic shoemakers; who commissions quality suits from the quality gentlemen's tailor; who reveres top-drawer cars; who professes admiration for the nonchalant ease of the upper classes. Leisure and philanthropy, coolness and class draw Ian to Prince Charles and the English gentleman, mythical, ambiguous or archaic notions though they may be.

Both Ian Wrights are fundamentally loyal to friends, family, colleagues and club. But where Wrighty is ambitious, Ian is aspirational. Where Wrighty wraps himself in the British flag, Ian has a more complex take on his cultural identity.

There are mixed black and white pop groups, marriages, football teams . . . It's a better world in some ways than the one Ian grew up in, but only just.

As a black man, Ian knows he's he'll never be allowed entry to the English gentleman's club – the cricket race row during the summer of 1995 was another illustration of that. Two things you're prohibited from buying into are nationality and class.

The more successful he has become, the more intense the public gaze, the greater the search for a fatal flaw and the prospective fall from grace amongst certain sections of society. And the harder it becomes for him to carry off the street ragamuffin image, especially leading such a comfortable life of luxury protected by sophisticated burglar alarms.

Like so many black people, Ian has been harassed by the police all his life. He may not get picked up on 'Sus' any more, but he's well aware that a younger generation is. Ian's celebrity brings no immunity from persecution either. The same bigots, who hassled him as a youth, abused him as a teenage footballer and threw bananas at him as a professional footballer, persist.

Ian is picked up by police in his car all the time. A black man in a Jeep is, in the eyes of the law, a drug dealer; a black man at the wheel of a Jaguar XJS is a more successful drug dealer. Linford Christie complained recently that he was never taken seriously as a top athlete because of sexual allusion. He could just as easily have revealed the disturbing behaviour of many boys in blue as meted out to the few high-profile Afro-Caribbean people of this country. A typical example happened in the early summer of 1995. Ian was driving home with friends and in-laws in his car. The police saw him going by and pulled him over. They were surly. They acted like South African cops during apartheid.

Ian was wearing a leather jacket emblazoned with the Arsenal badge. 'Right then, sunshine,' they said. 'How many more of those have you got in the boot, then?' Ian told them he was an Arsenal player. They made out they didn't know who he was. They said, 'We're all rugby fans. We don't like poofy sports.' And they wound him up knowing he had to take it, humiliated him in front of his peers, just to prove that no matter how successful he was he was still inferior to them, still worthless.

Ian Wright isn't one to founder on such contradictions in his life. But he has to play the game like everyone else because he's powerless and he's known that scenario his whole life. He gets his own back in a way.

Like when he was shooting the video for 'Do The Right Thing' a couple of years ago. It was in Portobello Road, north-west London, brothers' territory, and the scene of the Notting Hill Carnival battles between police and black youths. As he was executing a stroll towards the camera, a police van prowled the road next to him. He suddenly broke away from the lens, wheeled round and yelled 'Babylon!' into the faces of the shocked officers.

So do the police particularly enjoy bringing him down because of his image? It is highly possible. Lots of people lose their temper in sport, but present a more amenable personality in other ways. He is a caring father, a sensitive, loyal and thoughtful man, always keen to help out his friends, and he often spends time working for worthy causes but that side of him doesn't fill many column inches.

His public profile has largely been constructed by the media in the heat of his dazzling, temperamental career. He has been poorly advised in that department. No such thing as bad publicity, he was told.

Ian has been ill-served as a person by such advice, and it is a source of frustration for him. One of the most enticing prospects for the future is how Ian Wright is going to change over the next few years. Will he learn to believe in himself in a less demonstrative, deeper way than before? Will he show more of the immensely likeable private man rather than cash in on the firebrand reputation?

There is one who is well-placed this season to have a hugely positive influence on Ian Wright, if only he feels inclined. He could channel the 'fire in the belly', help present a more fitting public profile and inspire him towards the Golden Boot. Step forward the man himself, Ian Wright.

Wherever the future takes him – another Premiership side? Japan's J-League? – Ian's in a stronger position than he's ever been to decide his own destiny.

The ages of life are like those of rivers. He's had the turbulent beginning, the struggle to cut his own furrow and he's now experienced the fastest, most incisive and effective phase. Soon he'll slow, spread himself, meander where he fancies, develop the intellect that was suppressed by boredom at school, continue the stimulation he has recently found in literature and other arts – especially music.

Ultimately, kin for Ian Wright overrides any other consideration, no matter what hitman thoughts run through his mind as he springs out of the players' tunnel or as he rummages proudly round the trophy room at home. His family, and the boys he cares for so much, are more important than anything.

When he eventually does hang up his boots, when Ian Wright dons his classic leather, sparks up his Harley-Davidson and when he roars off into the sunset for that grand tour of Europe, don't rule out a sidecar.